THE BOOKMAN SONG
a memoir

BY **Tad Simons**

The Bookman Song: A memoir

Copyright © Tad Simons, 2020

All rights reserved

Published by Pembroke Press

ISBN: 978-0-9961110-1-0

Publisher's Note: This is a work of non-fiction, meaning that the events related in the narrative did occur in the real world, in the space and time described, and that the story is as true to the author's memory as he can make them. In order to shape that narrative, however, techniques of narrative fiction were used in the writing of it, because no, the author has not carried a tape recorder around with him his entire life.

No part of this publication may be reproduced, stored, or transmitted, in any form or by any means (electronic, mechanical, photocopying, recording, or otherwise), without the prior written consent of copyright owner and publisher, who—to make it really easy—happens to be the same person.

The scanning, uploading, and distribution of this book via the Internet or any other means without the permission of the publisher may be tempting—but it is illegal and punishable by law. Please purchase only authorized electronic editions and do not participate in, or encourage, electronic piracy of copyrighted materials. Your support and respect for the author's rights is appreciated.

Cover Design: DaisyMaeDesign

Interior Design: DaisyMaeDesign

Editorial assistance: Elisabeth Rose

Printed in the United States of America

For My Wife

Who graciously reads between the lines

INTRODUCTION

Dear Reader,

Believe it or not, this is a true story.

I am only telling you this because in this age of trickery and deceit, when seemingly everyone is a truth-twisting bullshitter, it seems necessary to clarify—to insist, really—that the events contained herein did actually happen in real life, not in some dank corner of my imagination.

And the reason it feels necessary to emphasize the veracity of my account—to declare right up front that every word of this book is as true as I can make it—is that some parts of my tale may strike the reader as unbelievable.

I know this because over the years I have told bits and pieces of this story to people at parties and in polite conversation, and have gotten people slapping their knees and banging their foreheads, saying, "No way!" "You're kidding!" "That's incredible!" Apparently, their own lives are not filled with weird characters and improbable events, so they are astounded when they hear about things that fall so far outside their personal experience.

I understand this reaction completely. There are things that happened to me during the summer of 1979 that I still can't quite believe.

"The Truth" is a slippery concept, however—one some people would say doesn't even exist. Which is understandable. We live in a world of unreliable narrators. Liars and cheaters are everywhere, running everything, so much so that irony and obfuscation have become the language of the realm. There are many people who, when you tell them something is true, will immediately assume it is false, because that's the smart thing to do. Trust is for suckers, they think, and believing in something, anything, is a sign of intellectual weakness. Therefore, they can't allow themselves to believe that a story like mine is true, because that would make them a gullible idiot.

I don't blame them. No, I blame the Coen Brothers. In the opening credits of their movie *Fargo*, they used the same words I used just a few paragraphs ago: "This is a true story." Only it wasn't. The Coen Brothers trusted that their audience was smart enough to figure out they were joking, and to understand that making fun of the truth is, in this day and age, just another layer of entertainment. By declaring the thing "true" when it obviously wasn't, some went so far as to suggest that the Coen Brothers were creating a kind of meta-narrative of fictional authenticity by planting an ironic signpost at the very beginning of their narrative, a wink to the cognoscenti indicating that the story itself is not to be taken seriously.

My use of the phrase is precisely opposite that of the brothers Coen. So, while we may be using the same words—this is a true story—their meaning is entirely different. Mine is a true story, dammit, even the parts that may strike the reader as crazy or implausible. Furthermore, the telling of it is as close as I can come to an honest recollection of the events that befell me that fateful summer. Nevertheless, because so many years have passed, and the fog of age has no doubt affected the clarity of my recollections, to say nothing of the trustworthiness of my memory or the extent to which I am inclined to twist or shade narrative in one direction or the other to make myself or others in my tale look better or worse than they "really" were, it is perhaps in the reader's best interests to remember that telling the truth is a very difficult thing. Most people can't do it, even if they try—even if they are paying someone to pry the truth out of them, session after session, like a rotten tooth or an old, rusty nail.

Trust me or not, that's your choice. But I'm telling you, once and for all, a truer story than *The Bookman Song* has never been told, no matter how hard it may be to believe.

CHAPTER 1

There are pivot points in everyone's life, hinge moments when the universe shifts, events collide, and the great unfolding from that point forward feels like the insistent pull of fate. For me, one of those moments was the first day of college, when I learned that my assigned roommate, the fellow I would be living with for the entire upcoming year, was a 39-year-old Mormon missionary.

Let the horror of that revelation sink in: After years of high-school college-prep courses, the usual battery of standardized tests, months of rigorous research, several scouting trips to various institutions of higher learning, and a careful assessment of the weather and "culture" at my college of choice, I ended up at the University of Arizona in Tucson, trapped in a dorm room with a man twice my age who wore strange underwear and held even stranger beliefs. My father was only forty years old at the time, so I had essentially been sentenced to live with a man who should have been living in the suburbs raising kids in a three-bedroom rambler, not bunking with them in a college dormitory.

His name was Dan. He was from Ramona, California, a farming community east of San Diego, where, I gathered, his family owned some modest acreage and raised an assortment of cows and horses and chickens. So, in addition to being a Mormon, Dan was also a cowboy. The day I met him he was wearing black leather cowboy boots, greasy black jeans, and a red-and-black checkered shirt that looked as if it had been washed several-hundred times in a muddy stream. Underneath it all he wore the weird underwear of his faith, a pair of Dickensian long-johns rendered even weirder by the fact that it was 112 degrees outside. Sun-damaged skin and a pronounced limp made him look ten or fifteen years older than he was, and all of his belongings, save for an old guitar, fit into a beat-up black leather suitcase with a broken handle that he'd tried to repair with silver duct tape.

The second we met, both of us knew the score. He knew he shouldn't have been there. I knew it too. And yet there he was. And so was I.

Shit.

In retrospect, perhaps I should have had more compassion for the man. After all, no one in his right mind would choose, on the cusp of forty, to live amid a horde of teenage egomaniacs hopped up on hormones and high on the most powerful intoxicant of all: freedom. And not just freedom from parental supervision and annoying siblings, but freedom from the person we used to be in high school, the confining boxes and labels of our former selves (soon to be replaced of course by the boxes and labels of our college selves, then our professional selves, then all the other selves we all long to discard before finding the one true self that constantly eludes us).

Dan said he was there to "save money" while he finished his degree in biochemistry. He wanted to be a veterinarian, he told me, but his grades weren't good enough to go to a vet school in America. So his goal was to go to vet school in Mexico, where admission requirements were more forgiving, then return to the U.S. and start a practice. Living in the dorms was the cheapest way to put a roof over his head while he pursued his "dream."

So the man had a plan. Not a good plan, but a plan nonetheless. Still, I had no interest in being part of it. Whatever sad set of circumstances led poor Dan to seek shelter in a dorm full of college freshmen, I did not care. All I knew at the time was that a horrible mistake had been made. He and I together, in the same room, was a tragic wrong that needed to be righted.

Immediately.

To resolve the matter, I headed straight to Housing Services and explained the situation. A large man with unruly hair and a ribbon of sweat on his upper lip sat behind the Housing Services counter reading a Robert H. Heinlein novel. From the look on his face, I gathered that he did not appreciate being interrupted. He cocked his eyebrow at me in a way that said: "This better be good." I explained to him that a forty-year-old man had somehow slipped through the cracks of the university's rigorous screening process, and that he had mistakenly been assigned to bunk with me, an eighteen-year-old freshman with my entire life ahead of me and a deep, abiding desire not to live with an old religious person who plays earnest folk songs on the guitar. Surely there was a more appropriate roommate on their roster for both him and me, I ventured—and that being the case, wasn't it in everyone's interests to switch our room assignments as soon as possible, before any of us had actually unpacked?

The Housing Services guy looked at me with tired, droopy eyes and said, "Sorry, all room assignments are final. In college as in life, students must learn to get along with all types of people," he opined. "As a matter of policy, the University of Arizona believes it is in your best interests to suck it up and figure it out, because learning to live with someone you don't like will improve your character and better prepare you for the shit-storm of disappointment that awaits you after graduation."

Or words to that effect.

"But the man is forty years old!" I protested. "And he's a Mormon. And he gives me the creeps."

"And?"

"And . . . I'm pretty sure he has some sort of communicable disease. He's got awful skin, and when I saw him last, his eyes were real watery. I think he might have hepatitis."

"B or C?"

"D, I'm guessing. Or E, possibly. Whatever's worse."

The guy gave me a well-practiced "get out of here" stare, and I tried one last gambit.

"What if he's a child molester or a murderer?" I pointed out. "How's that going to look in the news? 'University of Arizona allows child-molesting murderer to live in dorms. Residents say they are lucky to be alive. The school was warned, say sources close to the investigation, but those warnings—given to Housing Services by a solid B-plus student who is only three merit badges away from being an Eagle scout—were tragically ignored.'"

Instead, he ignored me.

I tried with Dan, I really did. And it would have been okay if he stuck to his business and allowed me to stick to mine. Unfortunately, at some point during the semester he decided that God had placed him in that dorm room for the specific purpose of converting me to his faith, the Mormon faith, a faith I had become all-too-acquainted with during an ill-advised high-school romance with a girl who, one might say, put the "more" in Mormon.

The problem was my soul. It was clearly troubled, he could see, and to prove it he would read to me passages from the Bible that he thought applied to my situation. I'd be sitting at my desk, doing homework, and he'd turn to me, Bible in hand, and read something like James 1:14-15: "Each person is tempted when they are dragged away from their personal desire and enticed. Then, after desire has conceived, it gives birth to sin; and sin, when it is full-grown, gives birth to death."

Or, when he learned I was enrolled in the business school, he read Timothy 6:9: "Those who want to get rich fall into temptation and a trap and into many foolish and harmful desires that plunge people into ruin and destruction."

Or, if he heard me talking to someone else on the hall about going to a party and meeting some girls, he'd read me something from second Timothy 2:22: "Flee the evil desires of youth and pursue righteousness, faith, love, and peace, along with those who call on the Lord out of a pure heart."

I was just getting acquainted with the evil desires of youth, of course, and my sole intention at the time was to flee toward them as fast as possible. To put brother Dan off, I did everything I could think of to prove to him that my soul was beyond redemption. I left *Playboy* magazines conspicuously open on my desk. I played the most demonic records I could find—by The Grateful Dead, Santana, Black Sabbath, The Rolling Stones, Led Zeppelin, Alice Cooper—and wore my turntable needle to a nub playing songs that had the word "devil" in them. From the library I checked out books like Bertrand Russell's, *Why I am Not a Christian*, Ayn Rand's *The Virtue of Selfishness*, and Austin Osman Spare's *The Psychology of Ecstasy*. I kept a pack of cigarettes on my desk, even though I didn't smoke. In conversation, I lied about sexual encounters I'd had at parties, about how much I liked to drink, and how many dangerous drugs I'd done—all to emphasize how much fun it was not to be a religious fundamentalist. I wore black t-shirts with skulls on them. I made up lurid dreams, about clown orgies, swimming in a sea of snakes, drinking the blood of a thousand bats, having sex with a chimpanzee, being trapped in a forest full of albino leprechauns.

Nothing worked. The darker I painted my soul, the more convinced he became that I needed saving. And he was right, I did need to be saved. From him!

I needed out. And so, I began to plan my exit strategy.

CHAPTER 2

At the University of Arizona, the only way a freshman could avoid living in the dorms was to pledge a fraternity or sorority and live in one of their houses. I'm not normally a "joiner," and I've never been all that keen on parties or drinking to embarrassing excess, but my situation with Dan the Merciless Mormon forced me to explore options I might otherwise not have considered.

Though my father had been in a fraternity, and had fond memories of his college years, the idea of living in a fraternity house did not appeal to me for many reasons. For one thing, the movie *Animal House* was released in the summer of 1978, about a month before I set off for college, searing into my consciousness a vision of Greek life that reinforced and amplified every imaginable stereotype of frat-boy smugness and collegiate degeneracy ever devised, plus a few new ones. For those of us who saw *Animal House* in the summer of 1978 and were headed off to college that fall, the movie also served as a cautionary instruction manual. It was funny, sure, but also terrifying. Seeing *Animal House* only a few weeks before setting off for college, as I did—when the apprehension and anxiety about this new phase of life is at its peak—was like peering down Alice's rabbit hole into a topsy-turvy world where the rules of normal life did not apply. In much the same way *Alice in Wonderland* might teach you how to throw a tea party, *Animal House* taught us what college might be like if everything in our lives went terribly, disastrously wrong. *This* is what happens if you aren't careful and you allow yourself to succumb to peer pressure, I thought. *This* is what happens if you allow yourself to have too much fun. More to the point: *This* is what happens if you allow yourself to join a fraternity.

By "this," I of course mean waking up half naked in a pool of vomit wondering how many laws you broke the night before, and whether your life from here on out is completely, utterly ruined. That's what happens when you mistakenly travel down what my father would call the "wrong path." But life—my life, at least—has never been guided by reliable signage, so picking "the right path" has never been as easy as some sages pretend.

Like many big universities, the U of A has a large and very active Greek system. (In fact, the *Animal House* sequel *Revenge of the Nerds* was filmed there, a cringe-worthy fact if there ever was one.) Dozens of fraternities and sororities sit side by side on the campus's Greek row, most of them large, dormitory-style "houses" built specifically for groups of fifty to a hundred marginally civilized young people to live together and run their own affairs. In practice, most fraternities and sororities operate like independent businesses. All members pay monthly dues, and those who live in the fraternity house itself pay additional rent. In turn, that pot of money is used to buy food for meals, fund parties and other social activities, and maintain the building itself. At the U of A, it was actually cheaper to live in a fraternity house than to live in the dorms, a perk that, combined with brother Dan's insufferable proselytizing, tipped the scales further in favor of joining a fraternity.

But which one?

That's the question facing every college kid who wants to join a group of people who are already friends, who have already developed their own culture, and who may or may not like you, depending on some mysterious criteria of which you are woefully unaware. Fraternities are basically cliques organized around an idea. The idea might be a formal part of the charter—pre-med, pre-law, business, music etc.—but most often it's an informal, rather vague agreement among the current members about what their group identity is and how far they are willing to stretch that identity to accommodate new members. For example, jock fraternities tend to attract guys who like to play sports, but jock fraternities don't like to be labeled that way, so they might "diversify" their membership with guys who are good at something else, like fashion merchandising or interior design (just kidding). Likewise, there are plenty of "party" houses whose members are seemingly dedicated to the proposition that deciding which mind-altering substances one prefers, and in what combinations, is the *sine qua non* of a college education. Such houses do need a few members with passing grades, however, so they might accept someone who has a legitimate prescription for Adderall rather than someone who simply takes it recreationally. (Again, kidding. Adderall did not exist in 1979. But you get the idea. Like attracts like in the fraternity rush game—until it doesn't, at which point they send you on your way.)

Logically, any group of more than a dozen guys is going to be filled with different sorts of people, of course. But fraternities traffic in a specific kind of different, and they live or die by their ability to find, recruit, and retain the sorts of people who fit their idea of themselves. So-called "rush week" is when fraternities and sororities throw open their doors and invite outsiders and potential new members in to meet "the group." These events are billed as parties or "mixers," but they are really social auditions. Both sides are giving a performance of sorts, presenting the "best" version of themselves they can muster. For those who want to join a fraternity, rush week is about finding the group that best fits one's idea of oneself or, more importantly, the kind of person one wants to become. For the fraternity, it's about finding people who will add something to the mix of talents and egos and personalities they've already collected, without diluting the purity of the idea that binds them, whatever that happens to be. The trick is matching the two. Like any relationship, a good match can be wonderful, and a bad match can be a disaster. The person seeking to join is at a distinct disadvantage, however, so it's the responsibility of those who are already in the fraternity to weed out guys (or girls) who won't fit in and identify those who will.

Most people have an instinctive dislike for this kind of social sorting, even though it happens everywhere in different ways. Deciding who to marry, where to work, where to live, where to send the kids to school, which car to buy, what kinds of shoes to wear, etc.—it's all social sorting based on one's sense of identity, and fraternities are just one way in which that dynamic plays out in real life. The irony, of course, is that most people think of themselves as distinct individuals who can't be put in a "box," even as they secretly long to find a box they can comfortably put themselves in.

On my first night of rush week, I had serious doubts about finding a group of guys to whom I could sincerely "pledge" my allegiance. Students who are not in the Greek system are called "independents," after all, and being independent was something I prided myself on, even though the word doesn't actually mean anything when you are spending your parents' money to have a school shelter, feed, educate, entertain, and protect you. Still, maintaining the illusion of independence is important to an eighteen-year-old free-thinker. And, since fraternities require a certain amount of conformity, or so I assumed, I wasn't sure finding one that would embrace my own unique attributes as a human being was even possible. That assumption was due in part to the fear that I had no unique attributes—that I was far too average in every way, and my triumphs thus far in life were pretty much non-existent. I could whistle loudly with my fingers and knew how to make a potato cannon, but beyond that my résumé of personal accomplishments was a bit thin.

During rush week that year, all the fraternities seemed to be offering one of two propositions: Either they were an Animal House, or they weren't. Those that were prided themselves on their ability to party more or less constantly without getting kicked off campus. Those that weren't tried to appeal to the more serious, studious side of one's nature, always with the caveat that they did of course have plenty of fun, despite the conspicuous lack of girls in the room at the moment.

Going from house to house trick-or-treating down Greek row in hopes of finding some people who will let you live with them is a strange way to find an apartment, but it was the only option I had. As if his proselytizing wasn't bad enough, Dan had taken to bringing his girlfriend to the dorm and locking me out until all hours of the night. I could only entertain myself so long by wondering what sort of middle-aged man woos a woman by bringing her back to his college dorm room, and likewise, what sort of woman allows herself to be wooed that way? My anger was compounded by the fact that he wasn't in there having sex with her (that, I could have understood). No, according to him, they spent their time lying side by side in his bunk, talking about "spiritual matters" and listening to a Christian music station he'd found at the upper end of the FM dial.

I couldn't take much more.

After visiting eight or ten different fraternity houses, I was beginning to lose hope. I'd met some decent people, but I'd also met plenty of guys who fit the stereotypes I was trying to avoid, and many whom I just didn't like, and I couldn't imagine living with.

It was late on a night near the end of rush week, and I was about to throw in the towel when I decided to visit one last fraternity before heading back to my dorm. I had avoided the Delta Chi house because it was one of the largest fraternities on campus, which meant it was also one of the most popular, indicating to me that it had none of the exclusivity and character I was looking for. In my mind, the ideal fraternity was about fifteen or twenty guys who didn't make a big deal out of being a fraternity and could under other circumstances be called a "club," or a "softball team." It was not a hundred-and-twenty guys living in a fraternity-industrial complex that took up a whole city block and, come the revolution, could fund its own militia. Also, the legendarily sordid fraternity in *Animal House* is named Delta Tau Chi, and that was a little too close for comfort. I feared there might be other similarities, and so was predisposed to hate the place before I even set foot in it.

When I finally did step inside the Delta Chi house, however, I was greeted by a peculiar sight. The president of the house introduced himself as Jim. The thing about Jim—the thing you could not avoid noticing about Jim—is that he was a dwarf. Short arms, short legs, big head, he wasn't much more than four feet tall, but when I shook his hand, his grip felt like a strong pair of pliers. Jim also wore a ROTC uniform, and, I soon learned, was a "tank commander" who could throw his voice like a grenade, with eerily similar results.

Standing beside Jim was the vice president, a guy named Russ who was about six-foot-six but looked much taller standing next to the diminutive Jim. Russ wore a nicely tailored blue blazer, white shirt, and a red tie, the original "power" combo before it became a meaningless business cliché. The thing I remember most about that meeting—and it is an odd thing to remember—is the knot in Russ's tie. Most guys tie a tie using what's known as a "four-in-hand" knot or a half-Windsor, which results in a sloppy, asymmetrical knot, and the tie itself hangs with a noticeable crease or indentation at the top. Russ's tie had a small, tight, perfectly symmetrical triangle for a knot, and the tie itself hung down with no hint of a crease. I'd never seen anything like it. I actually found myself admiring it, even though I hated suits and ties and everything they represent. Still, I spent a lot of time sailing as a kid, and could appreciate a good knot. The knot in Russ's tie was the best I'd ever seen.

They were a strange pair, Jim and Russ. But the moment I met them, I thought: If there's enough room in this place for a dwarf soldier like

Jim and a sartorially savvy giant like Russ, maybe there's room for me here too.

CHAPTER 3

Turns out there was. Or at least they seemed to think so.

I moved out of the dorm and into the Delta Chi fraternity house immediately after the Christmas break. Sixty or so members lived on the property, in the house, while another fifty or so lived elsewhere. As a "pledge," I lived on the top of three floors, but occupied the lowest possible social rank: "Scum," a designation given to me and the dozen or so other fellows who pledged at the same time. We were treated accordingly.

As Scums, our job was to mop the halls, clean the bathrooms, and take care of all the other unpleasant tasks necessary to prevent the place from descending into anarchy. The morning after a party, for instance, the floors in the main room were always sticky with spilled beer and soda, and the stale stench of cigarettes and booze hung thick in the air like a noxious fog. Hundreds of plastic cups were strewn around the house, many of them still half-full, along with empty bottles of Jim Beam, discarded pints of peppermint schnapps, and, owing to Arizona's affinity for all things cowboy, countless soda cans brimming with chewing-tobacco spit. Sometime during the previous night's festivities, at least one unsuspecting idiot inevitably spied a Coke can and, thirsty, shook it to see if there was anything in it, then took a gulp. The resulting pile of vomit was our duty to clean up as well, along with the carpet of popcorn, peanut shells, sunflower seeds, peanut M&Ms, and pretzels crushed into the floor, and whatever gooey substances were smeared in the walls, including (but not limited to) feces and blood.

For me, these indignities were a small price to pay for the privilege of not having to live with a middle-aged Mormon. In exchange, I got a room, a non-religious roommate, meals, an instant social life, and plenty of new friends.

Though Delta Chi had a reputation for epic parties, its vision of itself—the binding "idea" of the organization—was much more ambitious. Many people who have never been in a fraternal organization tend to dismiss their higher ideals as a kind of altruistic smokescreen to prevent campus officials from peering too deeply into the heart of darkness at the center. But in the world of Delta Chi, many of the members took the group's larger mission—to build character, serve the community, and lay the moral foundation for future success as an individual and as a citizen—quite seriously.

Once, at a weekly chapter meeting, Jim, our tank-commander president, stood in front of the assembled brothers holding a plant in his hand. It was a sprig, barely a foot long, but the leaves were slender and pointed, and, after a few seconds of silence, all of us understood that it was a marijuana plant. Pot was not nearly as common on campus then as it is now. Out of the hundred or so people in the room, less than half-a-dozen smoked it regularly, so the likely culprits weren't difficult to deduce. Jim held the plant up for all to see, and explained that he had found it growing in front of the house, where "anyone could see it." He then began launching verbal grenades, condemning whoever was stupid enough to plant a seed like that, screaming at the gigglers that it was no joke, and reminding us that it was mindless indiscretions like this that get fraternities kicked off campus. "Do you want that??!!" he screamed, his face red with menace. "Do you want that to be your legacy?!" He then went on a ten-minute tirade about what it meant to be a Delta Chi brother, why we were there, and proclaimed that the consequences of another such infraction would be immediate banishment, forever. He reminded us of the ideals we had pledged—but in this instance failed—to uphold, and challenged us to do better. Zero tolerance was the message, and anyone who wasn't on board with that was welcome to leave.

The hypocrisy of getting so worked up over a pot plant in a place where alcoholic inebriation was pretty much mandatory was ridiculous, of course. But it wasn't about the actual morality of smoking pot; it was about the perception of the fraternity as a place where high moral standards are upheld, and the legal consequences of breaking the law in such a way that this perception is compromised. In other words, it was about self-preservation. Jim himself was aware of the contradictions, I think, but I'm also certain he believed in the importance of reminding ourselves, once in a while, that in order for society to function, people can't just go around doing whatever the hell they want. There are laws, and if you ignore them, bad things will happen. In which case you have two choices: Either obey the law, or be smart about breaking it. Marijuana, he thought, was for degenerates. Alcohol, not so much. If you wanted to get legally shit-faced, the choices were clear.

Navigating the vast chasm between the fraternity's espoused ideals and the actual behavior of its members was a daily challenge, of course. But the structure and purpose of such organizations is largely to contain the excesses of spirited young men and channel it toward something constructive. Fraternities are in fact one of the first places where young men get to try their skills at self-governance. Like many other institutions in society, a fraternity's charter is drawn up, a "constitution" is written, by-laws are passed, and a leadership structure is put in place to enforce the rules, make decisions, manage business, and organize activities. Like I said before, fraternities are basically run like small businesses, and, social indiscretions aside, are intended to confer upon their members an appreciation for cooperation, citizenship, and respect for the greater good. Also, they give people who want to be leaders a chance to practice and develop those skills before applying them in the "real" world, where the consequences of screwing up are much harsher.

There was however one period during which all of the fraternity's higher ideals were completely and utterly abandoned: Hell Week.

Ever since the Masons donned robes and traded esoteric secrets by candlelight, fraternal organizations the world over have used initiation rituals as a gateway to membership. To devise the sort of initiation rituals endured by the members of Delta Chi, however, one must take the idea of a legitimate ritual, then twist, bend, contort, and pervert it beyond all recognition, add alarming quantities of alcohol and sleep deprivation, mix it with a sadistic sense of humor, and excuse it all under the comforting banners of "tradition" and "brotherhood."

Delta Chi was by no means unique. Almost all fraternities had—and still have—a version of Hell Week. Inventive forms of humiliation and abuse are the norm during these infamous rites of passage. When you hear news reports of someone going to the hospital or dying because of a fraternity prank gone too far, it's usually during Hell Week, when crimes against dignity are typically committed to a chorus of hoots and hollers and several chugs of that region's cheapest beer.

"Hazing" is the term most people use to describe such behavior, though fraternities themselves prefer the term "initiation," for obvious reasons. Hazing incidents are responsible for most of the negative press fraternities receive (when they aren't being investigated for sexual assault, that is), which is why it has since been banned and/or outlawed (though by no means eradicated) at most colleges and universities, along with consumption of alcohol and drugs. In the late 1970s, however, hazing was more popular than ever, and no one embraced it more passionately than the brothers of Delta Chi.

Though officially discouraged by the university proper, hazing was considered by many of our members to be essential to the brotherly "bond," the glue of commitment to each other that made us different from a mere social club or other, lesser organizations. Every fraternity has its secret handshakes and a history of high-minded nonsense that confers on its members a feeling that they belong to a special group, and Delta Chi was no different in that regard. Where my eventual brothers excelled was in the level of enthusiasm, creativity, and energy they devoted to the art of hazing. Physical abuse was an important component of it, naturally, but psychological torture was our house's specialty.

As pledges, we endured the standard embarrassments: having to wear goofy red outfits around campus, doing push-ups on command, not being able to shower or sleep, being abandoned in the desert in our underwear, etc. But these activities were a mere preamble to the flurry of mind-fuckery awaiting us at the end of Hell Week, when, exhausted and weary, the escalating humiliations reached their sadistic peak.

One evening, after three straight nights of almost no sleep, we were told that we would finally be given a chance to rest. About one in the morning, we were awoken by the crash of banging pots and pans and the wail of a police siren (a few alumni were actually in local law enforcement). Ordered to strip down to our underwear, we were ushered single file down to the house showers. The showers were the sort of open tile boxes used in school locker rooms, with four spigots on either side and nothing but open space and a drain in the middle. I and my cohorts were ordered to stand in the showers and get blasted with hot, then cold, water. After that, we were told to sit still, not to move, and above all, not to go to sleep. To make that last part a wee bit more difficult, music was blasted into the bathrooms at a deafening volume. And not just any music; it was one song, played over and over, for hours. Furthermore, tradition demanded that the chosen song be the most irritating song on the radio that year—which was, in our case, The Captain and Tenille's "Muskrat Love."

Think about that: a dozen guys, almost naked, sitting in a shower listening to "Muskrat Love" over and over again, ad infinitum, in a state of hallucinatory exhaustion. And, to keep them awake, you turn the showers back on every twenty minutes or so, bang some pots and pans, and wail that siren a few more times. The simple, elegant perversity of it is remarkable.

To this day, I cannot hear that song—"Muskrat Suzy, muskrat Sam, do the jitterbug out in muskrat land"—without flinching. For hours we sat, wet and weary, listening to that insipid chorus—"and they whirl and they twirl and they tango, singing and jinging a jango"—trying not to lose our minds. Personally, that last line almost put me over the edge. They what? Jango isn't even a word! Neither is jinging! If they needed to come up with something to rhyme with "tango," how about "eating a juicy ripe mango," or well, okay, nothing else rhymes with tango. But resorting to nonsense words? Is that necessary? For that matter, is a song about nuzzling muskrats necessary? Is it even legal? Shouldn't there be limits on artistic freedom to prevent travesties like this? I mean, how could you write that song and not think, wow, this is going to be the most annoying song ever recorded. How could you not think: you know, played over and over again at excruciating volume, this piece of putrid pop could be used as an effective form of torture. When, in 1989, the U.S. Navy attempted to force Panamanian dictator Manuel Noriega to surrender by blasting rock-and-roll music at his compound for ten days straight, I could have told them they were wasting their time assaulting him with the Doobie Brothers, Van Halen, and Oingo Boingo. If they'd just hit him with twenty-four hours of "Muskrat Love," the man would have crawled out of his compound on all fours, begging for mercy.

Every pledge class got a different song, its own special musical hell. And for every person in every class, that song ended up meaning something entirely different than it did for the rest of humanity. Legend has it the class that had to listen to the Beach Boys' "Help Me Rhonda" had it worst of all, though the group that got Starland Vocal Band's "Afternoon Delight" always had a solid claim. For me, however, "Muskrat Love" will always occupy an especially loathsome place in a deep, dark part of my psyche that I'd prefer never, ever to shine a light on.

Another classic bit was called "Eat Shit or Die."

For this masterful mind-game, pledges are ordered to clean the bathrooms as thoroughly as possible. After they finish their cleaning, the pledges are lined up outside in the hall and a senior fraternity member enters the bathroom to inspect their handiwork. After a few minutes, the senior inspector emerges from the bathroom enraged. He has found a renegade "turd" floating in one of the toilets, and demands to know who left it there? When no one confesses, he grabs the first pledge in line and pulls him into the bathroom. Inside, the lights have been turned off so that it's just dark enough to see shapes and shadows. The pledge is led to a toilet stall and ordered to kneel in front of the commode. In the toilet are what appear to be two logs of shit floating on top of the water. The pledge is then ordered to "eat shit or die." One of his pledge brothers has taken an illicit dump and failed to flush it, so now he must pay by taking a bite of his brother's insubordination. When the pledge refuses, his head is pushed closer to the toilet and he gets yelled at to "be a man" or, conversely, "don't be a pussy." When the pledge continues to resist, an elder brother reaches over his shoulder in disgust, grabs a log of shit out of the water, and takes a bite himself. Having proven that a real man will indeed eat the shit of his beloved brother, he throws the log back in the water and demands that the pledge himself now prove his worthiness. When the pledge reluctantly (but inevitably) reaches into the water and pulls the shit log to his lips to take a bite, the lights suddenly go on and the pledge sees that he is not in fact holding someone else's shit in his hand; he is holding a banana. Laughter all around, ha ha ha, slaps on the back, etc. Then some chocolate sauce gets smeared around the pledge's mouth, and his job—now that he's in on the joke—is to leave the bathroom gagging and coughing in order to sell the bit to the next poor schlub in line. And so it goes, until everyone has experienced the terror and hilarity of a near-shit-eating experience.

A similar trick involves coaxing pledges to jump on a nail to prove their commitment to the fraternity. But the nail is made of tinfoil, so if anyone is actually stupid enough to do it—as some inevitably are—the nail crumples harmlessly under their heel.

The truth is, much of what passes for fraternity "secrets" is this now-you-are-in-on-the-joke camaraderie. That and a healthy dose of shared personal humiliation are what constitute the special bond that fraternity brothers share. The sick part is that it actually works. After you've gone through all of these ordeals with a group of guys, you do feel closer to them. And the fact that everyone else in the fraternity has endured the same ego-crushing experiences, even the muscle-bound psychopaths and take-no-shit hard-asses—well, it does create a deep sense of kinship, the feeling of connection that fraternities call brotherhood.

The question is, why would any self-respecting human being allow themselves to be treated like this? What craven need is filled by it? And why, oh why, would anyone want to belong to an organization that requires you to check your dignity so far outside the door?

The answer—for me, and I suspect many of my brethren—was the sheer, brazen fun of it.

Yes, fun.

To outsiders, that sounds ridiculous, I know. How can a continuous assault of physical and psychological abuse be fun? But it is. And it's fun because, whether they want to admit it or not, there is nothing an eighteen-year-old boy wants more in the world than to be pushed to his physical and emotional limits. And, since most boys that age are incapable of pushing themselves to their own limit, they need someone else to help them do it. That's why athletes have trainers and coaches. So, while the external details of a particular initiation ritual may sound sick and twisted, the experience of going through it is "fun" because it tests you, it pushes you into a psychological space you could never get to on your own. It's enervating in a weirdly joyous way, because no matter how bad things get, there's always a choice: you know deep down you could decide you've had enough and walk away. And some people do.

In the pledge class following mine, there was a guy who elected to un-pledge himself, and we were all glad he did. He was easily the largest, strongest guy I'd ever seen—a body-builder hulk of a dude who had a brooding personality and didn't take kindly to being ordered around by people who, in a different setting, would never dream of goading him. Whenever he had to do push-ups, he did them with one arm as a kind of symbolic "fuck you" gesture. With his other hand, while he was pumping away, he'd flash an actual "fuck you" gesture. Everyone thought it was hilarious. And he put up with most of the nonsense dished out during the semester without much fuss. But on the first day of Hell Week, he simply disappeared. According to his pledge brothers, the guy said he'd left because if he didn't, he was afraid he was going to kill somebody. Later, a rumor started that the reason the guy wasn't around on weekends (a sore spot in terms of party participation points) was that someone had tried to shoot him during a bar fight in Flagstaff, and he drove up there every weekend to track the shooter down and kill him.

So no, that guy never made it to the showers, never got a song, and never ate banana shit. And, in retrospect, it's a good thing he didn't.

Defections were rare, though. Peer pressure might have been a factor, of course, but then again, a great deal of misery can be endured, and even enjoyed, when it's shared. That's why a football coach can get his players to run until they puke, but their mothers can't even get them to take out the trash. The fact is: surviving something you didn't think you could handle, or pushing yourself past what you thought were the limits of your own endurance, is . . . fun. Even, and sometimes especially, when people are yelling at you.

Then there's the psychology of it. Everyone knows it's a game, so there's an element of sportsmanship involved. These are the rules: play by them and you will be rewarded, break them and you will be penalized. But above all: enjoy the game.

I remember the night we were ordered to strip to our underwear, then driven out into the middle of the desert, abandoned, and left to our own devices to get back to campus. This is a fairly common fraternity prank, but the sense of loneliness and isolation is especially acute when you're standing alone in your underwear in the middle of the Sonora desert.

The moon was almost full that night, and cast a bluish hue across the landscape. The air was perfectly warm, 80 degrees or so, and there was a slight cooling breeze. Huge saguaro cactuses stood like shadow people all around me, pointing their fat, mangled arms in every possible direction. Bats flew in and out of my field of vision, and there were so many stars that the Milky Way looked like a long, hazy cloud that stretched from horizon to horizon. Yes, I could have been bitten by a rattlesnake, or stabbed in the leg by a cholla cactus, or attacked by a wild pig, or been bitten on the foot by a gila monster. But those threats didn't concern me. From where I stood, I could see the outline of the mountains around Tucson, and I could tell by the city lights which direction to go. I wasn't scared. In fact, the word that comes closest to describing the feeling I had when I looked out across the desert at all those miles of desolate nothing was: freedom.

I didn't have to go back to the fraternity house, after all. I thought about disappearing for a couple of days and making those bastards think I had gotten lost in the desert. Put a scare into them, make them think I might be dead—that they might have killed me. But the moment passed. One of my pledge brothers appeared out of nowhere, then another, then another. We walked until we found a dirt road. Then we followed the road to another road, where we somehow convinced someone to give us a ride. The whole thing was a grand adventure, a shared experience that otherwise never would have happened.

And yes, it was a helluva lot of fun.

CHAPTER 4

During my semester as a pledge, one of the people who made things more fun than not was Russ, the tall, lanky fellow with the perfect tie knot I'd met that first night at the entrance of Delta Chi.

Russ had the right attitude about everything. There are some things worth taking seriously, his demeanor suggested—such as school and public service and basketball—but extracting as much enjoyment as possible out of everything else seemed to be his goal in life. He was the guy who rallied people to do crazy things, like build water-balloon launchers out of surgical tubing and a plastic funnel, then climb on the roof and rain water bombs on the guys sunbathing on the roof of the neighboring fraternity. Or he might instigate a bottle-rocket war inside the halls of the fraternity house, or rally as many people as he could to go from sorority to sorority singing Christmas carols (the sappier the better). Fun was his middle name. As a pledge, even if he was harassing you or giving you a hard time, he let you know with his eyes and a gentle smirk that he didn't really mean it. He was just messing with you. So don't take it seriously. Attitude is everything, his own attitude seemed to suggest. If you're not enjoying yourself—if you're miserable and angry because you're being treated like the scum you are—either your attitude needs adjusting or you're in the wrong place.

Russ was also very good at things I was not. Like dancing.

One of the curious things about attending the University of Arizona is that, as every freshman soon learns, in order to participate fully in the campus's social life, one must learn to dance. Really dance. Country Swing is the dance of choice in those parts, and the importance of knowing how to do it becomes apparent at every party. Things might be going along normally, with people chit-chatting and having a good time. And you might be talking to a pretty girl, thinking you're making some headway, when a "country swing" song suddenly starts to play. (The Marshall Tucker Band's "Fire on the Mountain" or "Can't You See" were staples back in the day.) The young lady you were talking to would then get an excited look on her face and ask you if you knew how to swing? If your answer was no, that would be the last you'd see of her. She'd immediately leave you and go pair up with someone else—usually an older guy who knew what he was doing—and proceed to twirl and spin and strut with that guy, not you.

That never happened to Russ. Because one of the things Russ was famous for on campus was his prowess on the dance floor. By the time I'd met him, he'd already won the campus-wide Country Swing contest twice, and was practicing to defend his title for an unprecedented third year in a row. His dance partner was a tall, gorgeous, long-haired blonde from the popular Gamma Phi Beta sorority, and together they were something to behold. Often, at parties, people would simply clear the floor and form a circle to watch them dance. Country Swing is full of various moves—some simple, some complicated, and some insanely convoluted—that require a certain amount of dedication and practice to master. (When Russ and his partner were getting ready for competitions, they practiced so much they got blisters on their hands. She had sense enough to wear gloves, but like a boxer or basketball player, Russ wrapped his fingers in white adhesive tape to emphasize the fact that he was "training.") Most of the guys I knew were lousy at Country Swing and wanted to get better, because dance skills at the U of A were an important form of social capital. Watching Russ and his partner dance was like attending a master class. Russ and his partner not only knew all the possible moves in the Country Swing repertoire, they made up moves of their own (that's how they won so often), moves so intricate and ingenious that only a fool wouldn't try to steal them.

As a member of Delta Chi, however, I didn't have to steal Russ's moves. All I had to do was listen to him. Every semester he taught Country Swing classes for incoming pledges. But he didn't do it out of the kindness of his heart. He did it because he recognized how socially powerful Country Swing was at the U of A, and he wanted our entire fraternity to be known campus-wide for its superior dance skills. Why? Because that sort of reputation would attract the prettiest girls, yield the best parties, and elevate our fraternity to the top of the school's social pecking order. In other words, it was a strategic move on his part to leverage his skills as a dancer to improve Delta Chi's collective reputation on campus. That, in turn, would attract the highest-quality pledges, which would ensure our house's social dominance on campus for years to come.

To my mind, there was a kind of genius in this plan. And at the same time, I was looking for someone to admire and emulate, someone to model myself after, since I didn't yet know who the hell I was or what I was doing with my life. Russ, on the other hand, seemed to know exactly who he was, what he was doing, and where he was going. To me, he embodied a kind of success I envied. He wasn't just going along with the crowd and doing what everyone else did. He was succeeding on his own terms, in his own way, and doing it with style, charisma, and joy. That, to me, was leadership. That, to me, was strength and character, vision and creativity. He didn't take the easy path, either; his success on the dance floor, and in other areas that interested him—basketball, photography, business, politics—was largely the fruit of discipline and hard work. Those were also the character traits I most wanted to develop in my young self.

At some point, I don't know exactly when, I decided to ally myself with Russ and learn everything I could from him. I consciously chose him as a role model, because of all the people I'd met in college he exhibited the qualities I most admired. He was an iconoclast who was driven to succeed, a genuine character who approached life with more energy and originality than most of the people I knew combined. He was one of those rare people who made life for everyone more fun (unless you happened to be competing against him, in which case he could make your life miserable), and who made you feel better about yourself by simply knowing him. Whatever cocktail of ambition and fortitude and charisma he was drinking, I wanted to drink it too.

The idea of admiring someone, copying them, and integrating character traits of theirs into your own approach to life is not new, of course. Sons copy their fathers. Artists steal ideas and techniques from each other. Athletes and dancers copy each other's moves. It's all part of the give-and-take of personal development, of trying things out in life and finding what works for you. Do it right and you end up assimilating the good, discarding the bad, and forging a unique path of your own. But first, you have to walk a few miles in the other person's footsteps to see how it feels.

Walking in Russ's footsteps wasn't easy. First of all, you had to be willing to make a fool out of yourself at any given moment. One of the greatest (and most infuriating) things about him was that he could pull you out of your own ego, usually by insisting you do something embarrassing or silly, and making you feel like a killjoy if you refused to play along. So, for instance, if you didn't really feel like going out and buying a pumpkin, carving it, putting a speaker in it, placing it on the front stoop, and saying funny things to people as they walked up, he'd be disappointed. But if you caved and did it, he'd make it worth your while by turning the whole thing into a hilarious caper that, in retrospect, you'd be glad you didn't forego.

He was also generous with his time and expertise.

One day, in the spirit of emulation, I asked him to teach me how to tie a tie the way he did. He seemed surprised.

"What, your dad never taught you how to tie a tie?" he chided.

"No, my mom did," I told him.

"So you're using a mom knot?"

"The truth is, I don't wear a tie very often, so I always forget how to do it," I admitted. "I just like the way your tie looks, and was wondering if you could show me."

"Sure," he said, and grabbed two ties out of his closet—one for him, and one for me. He then spent the better part of an hour showing me the knot, and making me tie and re-tie it until I got it right. As it happens, he knew everything there was to know about his tie knot—"It's a full-Windsor, but you have to use the narrow part of the tie and pull it really tight in order to get the length to fall right, or else you end up with a fat knot and the tie comes up short"—and I think he was probably a little flattered that anyone even noticed. He'd learned the knot from his father, who was a lawyer, and he was happy to pass it on to me. To this day I tie my ties the way he taught me that day, and I have yet to meet anyone else on this Earth who does it the same way.

CHAPTER 5

Shortly after my pledge class was initiated, Russ was elected president of the fraternity, to no one's surprise. What was surprising, to me at least, was that I was elected as his secretary. This meant that after the summer break, I would not only be a member of the Delta Chi fraternity, I would be helping to lead it.

Taking such a position was totally uncharacteristic for me. It meant extra duties and responsibilities (more work!), as well as a "seat at the table" for upcoming decisions about the fraternity's future. As I said before, I never was a joiner, nor did I see myself as a follower. But I also didn't see myself as a leader, or the kind of person who aspires to leadership. Like most people, I always assumed I could do a better job than whoever else was in charge, from the president of the United States on down. But—again, like most people—I was never very eager to put my high self-regard to the test. This time I did, however, because it meant building a strategic alliance, and possibly even friendship, with Russ, my new mentor.

A few days after the election, Russ and I were sitting in his room talking. The semester was ending in a few weeks, so I asked him what he was going to be doing over the summer. He wasn't sure, he said, but he thought he might be selling books door-to-door.

"Books? Door-to-door? Why?" I asked.

"I need to make $3,000 this summer," he answered. "Besides, lots of successful people have sold stuff door-to-door. Johnny Carson sold vacuum cleaners."

"Who else?"

"I don't know. But it's supposed to be a great way to develop your sales skills and get used to rejection," he said.

"Why would anyone want to get used to rejection?"

"So when the world kicks you in the ass, it doesn't hurt so much," he replied. "What are you doing this summer?"

"I have no idea," I said.

"Do you want to make $3,000?" ($3,000 in 1979 was equivalent to almost $12,000 in 2017.)

"Sure, if I could."

"Then you should do it too," he said.

"No thanks," I said. That summer, another lucrative opportunity awaited me somewhere, somehow, I was certain. I just hadn't quite arranged it yet.

Russ could be very persuasive, however, and he already had more influence on me than was probably healthy. So it didn't take long before I started thinking that if Russ was selling books door-to-door this summer, maybe I should consider doing it too, crazy as it sounds. "Emulate those you admire" was the only surefire key to success I knew of at the time, so it suddenly didn't seem like such an outlandish idea.

"Tell you what," he said. "There's a meeting tomorrow where they explain everything. If you like what you hear, great. If you don't, that's fine too. But there's no harm in hearing them out, is there?"

If my current self could give a tiny piece of advice to my former self, it would go something like this: When someone appeals to your sense of reason by claiming there's "no harm" in something, beware, because what they're really doing is calling you a coward. The question might as well be, "Are you such a coward that listening to someone is going to hurt you?" The answer might very well be yes, but adding that tag question "is there?" puts you on the spot. If you disagree, you have to come up with an immediate example of the harm that could be caused. But the harm itself might be unimaginable, which means you literally can't imagine it. Disagreeing also puts you on the defensive, because they can double-down on the cowardice angle and tell you that you're making a big deal out of nothing. It's another way of saying, "Don't be a wuss." If you agree, on the other hand, that no harm can come of it, the tag question makes it seem as if the whole "no harm" thing was your idea, and that the harm itself couldn't have been foreseen. So when the harm comes—the harm that previously couldn't happen and no one could foresee—you have no one to blame but yourself.

Because you listened when you should have run.

CHAPTER 6

The meeting was held in an empty room somewhere in the bowels of the business building. About a dozen other students showed up, some holding the yellow flyer that had been been distributed all over campus posing the same question Russ had asked me: "Want to earn $3,000 this summer?"

The dude running the meeting was a soft-spoken, unassuming guy named Steve. He did not look at all like a paragon of success. He had longish, stringy hair, and wore baggy shorts and a t-shirt—an outfit I later learned was "strategic" because it made him look more like a student and less like a corporate shill. He introduced himself and said he had recently graduated from some school in the Midwest, where he'd paid his way through college by working summers for an outfit called the Southwestern Company. The company employed thousands of college students like us all over the country, he explained, and working for them was, he said, the best experience of his life. He'd come to the University of Arizona to share that experience with us, he said, then reached for a fat, gold book the size of a large dictionary.

The book was called the *Volume Library*, and he explained that it was like a mini-encyclopedia, one that distilled an entire high-school education into a single, miraculous volume. It had sections on American history, world history, math, physics, geology, astronomy, and a number of other subjects, all illustrated with captivating photos and printed on the highest-quality paper. As he flipped through the sections, he asked questions like, "How much easier do you think high school would have been with a book like this in your house?" and "Can you see how a book like this would be useful?"

It was impressive. To understand how impressive, you have to imagine the world the way it was in 1979. The Internet and personal computers did not exist. The only way to accumulate knowledge of any kind was to read magazines and newspapers, watch TV, check out a book from the library, or consult the almighty encyclopedia. Before the internet came along in the mid-1990s, most middle-American homes had a bookshelf dedicated to either the *World Book* encyclopedia or *Encyclopedia Britannica* (EB). I grew up with the latter, a 28-volume set of authoritatively bound volumes that took up an entire bookshelf in our house. The complete set contained roughly fifty-million words, weighed about 130 pounds, and cost more than a thousand dollars.

The value of having a set of encyclopedias in your house was that it gave you entry into worlds of knowledge that were otherwise difficult or impossible to access. The *Encyclopedia Britannica* was the Google of its day. If I ever had a question about anything my parents couldn't answer, their reflexive admonition to me was "look it up." If I was ever bored, my dad would hand me a volume of the EB and give me the same advice that Merlin gave King Arthur, "The best antidote for boredom is to learn something." (Regarding boredom: The other thing you have to imagine is a world without video games, a world where, on a rainy day, there was absolutely nothing else to do but pick up a book or play a board game, of which there were only three: Clue, Risk, and Monopoly. For a kid in 1979, battling boredom was a constant fight, and sometimes leafing through the EB was the best way to alleviate it, if only for an hour or so.)

The EB was also helpful for writing school papers and settling arguments. It contained facts. It had authority. If you read it in the EB, you could trust the information was accurate and true. And if, by reading the EB, you knew things other kids didn't, it made you "smarter" than them, though not always more popular. If you read too much of the EB, people might start calling you a "know-it-all," because you had the magical ability to pull arcane bits of knowledge out of thin air—knowledge that, when challenged, could be backed up by the EB itself. So if, for instance, you were arguing with a kid who did not have access to an encyclopedia, and did not see the value of alleviating one's boredom by flipping randomly through its glossy thick pages, chances are the argument would end with him calling you an "egghead" or "Poindexter," or "nerd," right before he hit you. Knowledge has always been a dangerous thing, because it leaves you defenseless when the fighting starts.

I'm sure my parents bought the EB believing that such a valuable educational tool would give me, their son, a competitive advantage in both school and life. Indeed, the EB's stated goal wasn't just to provide folks with a handy educational tool, but to "systematize all human knowledge." According to our man Steve, the *Volume Library* performed a similar intellectual miracle by consolidating all the important stuff one learns in high school into a single, easy-to-use book that sold for a fraction of the cost of a set of encyclopedias.

"How much do you think a book like this is worth?" he asked.

"$200?"

"$300?"

"What if I told you this book could be yours for $79? Does that sound like a fair price?" he asked, subtly nodding his head yes.

Several of the assembled students nodded yes along with him. "At a price like that, how many of these books do you think you could sell in a day?" he asked.

"Ten," someone offered.

"Fifteen, maybe."

The guesses went all the way up to twenty books a day. Who wouldn't want one?, the thinking seemed to be. It was a no-brainer, especially if you couldn't afford a whole set of encyclopedias.

"Do you think you could sell two a day?" Steve asked. Everyone laughed. Of course! Two a day would be a piece of cake!

"Well, if you want to make $3,000 this summer, that's all you have to do," Steve said matter-of-factly. "Two books a day is all it takes." He went on to explain that selling ten a day was unrealistic—that a feat like that would put you in the Southwestern Company Hall of Fame—but that he and a lot of other veteran booksellers averaged five or six volumes a day, which meant they made closer to $10,000 in a single summer.

By conventional estimates, $10,000 in 1979 dollars is equivalent to about $31,000 in 2017 dollars. But in 1979, before the Reagan Revolution and its accompanying decimation of state support for higher education, that kind of money went a lot further for students. Out-of-state tuition at the University of Arizona was only $1,100 a semester at the time, and in-state students could practically pay for college with the spare change in their parents' ashtray. Unfortunately for students in 2017, out-of-state tuition at the U of A has ballooned to $36,017, and the total estimated cost of attendance is now $51,417 per year. Even Bill Gates's ashtray can't pay for that.

In 1979, however, it was entirely conceivable to pay for a year of tuition with the earnings from a decent summer job. One that made, say, $3,000.

But $10,000? That was an unthinkable amount of cash. And yet, here was this conspicuously unimpressive fellow telling me it was not only possible, but that he'd done it! As I sat listening to his presentation, I was one of those who figured I could sell about ten Volume Libraries a day, if I put my mind to it. If this guy could do it, I could sell five or six a day too, I was sure, given that I had everything he didn't: clean tennis shoes, better-fitting shorts, a shirt with a collar, and a decent haircut. I also had experience: I'd sold magazine subscriptions door-to-door, and for years had a paper route that required knocking on eighty doors a month to collect the money customers owed me. I didn't like it, but I'd done it, and figured I could do it again.

Steve went on to explain how the program worked. First, we'd receive a week of sales training at the company's facility in Nashville, Tennessee. Then, after completing our training, we'd be assigned to a city somewhere in the Midwest (he couldn't say exactly where), and taken in by a family that would lodge us practically for free out of the goodness of their hearts, with continuous support from a "regional manager" who would make sure our "experience" was as rewarding and profitable as possible. He added that Southwestern book-selling experience on a college graduate's résumé was a surefire way to rise to the top of the heap in the great American job hunt, since there are companies that look specifically for that type of experience when hiring. If you could sell books door-to-door, the implication was, you could do anything.

So, to recap: $3,000 to $10,000 for three months of work, invaluable sales experience, professional kudos up the wazoo, all for selling something we, as college students, obviously believed in: the value of a good education. Plus, the job itself was a gateway to future success; all we had to do was walk through those gold-bound gates, and the American Dream was ours for the taking.

I left that meeting pumped, jacked, intoxicated by my own personal potential. Here was a kick-ass opportunity to go out and do something extraordinary, something other college students could only dream of. All it took was a little hard work and a willingness to ignore that nagging voice in the back of my head alerting me that possibly, just possibly, the whole thing sounded a bit too good to be true. This was not difficult, because at that point in my life the little voice that should have been warning me was annoyingly faint, barely a whisper, an unreliable guide if there ever was one. Instead, there was another voice shouting quite loudly that *I could make $10,000!* just by convincing the good people of the Midwest to read a little more. How hard was that? Not hard at all, especially for someone with my extraordinary talents. And even if it did get hard, I had just survived Hell Week, for chrissakes. I was, for all practical purposes—and even some impractical ones—invincible.

After the meeting, Russ and I met and compared notes. He was less fixated on the money than the fact that door-to-door sales would be "good experience" and look impressive on his résumé. I was more attracted to the possibility of making a ton of dough, and to the idea of making a decision that would appear to others as if my life suddenly had purpose and direction. We both had reservations about this Steve guy, but we both agreed that if he could sell books, so could we—only better.

Then, the kicker. "Hey, let's do it together." Russ proposed. "Let's tell them we're a package deal. Wherever you go, I go, and vice-versa. It'll be fun. It'll be an *adventure*."

That word: *adventure*. Is there a more intoxicating word in the English language? The promise of adventure is the promise of surprise, of exhilaration, of life lived to the fullest. It's a road trip, safari, and beer commercial all rolled into one.

Suddenly, what appealed to me most of all about the idea of selling books door-to-door in some godforsaken town in the Midwest was that it would be an adventure with Russ. We'd be in it together. By spending the summer in each other's company, I'd get to know him better, he'd get to know me, and by the end of it we'd be the best of friends. Buddies! And whatever happened, however weird or whacked, from the surreal to the sublime, we'd come back with money in our pockets and a *story to tell*.

CHAPTER 7

"So, does this mean you won't be coming home *at all* for the summer," my mother asked, followed by, "and does that mean we won't see you until *Thanksgiving*?

"Are you *sure* this is what you want to do?" was my father's question.

Neither of my parents seemed too concerned that I planned to drive half-way across the country with strangers to meet some more strangers who were going to be sending me out in the world to spend my days meeting still more strangers, some of whom might not take kindly to a white kid banging on their door and trying to sell them something. I'm not sure they understood what I was going to be doing, which may have been partly due to the fact that I didn't really know what I'd be doing either. Or perhaps they did understand, but figured I'd flame out in a couple of weeks and come home, so it wasn't worth getting worked up about. My father allowed as how he'd tried to sell vacuum cleaners door-to-door once upon a time, but it didn't go well.

"I lasted a day," he said.

As rites of passage go, selling anything door-to-door used to be thought of as something so difficult that few people could endure it, let alone succeed at it. Many people tried, and most, like my father, failed. The very idea of knocking on doors and talking to people terrifies most people. For my father's generation, that fear may have had something to do with Arthur Miller's disturbing play, "Death of a Salesman," in which the traveling salesman Willy Loman slowly succumbs to irrelevance, dementia and, eventually, death.

Nobody wants to be Willy Loman.

But for my generation, door-to-door sales straddled a curious paradox of capitalism. On one hand, door-to-door sales offers anyone the opportunity to embrace the so-called "entrepreneurial spirit" by "starting their own business," becoming their "own boss," in pursuit of the "American Dream." On the other hand, it does not offer a guaranteed salary (most door-to-door businesses are run on 100% commission), it requires a great deal of dedication, especially in the beginning, and the only way to succeed at it is through an extraordinarily high level of self-discipline. When door-to-door sales were at their peak, there was no excuse not to have a job, because you could always sell door-to-door. But the fear of selling door-to-door, particularly the humiliation of constant rejection, was enough to motivate generations of men to look for other, steadier work—work that didn't require so much self-motivation. Most people, it seems, would rather hate their boss than hate themselves.

Nevertheless, before the days when one could click on a computer screen and have the object of their desire arrive the next day, many products were sold primarily by salespeople traveling door-to-door. If a smartly dressed adult knocked on your door in the middle of the afternoon, chances are they were selling Encyclopedia Britannica, Electrolux or Kirby vacuum cleaners, Fuller brushes, Amway cleaning products, or Avon cosmetics. Electrolux salesmen were famous for dumping fistfuls of dirt onto people's carpets, then sucking up the mess in a demonstration that took people from horror (that man just poured dirt on my carpet!) to relief (whew, that man just cleaned my carpet), to amazement (that vacuum cleaner costs how much?). Likewise, the "Avon lady" was famous for giving bored housewives a "free" makeover that was impossible to replicate without a drawer full of Avon products. Alternatively, you could get your mascara and skin-tightener from the Mary Kay cosmetics lady, who, if she was a top salesperson, would roll up in a custom-painted pink Cadillac. The car itself was a strange sort of status symbol for women, because the only way to get one was to rise to the top of the Mary Kay food chain, and if you could do that, it meant you were a woman of independent means, unconstrained by the sort of person who would drive, say, a black Caddy. This was back when the Cadillac brand was the ultimate symbol of wealth, and wealth itself was the domain of men. In many ways, driving a pink Cadillac was the ultimate feminist fuck you, a powder-puff repudiation of the dominant male power structure. To own one meant you weren't owned by a man. Except that so-called Mary Kay "Grand Achievers" did not actually own their cars; they simply earned the right to drive them as long as they kept their sales numbers sufficiently high. If they didn't, they lost the car and the prestige that came with it, forcing them to endure the shame of life at the wheel of a more prosaically colored vehicle. If you were a Mary Kay salesperson who drove a blue Toyota, you clearly had work to do.

Allowing such people to come into your home to deliver a sales presentation was not unusual in the 1960s and 1970s. The airwaves had yet to be saturated with stories of murder and mayhem, and stories of child abduction, pedophilia, human trafficking, and other assorted human perversions were mercifully rare. The most popular song in the country at the time was "Hot Stuff" by Donna Summer, a thumping disco number about a lonely woman who wants a man, any man, to sleep with her: "Wanna share my love with a warm-blooded lover, wanna bring a wild man back home," she croons, her only apparent stipulation being that he is not an actual reptile. Likewise, the most popular TV show in the land was *Three's Company*, a comedy about a straight man living with two beautiful women and *not* having sex with them, ha ha ha. Everyone thinks Jack is gay, but surprise!, *he's not*!

It was, as they say, a more innocent (though some might say ignorant) time. A housewife trapped in a suburban tract home all day with three young children and a yappy dog did not immediately assume the man in the suit knocking on the door was going to rape and murder her. On the contrary, he was often invited in as a welcome break from her oppressive monotony. And, as his true purpose was to help make her life easier, she might even feel grateful that he stopped by, considering that opportunities for her to go out and shop for a vacuum cleaner were few and far between. Amazon did not exist then, nor did Target, Best Buy, Costco, or Sam's Club. Walmart had yet to carpet the landscape with megastores. K-Mart was just getting started. Indeed, if you didn't live within fifty miles of a Sears & Roebuck store, buying something as simple as a vacuum cleaner could be a significant logistical challenge. Sure, you could order one from the Sears catalogue, but you never knew what you were going to get. The thing might be a piece of junk. So if some nice salesman was willing to schlep the thing to your door, and gave you a chance to see the machine in action (Electrolux vacuums had an excellent reputation), why wouldn't you at least hear him out?

Certainly, there were some door-to-door visitors who were not always welcome. In the Midwest and South, so-called "Bible thumpers" often roamed the neighborhoods selling Bibles. Which was fine if you needed a Bible, but not so great if you already had one, didn't need another one, and it had been a while since you picked up the one you already own. Likewise, Jehovah's Witnesses and Mormon missionaries were deployed door-to-door to proselytize for their cause. These folks were easy to spot, because they usually dressed in black suits with white shirts and shiny black shoes, exactly the sort of footwear most people would not pick to walk around in all day. They also traveled in pairs. If they approached you, you got a double dose of righteousness tempered only somewhat by the fact that these kids were barely out of their teens and hadn't yet experienced many of the cruel ironies their God is so fond of.

But in the late 1970s, the people to watch out for—the ones who most Americans were genuinely afraid of, and who marked the beginning of the end of door-to-door enterprises of all kinds—were the Moonies.

"Moonies" was the celestially pejorative term used to describe followers of the Rev. Sung Myung Moon, a South Korean minister and founder of the Unification Church, whose spiritual teachings began infiltrating the American consciousness in the mid-1970s. Moon's name alone was enough to cause alarm in certain parts of the country, since California was being governed at the time by Jerry "Governor Moonbeam" Brown; the counterculture's most outrageous musical anarchist, Frank Zappa, had named his child Moon Unit; and the moon itself was as far as humans could imagine traveling without being sucked into the inky void of intergalactic nothingness. The moon was way "out there," and so was Rev. Moon. He offered a version of Christianity tinged with Eastern mysticism that appealed to young people dissatisfied with traditional Western religions. In 1974, Moon gave several speeches in New York, at Madison Square Garden and Yankee Stadium, that attracted thousands of current and would-be followers. He then doubled-down on the spectacle by holding a series of mass weddings, during which thousands of couples were married at the same time. The hard-to-swallow part was that most of these unions were hand-chosen by Rev. Moon himself, and many of couples had not even met until the day of their wedding.

Images of these vast swarms of people—men dressed in black, women in white—appeared in every newspaper and news program in the country. The images themselves were threatening because they smacked of communism (even though Moon deemed communism "evil,") and represented a direct threat to the idea of a conventional Christian wedding, wherein one man and one woman are united through God, not thousands. Also unnerving was the fact that those attracted to the teachings of the Unification Church tended to be middle and upper-middle-class white kids who appeared to be turning their back on traditional American values. The church got so popular, so fast, that it was deemed a cult by most people. So when a Moonie knocked on your door, the smart thing to do was hide, lest you be sucked into their intoxicating vortex and lost to your family and friends forever.

Fear of Moonies was magnified by the fact that Moonies tended to be young, attractive, zealous, and slightly creepy. The creep factor came from the beatific look on their faces, a look that suggested they were intensely happy. Way too happy. So happy it was scary.

In America, the right to pursue happiness is one of the country's founding principles, but those who claim to have found it are immediately suspect. They must be brainwashed, or on drugs, or a little too fond of the bottle. What else could account for their apparent lack of misery? Spiritual happiness is the most suspicious happiness of all, because it suggests that the happy person is no longer struggling with the eternal tension between good and evil, and is no longer being tortured by life's constant agonies and disappointments. To be sure, nothing is quite so off-putting to a middle-aged adult than a cheerful young person who thinks they have found the "answer" to life, and is eager to share the joy of their nascent wisdom. In the late 1970s, thousands of such youthful proselytizers for Moon's church blanketed the countryside, knocking on doors and generally confirming people's suspicions that an evil cult of intolerable happiness was overtaking the country. For those of us trying to sell other paths to happiness and fulfillment (i.e., reading, knowledge, education), the worst thing that could happen was to be mistaken for a Moonie.

CHAPTER 8

The day after finals ended in the spring semester of 1979, Russ and I climbed into the back seat of Southwestern Steve's brown Dodge Dart for the 1,613-mile drive across the country to Nashville, Tennessee, where we were scheduled to be trained and, a week later, deployed to an unnamed city "somewhere in the Midwest."

As I recall, Steve's car was at least ten years old, and the stitching in the seats was starting to rip. For someone who claimed to make as much money as he did, it was not the sort of car one would expect him to be driving. The car's drab, utilitarian shade of brown—somewhere between a shopping bag and pile of mulch—was particularly depressing. It was the color of boredom, a chromatic confession that the driver had succumbed to the forces of stagnation and compromise, a statement of complete and utter neutrality. It was not a "notice me" color; it was a "please don't look at me" color, an "I am ashamed to be alive" color, a hue intended to divert attention rather than attract it.

This was entirely intentional, as it turned out. I know this because I asked Steve flat out, in a joking way, "If you're such a great salesman, why do you drive such a shitty car?"

He laughed, then explained the logic behind it. According to Steve, his specialty was selling books to people in rural areas, particularly farmers. Driving up to a farm in a flashy car would be counterproductive, he explained, because it would be too conspicuous and immediately make people suspicious of him. "There's usually a dirt road, and they can see the dust from my car a quarter of a mile away," he said. "They don't like people arriving unannounced, and they especially don't like 'city people' driving up out of nowhere. The more unassuming your car is the better."

I had to hand it to him: If driving an unassuming car was his goal, he had achieved it.

"So who else is coming?" I asked as I buckled my seatbelt.

"You're it," Steve said cheerfully.

"We're it? As in, the only ones?"

"Yep."

"Does that make us special or stupid?" Russ remarked.

"Maybe a little bit of both," Steve said with a friendly chuckle. "We'll find out."

So, after dozens of meetings with hundreds of people, it appeared that Russ and I were the only students from the University of Arizona that Steve had managed to recruit. When you learn a thing like that at the beginning of a 24-hour drive, you have a lot of time to reflect on what it might mean. Did all of those other kids know something we didn't? Were we the bravest people on campus, or the most gullible? Did all those other kids find better summer jobs, or did they all simply recognize that this was the worst possible option available to them? Were we climbing the ladder of ultimate success, or scraping the bottom of the desperation barrel?

"Book-selling isn't for everyone," was Steve's take, a master-of-the-obvious answer given his apparent lack of recruiting success. He told us we were made of "stronger stuff" than most college students, that we were obviously "ambitious," and that it took a great deal of "courage" to do what we were doing.

There is often a fine line between courage and stupidity, however, and I feared we had crossed it somewhere. I did not feel courageous; I felt like a guy who was well on his way to doing something he might very well regret. It was the summer after my first year in college, after all, and back home all my high-school friends were going to be getting together for party after party, comparing notes and wondering (I imagined) why I wasn't there. I grew up a few blocks from the beach in a little seaside village twenty minutes north of San Diego. Our summers were spent going back and forth between tennis courts and the beach, with the occasional sailing trip to Catalina Island thrown in, and at least two or three excursions south of the border into Mexico, where we feasted on lobster and beer, made bonfires on the beach, and swam naked in the Pacific Ocean, whose warm waters bathed us in their amniotic bliss. That's what I was missing. Day after day of idyllic idleness. Girls in bikinis tanning themselves, slick with oil, their top straps seductively undone. Surfing every morning and evening, when the sea is calm and the swells are high. Searing crimson sunsets and evenings walking barefoot on the beach at the edge of the surf line, where the water comes just close enough to kiss your feet, then returns silently from whence it came. The smell of the sea, thick with salt mist and eucalyptus. Tender kisses under the moonlight. The strum of a guitar. A gentle beer buzz. Stars over the ocean and, in the distance, the green light of a ship crawling slowly across the horizon.

Yes, that's what I was missing—all that and more.

It did however give me a certain perverse pleasure to think of my high-school buddies gathered around a campfire at the beach discussing the mystery of my absence.

"He's doing what?"
"That's all I know."
"Where?"
"Dunno."
"Why?"
"Dunno."
"When's he coming back?"
"Dunno."
"Door-to-door, you say?"
"Yep."
"That sucks."
"Yes, mightily."
"Glad I'm not him."
"Me too."
"What's he thinking?"
"Dunno."

No one would understand, I was sure. My home town is the sort of place people try to get to, not run away from. And yet here I was, hurtling across the desert at eighty miles per hour in the opposite direction. Why? There was no easy answer, just a constellation of circumstances that somehow landed me in a car traveling across the country with two guys I barely knew, only one of whom I actually trusted.

CHAPTER 9

I-10 from Tucson to Dallas is the dullest, most desolate stretch of interstate in the country. It's a highway designed to sap people's spirits and make them question not only the meaning of life, but the very existence of it. If the road weren't there, and you weren't in a car, chances are you'd be dead in a day. Once the Sonora desert's saguaros recede in the rearview, there is nothing taller than a tumbleweed for two hundred miles, and the sun hurls hot daggers of misery from above. For hours, the only movement in your field of vision might be a small dust-devil tornado or a lone hawk in the distance, riding the wind in search of a critter without enough sense to hide under a rock until the sun goes down. How anyone in history ever survived this trek without a 64-ounce Gatorade between their legs, I do not know.

The hiss of tires on asphalt; the roar of wind through an open window; REO Speedwagon playing too loud on the radio, too often—these are the sounds I remember from that journey. We talked, I'm sure, but about what I could not tell you. In those days, there were no handy devices available to pass the time, no games to play, no distractions other than conversation and music. You either listened to the stereo or you didn't. You either talked or you didn't. On long drives across the country, mostly you just stared out the window and, like that hawk, rode the current of your thoughts wherever they took you. People have mostly lost this ability to be bored and not bored at the same time, to suspend their need for entertainment in a zen-like state of pointless contemplation, simply because there is nothing better to do. More's the pity, because knowing how to combat boredom with the power of one's mind is a handy skill to have.

We started driving in the morning, so I assumed we would be stopping somewhere along the way to sleep for the night, probably in Dallas or somewhere thereabouts. When the subject came up a few hours into our trip, however, Steve informed us that no, we were going to be driving straight through, rotating in three-hour driving shifts, because there was a meeting in Nashville at ten a.m. that we needed to attend. If we stopped only for gas, and didn't dawdle, he estimated we could make it there with an hour to spare, barring any unforeseen complications.

And so we drove.

At 3 a.m., somewhere near the border of Texas and Arkansas, Russ pulled over to the side of the road and punched me in the shoulder; it was my turn to drive. We wasted no time on these changeovers. The rule, however, was that the driver-to-be had to do twenty pushups and run in place for ten seconds before getting behind the wheel. In the glare of the headlights I did my twenty, hopped up, ran in place for a few seconds to get my blood flowing, then slipped into the driver's seat.

I didn't mind the 3 a.m. to 6 a.m. shift. In fact, I volunteered for that time slot. In my early teens I had a newspaper route that required waking up at 4:30 a.m. and riding my bike a mile away to deliver the *San Diego Union*, alone, in the dark, in a manner that today would be considered unthinkable, immoral, and probably illegal. Every morning, I loaded eighty papers into my saddlebags and rode down a long, winding hill as fast as I could, wheels wobbling, wind in my face, in a daily attempt to beat my record delivery time. Being alone, awake, and active while everyone else in the world was asleep gave me the invigorating illusion that I had a head start on the day, that I had accomplished something before most people had even opened their eyes. The best part was right before dawn, when the blue fringe of the coming day would start to appear in the Eastern sky. Until then, it was always serenely quiet. The only noise was the soft rumble of the nearby surf, which in my home town was more-or-less constant, like the background hiss of the universe. Then a bird or two would chirp, the avian conversation would start, and soon it seemed as if every bird in town suddenly woke up to cheer the coming day. That was always a happy/sad moment, the sad part being that I had to give the world back to everyone else; the happy part being that I had finished my route and could now go get some breakfast.

By "breakfast," I mean stopping in at the 7-11 to pick up either a Hostess fruit pie (cherry usually, but sometimes apple) or a package of Suzy Q's, a close cousin to the Hostess Twinkie that was discontinued for many years but reintroduced in 2016 with the vaguely threatening catch-phrase, "She's Back!"

A Suzy Q was/is two rectangles of a chocolaty-ish spongy substance that isn't quite cake, but in a different way than the not-quite-cake-like substance of a Twinkie. The difference, if I had to guess, is that they put more rubber into the Suzy Q mix. In between these rectangles is a layer of creamy Crisco fluff stuff, which, to my tongue, always tasted different from the fluff stuff inside a Twinkie. It was supposedly the same, but I always thought it had a bit more body than Twinkie fluff, as if they threw a little extra rubber into that mix as well. Though Suzy Q's never enjoyed as much popularity as the Twinkie, in my view it was a superior snack cake because you could eat it by squishing the cakes together and running your tongue along the outside to lap up the fluff stuff that oozed out. It didn't have icing, like a cupcake, but it had size and heft, which, for a growing boy, made it an ideal illicit breakfast.

Anyway, since my paper route days I have always enjoyed those pre-dawn hours when the rest of the world is deep in REM, dreaming of the day to come, the day I am already living.

While Russ and Steve slept, I drove through an alien part of the country, on a stretch of road so dark it looked like a wormhole in space. There were no lights or other signs of civilization outside, just an endless ribbon of road that seemed to appear magically out of the infinite blackness ahead.

Around 5 a.m., I noticed that the needle on the gas gauge had dipped below a quarter of a tank, so I started looking for a place to pull off and re-fuel. It had been half an hour since I'd seen anything remotely close to a freeway exit, so I felt confident that a roadside oasis would be coming up soon.

Minutes and miles went by. The needle was now below an eighth of a tank. Still, nothing. Just darkness and road, save for the occasional semi across the median in the two lanes headed the other direction. We seemed to be the only car on the road headed east, and east was looking less and less like a promising direction every minute. Where was the Shell station in my imagination? The friendly gas-and-go outpost conveniently located a hundred yards off the freeway, in plain sight, with a mini-mart and a bathroom and a rotisserie of greasy hot dogs spinning for who knows how long, and coffee, much-needed coffee, in large Styrafoam cups with flimsy plastic lids that don't quite fit? The kind of freeway pit stop that appears with depressing regularity in every other part of the country. This is America, I thought—and in America, these places are *everywhere*.

Except here. Wherever here was. I still don't know. All I know is that when the gas needle dipped into the red danger zone, I woke Steve and Russ.

"Guys, I think we have a situation."

Steve was in the front seat, next to me. When I told him how low the gas was, he leaned over to see the gauge himself. "Yep, we've got a situation," he confirmed. "If we don't find a gas station in about ten miles, we're in some deep doo-doo."

The sun was just starting to come up at that point, illuminating the land around us. It was farmland as far as the eye could see, the kind of land where Steve's people lived. Vast tracts of corn and soybeans stretched to the horizon. Row after row of vegetation whizzed by like slats in a window blind. Every few miles there was a road, but it was inevitably made of dirt and went nowhere. Though we couldn't see any evidence of it, Steve assured us that there were people out there somewhere. He speculated that, if worst came to worst, we could hike to the nearest farmhouse and ask for some gas. Russ fretted that he had to "take a dump," and warned that if we were stranded on the side of the road he was going to be forced to defecate al fresco. I suggested that, rather than walk, we try to drive to the nearest farmhouse, wherever that might be. Steve didn't like that idea, however, because if we ran out of gas off the main road, we'd really be screwed.

Besides, he wanted to try something else first.

Under the dashboard was a CB radio, which until that point had simply been a box with some complicated-looking knobs on it with a microphone attached by a curly coil of thick black wire. Thus far Steve had not used the radio, and I didn't know how. He reached over and turned the radio on, then twiddled a couple of knobs. Occasional bursts of static hiss came from the box, and every once in a while a lone trucker blurted a couple of unintelligible words.

"Hey, we got a Kojak with a Kodak near the 23-yard line."

"Go ahead, lady breaker."

"I got a Wally knittin' sweaters."

In the days before the internet and cellphones, CB radios were how truckers on the nation's highways kept in contact with each other. They developed their own language, a sort of hillbilly slang that was virtually impossible for the average listener to decipher. Unfortunately, if you didn't know trucker lingo, it was considered bad form to get on the radio and just start talking in plain English. But we had no other choice.

Steve grabbed the microphone and thought about what to say. "I just bought this thing and I've never used it," he said. "But here goes."

He pushed the button on the side of the microphone and said, "Breaker, breaker, you got a noob here running on fumes. We need to find a gas station fast. Lookin' for some help."

A few seconds went by and it didn't sound like anyone had heard us. Then there was a crackle and some hiss, and a man's voice said, "Roger that, noob. East or westbound?"

"East on the I-20," Steve said.

There was a pause, then, "Noob, what's your lollipop?"

We all three looked at each other, puzzled.

"Did you say lollipop?" Steve asked tentatively.

"Your mile marker, noob! What's your mile marker?" the voice shot back, then the guy laughed like we were idiots. Which, in this realm, we definitely were.

We waited until a mile marker went by and said, "Looks like mile marker 132."

Then there was another crackle and the word went out: "Breaker, this is the Flying Dutchman. I got an eastbound noob sailing on air looking for go juice at the 132."

Ten or fifteen seconds of silence, then "Roger that Dutch, this is the Abominable Snowman. There's motion lotion a mile north of the slab at 134. Tell 'em to turn left and trust us," he added, chuckling.

"Thanks Snowman. Keep your black stack smokin'."

"Always, Dutch. Always."

The upshot of all that, according to the Flying Dutchman, was that there was a gas station about a mile off the road two miles ahead of us. All we had to do was get off at exit 134, turn left, and, like the man said, trust him. He couldn't guarantee they'd be open that early, but he did sort of guarantee that he wasn't messing with us.

Half a mile off the interstate, we weren't so sure. The road itself was a crumbling chunk of old concrete that had been patched a thousand times with squiggly lines of bubbling black tar. There were no signs indicating "gas, food" or any other indication that salvation lay in the direction we were headed. But we had no other choice. We were so low on gas we couldn't turn back. If the truckers had been toying with us, leading us astray for the cruel, wicked fun of it, we were screwed. We started scanning the landscape for some sort of building or other sign of civilization, ideally a farmhouse we could hike to for help if we had to. But there were no human structures; just a whole lot of green and nothing in between.

Then we saw it. A small gas station up ahead, precisely where the truckers said it would be. The owner was just opening up as we pulled in, and I'm pretty sure we rolled in on an empty tank for the last hundred yards or so. At least that's how I remember it.

Back on the road, Steve thought the courteous thing to do was get on the radio and thank the Flying Dutchman and the Abominable Snowman for their help. When he did, there was no answer. They were long gone, out of range, headed in the opposite direction. And we were on our way to Nashville, with no time to spare.

CHAPTER 10

In my imagination, we were going to roll up to the Southwestern Company headquarters at ten a.m. and enter a gleaming modern skyscraper with high ceilings and slick marble floors. A huge reception desk would guard the executive suites like the sanctuaries they were, and the company's logo would be etched on the wall in fat, gold letters that communicated power and permanence. In my mind's eye, the building was going to be a shining monument to the power of books and the importance of a good education, an edifice that reflected values I believed in and had pledged to support. Smartly dressed executives would welcome us with firm handshakes and invite us to join them in a private conference room stocked with mountains of gooey pastries and plenty of freshly brewed coffee, all free for the taking. (The fact that I was hungry and tired may have influenced the details of this particular fantasy.) There, these smart and dedicated professionals would share with us the secrets to book-selling success and fill us in on details of the business known only to trusted associates, people who had demonstrated their allegiance to company by, say, driving 1,600 miles across the country in 24 hours with hardly any sleep to attend a meeting that would have made everyone's life a lot easier if it had simply been scheduled a day or two later.

Instead, we pulled into the parking lot of a roadside motel so innocuous that Best Western hadn't even endorsed it. The walls and doors were painted toothpaste blue, and the steel pillars holding the structure up were orange, as if the motel's management had bought their paint from a store specializing in 1950s clichés. There was no pool. There were no amenities to speak of other than "color TV." The rooms smelled like disinfectant—suggesting, of course, that something had been infecting them. It was the kind of place a Hollywood location scout would think was perfect for scenes involving sketchy characters who rent rooms by the hour, or where drug dealers on the run are holed up before the inevitable shootout.

We made our way to the lobby, where a few dozen other bedraggled students were assembled, waiting for something to happen. Tired, bored, dirty, and disheveled, it looked more like a scene from a Dickens novel than a collection of America's most ambitious and amazing college students. Many of them wore t-shirts or sweatshirts from their alma mater—Kansas State, University of Illinois, Old Dominion, George Mason, Butler, Texas Tech, etc.—but most chose not to advertise their school affiliation. There were no Ivy-leaguers present, either, a puzzling discrepancy given the company's alleged reputation for enhancing collegiate résumés.

Russ took one look at this bunch and remarked, "So this is the A team?"

It was a motley-looking crew, to be sure. But one of the reasons I admired Russ was his ability to see the best in people, to look beyond the surface of their skin or the cost of their clothes and recognize their potential, the part of themselves that most people hide beneath layers of pretention and bullshit. He seemed to see it in me, and I appreciated it. Hell, I gave up my summer to get more of his validation, to bathe in the aura of someone who, I thought, could bring out the best in me as well. The more I got to know him, though, the more I realized how fundamental this character trait was to his essential nature, and why he had such an outsized impact on the people he met. When Russ met someone and shook their hand, it was as if he saw not just the person who stood before him, but the person they wanted to become. He sensed their insecurities, but the look in his eye was one of reassurance, a subconscious signal that he did not represent a threat. On the contrary, he somehow managed to convey in seconds, through eye contact and a smile, that he could help them become the best version of themselves. The weird part was that the people he spoke to also seemed to sense this, and wanted to become the version of themselves that Russ saw, the version reflected in his implicit faith and trust in them. It was more than charisma; it was an ability to connect with people in a way they secretly longed for but resisted most of the time. Somehow, in a matter of seconds, Russ could cut through a person's reflexive defense mechanisms and get them to let their guard down, to be more genuine and open with him than they would be with anyone else except a therapist or a priest.

It was kind of amazing to watch. Because in addition to all of that, Russ was also a glad-hander. A back-slapper. A schmoozer. A joker. An imp. He seemed to have a hundred more watts of energy than other people, and he had an extra gear or two of determination that he deployed when circumstances warranted. In that room, at that moment, was one of those times.

Faced with a lobby full of tired, bored, cynical college students, Russ immediately began walking up to people and introducing himself. "Hi, I'm Russ. This is my buddy, Tad. We're from the University of Arizona." Then he'd stop, sniff the air theatrically a couple of times, and say something like, "Oh, and that smell in here, the one you can't quite place, that's me. I just farted." Then he'd laugh hysterically at himself, and the person he was talking to would have no choice but to at least crack a smile, even if they found the whole display distasteful.

That was Russ's way. He was entertainingly unpredictable. Charming one second, irreverent the next. One never knew what he was going to say or do. He loved to say outrageous things to people just to watch their reaction. Often, his behavior was boorish and crude. If he met a pretty girl who seemed a little too full of herself, he might say something like, "Please forgive me. I seem to have sprouted an enormous erection. Please don't stare. It's embarrassing." He could get away with that kind of thing because he'd do it in this disarmingly humorous way that made his behavior, however appalling, seem harmless. Some people thought he was a little crazy. And he was, sometimes. But the more I got to know him, the more I realized it was a strategic kind of crazy. He wanted to see if you were willing to play along with him, to go along with the joke. If you did, he'd reward you with his attention and admiration. If you didn't, he'd reassess and find another way to break down your defenses.

In that room, that day, Russ immediately lifted everyone's spirits by pretending he was glad to be in a sweaty motel in Nashville, that he was glad to be one of them. We were all in the same situation, after all: We had all been recruited on our respective campuses and shuttled across the country to that hotel, at that moment, having invested all our faith and hope in a well-delivered sales pitch. We were all afraid, too—afraid that we had been duped, that we had made a horrible mistake, that nothing about this little adventure was going to work out quite the way we expected. Because the truth was: None of us knew what to expect. We had simply thrown ourselves on the mercy of this company and these people, and all of us were waiting to see what would happen next.

About thirty or forty aspiring sales associates were staying at our hotel, but we were assured that hundreds of other students were undergoing the same training elsewhere in the city, and that many more had already been deployed in the field. None of us knew where we would eventually end up; our territories would be revealed at the end of the week, we were told, as part of our graduation from sales school into full-fledged book men and women.

But first, a pep talk. One of many. Because the first thing aspiring booksellers learn is that you can never have too much pep.

I'm kidding. Pep talks are necessary because door-to-door selling is a brutally demoralizing activity that chews up pieces of your soul and spits it out, then forces you to eat it again, vomit it, and re-digest it, over and over and over. Pep talks momentarily replenish the part of your soul that has been eaten, so that you may continue this cycle of spiritual regurgitation ad infinitum. Without these occasional injections of inspiration, all your faith and hope and dreams would simply be devoured by despair. The only way to combat this problem, as any salesperson knows, is through the immense power of the motivational speech.

Since the 1970s, motivational speaking has of course become an industry unto itself. Every day, somewhere in America, large groups of people gather in the most uninspiring environments imaginable—usually a generic conference room, classroom, or convention-center auditorium lit with flat, fluorescent sterility—to hear someone with amazing credentials and boundless energy tell them how they, too, can become amazing, boundlessly energetic success stories.

The premise of these speeches is of course that the people in the audience are not yet as amazing or successful as they'd like to be; otherwise, they'd be up onstage holding the microphone or somewhere else, enjoying the fruits of their professional awesomeness. By definition, if you are in the audience yawning and sipping lukewarm coffee to stay awake, you have some serious work to do. Because you, sad sap that you are, have not maximized your extraordinary potential for success in both work and life. You are not jacked up like a methhead on the confidence that comes from buckling down, facing your fears, and making the most out of every minute of every day. You are just a poor schlub with a job and a wife and three kids and a mortgage and a mountain of credit-card debt who is carrying thirty extra pounds around his gut because most of the time you are too tired and depressed to do anything but work and eat before collapsing in bed to watch a little TV and, hopefully, get at least one night's sleep without waking up at 3 a.m. to do battle with the terrible anticipation of the coming day and the teeth-grinding regret of the life you aren't living, the life that escaped you, the life that someone else out there—that guy onstage!—is enjoying, not you, because you lost your way somehow, zigging when you should have zagged, sending you on a long, pointless journey to nowhere, a journey that has landed you now, this moment, in this chair, listening to the one person in the world who knows the secret—the secret of saving you from yourself!

All motivational speeches are structured the same.

They start with a confession. After welcoming the audience, the speaker reveals that he was not always the paragon of success who now commands the stage. Once upon a time he was just like you, a sad lost soul adrift on the winds of fate, grinding through his days at a job he hated, trading his dignity for a paycheck and wondering what was the point of it all? Usually, the confession is told through a heart-wrenching story, one that may or may not include alcohol and drugs and land the speaker's former sorry self in a gutter somewhere, fighting off rats with a two-by-four and hallucinating a profound conversation with Jesus, who only seems to appear to people who could have used his help a bit earlier, before their unfortunate slide into the sewer.

The point of the speaker's story is that there is nothing special about him—he is just a regular person. Just like you, but worse. If he could pull himself up out of that gutter, so can you! The confession is supposed to establish a connection with the audience, to bridge the gap between student and sage, to convince everyone that he feels their pain. Before he can go on, his listeners must believe that he has been down that dark tunnel, and that he knows the way out.

The reason he knows the way out is that while he was lying in the gutter fighting off those pesky rodents, he had an *epiphany*, a flash of insight that told him what he was doing wrong with his life, and how to make it right. The clouds of doubt and fear parted, a beam of inspirational light shone through, and he followed it. The results were amazing. Life-changing. Transformational. And now he is going to share with you what he learned in that moment of divine revelation

(though if you want the full story and how to apply it to your own life, he recommends that you buy his book and/or the set of audio tapes at the back of the room, which are being sold at a discount for everyone in attendance.)

Through a series of anecdotes, aphorisms, and a gentle sprinkling of humor, he then proceeds to reveal the "secret" of his success. It usually starts with imagining what you want, then applying a mixture of goal-setting, self-discipline, positive attitude, and hard work to get it, all of which is possible through an unshakeable faith in a higher power that *wants* you to succeed (because massive wealth accumulation is what higher powers are all about). The important thing to remember is that no matter what obstacles you face in life, you can overcome them with the *power of your mind!* You can manifest your own destiny! Each of you has the secret to happiness, fulfillment, success, and wealth sitting on your shoulders, in that three-pound ball of jelly hidden behind your eye sockets. All you have to do is learn how to use it.

Motivational speakers are always light on specifics, unfortunately. They make their living by going around the country giving motivational speeches, after all, and it's much easier to get that gig *after* you've crawled out of the gutter. While you are still wallowing in the fetid muck of the life you want to escape, applying the principles of extreme motivation isn't quite so easy. In the world of wishful thinking, all things are possible. But in the life of an average American, wishes and dreams are often a luxury they can't afford.

On the first day of training, we gathered to listen to one of the company's vice presidents tell his story, and it was masterful. He remembered his first year selling books like it was yesterday. He told us how he went out on his first day and knocked on a hundred doors and didn't sell a single book! Then how he went out the next day and did the same thing, and still didn't sell a book! Then how he went his whole first week without selling a book (unimaginable!). How he beat himself up for being such a lousy salesman. How he felt like a failure. How he wept between houses, and came very close to committing the ultimate book-selling sin: he almost *called his parents!*

In those days, there were no cellphones and long-distance phone calls were expensive, so kids weren't in the habit of calling their parents anyway. If you did call your parents, it was usually for a reason: you needed money, you were in trouble, your tuition was due, or you got in a car accident and the paramedics needed to know your blood type. There weren't many reasons to call one's parents, though—one certainly didn't just call to "talk"—so admitting to an emotional breakdown that ended up in a call to mom or dad (especially mom) was, at that time, a powerful indication of how desperate you were. Indeed, *the point* of this guy's story was that it wasn't going to be easy out there, especially at first, but no matter how hard it gets, no matter how hopeless we feel, no matter how low in the gutter we have sunk—whatever we did, he pleaded, "do not call your parents." That, he claimed, would be the ultimate admission of failure. Think how ashamed your parents would be, he admonished. Think about how ashamed you would be about how ashamed they would be of you. (He really drove home the shame theme). So spare your parents the humiliation and heartbreak of having a son or daughter who can't cut it selling books. Call another book-person, call your district manager, pray to your higher power—whatever it takes. Just don't, under any circumstances, dial home. Oh, and if you have a boyfriend or girlfriend back home, don't call them either.

The reason the Southwestern company didn't want us calling our parents, of course, was that as soon as they found out what we were being asked to do, and how we were being asked to do it, they'd want to put us on the next plane home. (Nowadays, because of the cellphone revolution, Southwestern—now Southwestern Advantage—has reformed its practices somewhat by bringing parents into the fold and selling them on the idea of their son or daughter knocking on doors all summer. This is a smart strategy. By building an alliance with the parents, the company essentially co-opts them, so when those tearful phone calls come, the parents end up making the company's case for them.)

The rest of the speech was classic Motivation 101. He asked us to envision ourselves with that $3,000 (or $10,000!) check in our hands at the end of the summer, and to bask in the envy of our classmates when we returned to school. To the question, what did you do this summer?, we were the lucky ones who would be able to answer: "Made a shit-ton of money, pumped my erésume up on steroids, laid the groundwork for a lifetime of endless success, and learned how to beat the world at its own game. What did you do?" He told us that selling books was going to be hard, maybe the hardest thing we'd ever done, but the reward would be commensurate with the effort we put into it. By selling books, we were going to strengthen our character and find out what we were made of; we were going to overcome our fears, eliminate the obstacles in our way, and learn how to apply the principles of successful selling to ensure success in other areas of our lives.

And I believed it. I truly did.

Then again, college students are especially susceptible to a good motivational speech because their biggest insecurity is lack of accomplishment. They haven't done anything yet, so the prospect of getting over that hurdle—of actually doing something that can be catalogued on a résumé, and which the adult world deems impressive—is extremely exciting.

Russ and I were both very excited. Right after that speech we made a blood pact to never call our parents, no matter how hard it got. Never. Ever. And if they called us, we pledged to lie, to put a shiny face on everything and tell them whatever they wanted to hear. Somehow, some way, we'd find our own way through whatever problems we encountered. Short of actually dying, it was just a matter of enduring whatever heartaches and hardships came our way and figuring out how to deal with them.

The reason we could say this to ourselves was, of course, that if things got really, really, really bad, and if at some point we both agreed that the whole enterprise was a tragic mistake, guess what? We could always call our parents.

CHAPTER 11

The bulk of our training to become crackerjack door-to-door salespeople consisted of memorizing several basic scripts, twenty or so answers to "objections," and practicing them over and over again until, like an actor internalizing their lines, we could recite them spontaneously and effortlessly, without thinking. The acting analogy is apt, because door-to-door selling is really a specialized form of performance art. What's usually referred to rather dismissively as a "sales pitch" is really a carefully choreographed set of scenes designed to nudge the potential customer ever closer to saying "yes" to a sale. Each part of the "pitch" has a purpose, and is structured to lead into the next part, which is ultimately designed to convince people to part with their money. The "trick," if there is one, is to convince the customer that you are there to help them, and that the "cost" of your product—in this case, a book—is really an investment in their future, one that will repay itself many times over. This may or may not be true, but reality is not the salesperson's concern. Sales is about perception, about planting in the customer's mind a picture of the life to which they aspire, the person they wish to become, the image of themselves they want to project to the world.

Hotels are an ideal meeting place for prospective door-to-door salespeople for one basic reason: they have lots of doors. To learn the basics of the craft, each of us worked our way down the hall of our hotel, knocking on each door. Behind each door was a regional manager—usually someone who had been selling for three or four years—who pretended to be a different kind of customer. Sometimes they wore a costume, sometimes not, but they each represented a warped stereotype of some Midwestern persona: the grumpy farmer, the bored housewife, the angry construction worker, the skeptical husband, the rube who doesn't read, the know-it-all idiot. Our job was to convince each of these characters to let us enter their home and give them a demonstration, using the scripts we had memorized. We were not allowed to deviate from the scripts; we were instructed to deliver them word-for-word, the way they were written—because, we were told, decades of experience had resulted in these carefully constructed scripts, whose effectiveness had been proven by generations of book-sellers. Stick to the script and you will be fine, they assured us. Stray from it and you're in for a world of woe and heartbreak, because nothing you say off the top of your head could ever improve upon the persuasive genius of these time-honored texts. The scripts were our sacred scrolls, and we were to memorize and deliver them verbatim, or suffer the consequences.

This was not easy. First of all, the scripts themselves were impossibly cheesy. The language felt like it hadn't changed since the 1940s. They were also poorly written, with awkward sentences and phrasing. Try as I might, not a single word of these scripts felt remotely close to anything I would actually say. Every word felt false, and the unnatural rhythms of the speech I was supposed to internalize and deliver in a friendly manner, with smooth sincerity, proved to be a formidable challenge.

For example, the first thing I was supposed to say when someone answered the door was, "Hi, Mrs. _____?" (We got their names from the mailbox, or from a chatty neighbor.) "My name's Tad, and I'm talking to all the folks in the neighborhood. Everyone is really excited. Have you heard what all the excitement is about?"

The point was to be as vague as possible about your actual purpose in coming to their door, and to make them curious about all that "excitement." By asking them a question right out of the gate, the idea was to put them slightly on the defensive. Instead of telling you to go away, people feel like they need to answer the question. The answer is "no," of course—but that "no" gives you the opportunity to say, "That's great. Do you have a place where we can sit down?" Again, an idiotic question, because the answer is of course "yes, we own some chairs." But the point of the question isn't to get an answer, it's to put them in a "yes" frame of mind. It's also intended to confuse and fluster them. Because at the moment you ask the question, forcing their brains to momentarily short-circuit while thinking of a way to answer "no" to a "yes" question, you are supposed to break eye contact, reach down to pick up your sample case, point your shoulder toward the door and step toward it with your left foot. In other words, you're supposed to assume they are going to open the door. If they don't, you're supposed to continue the charade until you actually bang your head slightly against the door. If that happens, you're supposed to look up with a confused look on your face, as if to say, "Is there something wrong with your door?"

All of this struck me as rather deceptive and, if not outright aggressive, pushy to the point of obnoxiousness.

On my first day of training, I asked the obvious question: "Why can't we just be honest?"

All the experienced book people laughed. It was a stupid question, apparently, because if it were as easy as saying, "Hi, I'd like to sell you some highly educational books," anyone could do it. Though the *Volume Library* was allegedly so awesome that it "practically sells itself," it wasn't so amazing that it *actually* sold itself. Some persuasion was required. Several hurdles had to be jumped in order to break down people's resistance, and the first hurdle was their doorstep. If you could get inside their house, your chances of closing a sale increased exponentially. If someone lets you, a stranger, into their house, it means they already trust you not to rape or kill them. From there, you're only a fifteen-minute presentation away from collecting a check. Sure, there might be a few other hurdles in between, but that's what the "answers to objections" were for—to swat away any misgivings and reassure the potential customer that they are making a wise investment.

One of the hurdles was the name of the book itself: *The Volume Library*. While the average middle-class American loves the word "volume," they're not quite as keen on the word "library." Libraries are for nerds; they are where books are kept, where knowledge is housed, where intellectually curious people go to expand their minds and therefore confuse themselves about the proper role of God in their lives, not to mention the bedrock values of hard work and self-denial. In the abstract, "education" might be considered a virtue, but only if it is "practical" and leads to a reliable job. If, on the other hand, it leads one down the tragic path of the humanities, where the twin evils of moral relativism and liberalism reside, education can be dangerous. It can undo a lifetime of conscientious parenting, prompting children to question the authority and wisdom of their elders. It can glamorize the world of sin (i.e., sex, drugs, music, art), tempting children to indulge in deviant behavior. It can lead children to ask questions that simply should not be asked, such as "Is there a God?" and "Am I gay?" and "What exactly *is* a dildo?" In short, it can upset the natural order of things and cause good young people to stray from the clear path of righteousness into the tangled forests of uncertainty and doubt. Libraries are where eventual "elites" hang out, filling their heads with the sort of clever nonsense that gets them accepted to Harvard and Yale, where their heads are packed with more ingenious gobbledygook, which they then use to bamboozle the good people of the prairie and steal all their money.

Libraries also cause a great deal of guilt in people who don't use them. All their lives, non-library people have been told they should read more, and that the way to "get ahead" is by immersing oneself in the sacred texts shelved in that building they've never had the guts or inclination to enter. Education, they know, is the only solution for poverty. But school, of course, was not their thing. The act of educating oneself—paying attention in class, doing the homework, studying for tests, doing the assigned reading—is a lot of work. Work that, for whatever reason, many of them never got around to doing. Maybe it was boring. Maybe what they were being asked to study didn't seem relevant. Maybe they had a learning disability. Maybe they gave themselves a learning disability by smoking too much weed before class. Maybe they were clever and got others to do their homework and write their papers, successfully cheating both the system and themselves. Whatever the reason, deep down they know they should have read more books in school, and should be reading more as an adult. But they didn't and don't, because the bottom line is they don't *enjoy* reading. They like what reading is supposed to do for a person, but they don't like all the page-turning and thinking involved. It's painful. And tedious. There's not nearly enough violence and sex. And anyway, who's got the time?

In truth, the chief selling point of the *Volume Library* was that it wasn't a library, it was a handy informational shortcut for people who don't like to go to the library. It was the intellectual vegetables of an education served in a toothsome stew of expediency. It purported to be the essentials of a high-school education distilled into a single, easy-to-read volume. All the extraneous fat of a public education had been trimmed from it, leaving the delicious essence of knowledge—the vital, nutritious stuff that people really *ought to know*. Harvard scholars had supposedly vetted it (because even though middle-America hates "elites," they still respect Harvard), making the information therein as trustworthy as anything in the Encyclopedia Britannica, but much, much *shorter*.

The sales pitch for the *Volume Library* involved a deft bit of deduction and a certain amount of theater. If Mrs. Jones (as our generic fictitious housewife was called) acquiesced and let you into her home, we were instructed to scan the living room for signs of religious affiliation, the level of education she or her husband had already attained (from books on their shelves, memorabilia, or the kind of food they ate), and try to identify a key interest or two: a telescope in the window that indicated an interest in astronomy, say, or a World War II coffee book that suggested an interest in history. Since the *Volume Library* had many different sections, we memorized short demonstrations for half-a-dozen or so sections—Astronomy, Mathematics, American History, Biology, or whatever—which could be presented in any order. Using the information gleaned from the room scan, the idea was to make an educated (though not very) guess about what sections were most likely to light up Mrs. Jones's "buy" button. If no obvious clues were available, we were to fall back on a basic presentation that highlighted the book's strongest sections and, through a little gentle probing, find out what subjects their kids liked best in school.

The sweet spot was parents with kids in sixth to eighth grade. If the kid was home, and you could get him or her to sit still for the presentation, sales gold was all but assured. If a kid says to a parent that they want a book that might give them an edge in school—and hence an edge in life—the parent is pretty much obligated to buy the book. If they don't, they might look back on the moment the book guy offered them the golden keys to the world of adult independence and wonder: Maybe if we had just bought that damned book, our son wouldn't be living in our basement right now eating spicy Doritos and playing Nintendo, complaining how much the world "sucks" because he can't get a job that pays more than ten bucks an hour. And if he can't get a job that pays more than ten dollars an hour, he thinks, what's the point of working? Why not mooch off your parents for as long as humanly possible and hope the world ends in a fiery apocalyptic cataclysm before they boot you out?

The only way a kid sitting in can botch things is if they are completely indifferent or outright hostile to the idea of learning *anything*, or if they've played the "I want it, mommy" card too many times and have proven themselves to be greedy little cretins who waste their parents' money at every opportunity. In such cases, the smart thing to do is release the kid from his misery and tell them you want to talk to their mom alone. Then you pivot, establishing yourself as a sympathetic ally in the fight against youthful cynicism and stupidity, and suggest that the *Volume Library* isn't just for their kids—it is also a helpful reference to remind parents what they learned (or didn't) in high school, so they can help their kids with homework when the time comes. Sold as sort of a Cliff Notes guide to high school, the *Volume Library* appealed to people who did in fact use Cliff Notes in high school, so they could immediately see its merit.

The presentation itself also required a bit of staging. The ideal spot to make a *Volume Library* presentation was in front of a chair with five or six feet of space in front of it. Mrs. Jones's place was in the chair. Meanwhile, we carried with us a bright red sales case that contained our sales materials—chiefly a special truncated copy of the *Volume Library* (the whole thing was too heavy to lug around), some leave-behind brochures, and our order pad. The case itself was sturdy enough to sit on. So, while Mrs. Jones took her seat, we were supposed to position ourselves a few feet in front of her, open the case about a quarter of the way, sit on it, and—in one deft, well-practiced move—pull the shortened *Volume Library* out and start talking. The hard part was presenting the book itself. Because in order to show someone a book while you are sitting in front of them, you have to turn the book toward them, which means all the material in the book is, from where you sit, upside down and backwards. So, like a weatherperson working with a green screen, you have to know the material in the book so well that you can point to it, read it, and flip the pages in a natural way, all while delivering your memorized sales pitch.

Trust me, this is not easy.

It takes a great deal of practice to deliver a fifteen-minute sales presentation smoothly, with no mistakes, while also assessing the customer's level of interest and tailoring one's tone and tactics accordingly. Indeed, the better a salesperson knows their pitch, the less mental energy they must devote to it, and the more mind-muscle they can devote to scrutinizing the subtle facial cues and body language of the person they are trying to persuade. A good salesperson knows their pitch and product so well that they don't have to think about what they are saying at all. Their mouth is just a hole through which they deliver the necessary syllables; meanwhile, the rest of their consciousness is taking stock of the potential customer, assessing their level of interest and carefully calculating how they can get to the golden moment when, after all the words have been said and all their fears and concerns have been addressed, the customer finally breaks down and agrees to part with their money.

The hardest part about selling is closing the deal—or, as they refer to it in David Mamet plays, "the kill." It's one thing to give a nice presentation and provide people with all the information they need to make a decision; it's quite another to guide them toward the decision you want them to make, and still another to get them to pay you, on the spot, a mere twenty minutes after they've met you. Closing is an art all its own, which is why car dealerships have designated "closers," people who are so focused on making a sale that, like a sociopath seducing a co-ed, they see signs of resistance as a signal that they should push harder. Closers do not acknowledge the word "no." They see each "no" as a mere stepping stone to the "yes," and dispensing with the "no's" as a kind of game, a game they lose if you leave without acquiescing.

Closing is difficult because if, like me, you are the sort of person who is uncomfortable persuading people to do things they clearly do not want to, then your inclination is to back off at the precise moment when, during a sales pitch, you need to press forward and make the sale—to move in for the kill. To be sure, there is a predatorial aspect to the whole sales process that many people find distasteful. It feels like bullying. And it is, in a way. My job was to knock on people's doors out of the blue, worm my way into their home uninvited, convince them to buy something they probably didn't need, and pay for it with money they probably couldn't afford. In order to do all of that successfully, one either needs to believe so wholeheartedly in what they're selling that they can justify whatever angst and discomfort they cause by telling themselves that they are serving a greater good, or they need to be so sociopathically disconnected from the emotional side of the process that it doesn't matter to them. I existed in the ambivalent netherworld between: I believed in the value of education, but had doubts about the value of the *Volume Library*, and

I recognized the need to push people beyond my own comfort zone and theirs, but I hated doing it.

During our sales training, we also discovered that there was yet another layer of difficulty to overcome when it came to selling the *Volume Library*, and that was our inability to hand them the book once they'd paid for it. If Mrs. Jones decided to buy a book from us, we could not give it to her immediately, or next week, or even next month. No, we had to convince her to pay for the book now, on the promise that we would deliver the book at the end of the summer, in the last week of August. During the months of June and July, then, we were asking her to wait more than a month or two before she got her book. Talk about delayed gratification. So, in addition to making it through the door, delivering the pitch, answering objections, and closing the deal, we also had to manufacture an extraordinarily high level of trust. As in, "Trust me, if you give me $80 today, I will return in two months to deliver the book you bought, by which time you will probably have forgotten all about this transaction, in which case my arrival two months hence will be a happy surprise. Sign here, please."

These days, of course, such a request would be as absurd as it is intolerable. People expect to click their computer one day and receive a package on their doorstep the next. And the window of gratification is shrinking. In cities close to an Amazon distribution center, delivery within an hour is the new benchmark. Not content with that, technologists are also developing the "smart home" of the future, a house with appliances plugged into the internet that will automatically order supplies and groceries when stocks are running low. It's as if we're trying to engineer a world that anticipates all of our needs before we are even aware of them, then magically places the objects of our desire in front of us without requiring us to expend even a scintilla of conscious thought. How much lazier can we get?

In 1979, people had a little more patience. We were accustomed to waiting. If you sent a letter to someone, it took a few days for the Post Office to deliver it. Even if the recipient wrote back to you immediately, it would still take a week for their response to arrive in your mailbox. The whole idea of overnight delivery—of anything—was considered preposterous by many, not to mention unnecessary. What's the rush?, people thought. What's so important that it can't wait a couple of days?

At the time, Federal Express was still building its super-hub in Memphis, Tennessee, and lobbying Congress to change inter-state air traffic rules to enable it to implement its grand plan for nationwide overnight delivery. Federal Express's plan, which many thought was economic suicide, was to buy a fleet of aging jets and turn them into cargo planes. The Memphis super-hub operated as the central repository for all overnight packages. The planes were loaded with packages in the evening at airports across the country, then the planes flew to Memphis, where the packages were re-sorted according to their destination city. Then the planes were re-stocked and sent back to the cities from whence they came, where the packages were loaded onto a fleet of trucks and delivered by 10 a.m..

No such service was available for the *Volume Library*. In reality, we weren't selling a book, we were selling the idea of a book. And we had to sell the idea of the *Volume Library* so convincingly that it would sustain our customers through many weeks of doubt and suspicion. Doubt about the actual quality of the book. Doubt that they would ever really see the book. Suspicion that they had wasted their money. Doubt that they would ever see us again. Suspicion that the whole thing was a scam, that they'd been had, ripped off by a smooth-talking punk who was prowling their neighborhoods, taking advantage of good people whose biggest weakness was a willingness to invite strangers into their home and treat them nicely rather than slam the door in their face and tell them to fuck off.

To justify making them wait, we had to sell the thing as if it were an object of high art that took months to create. To hear me tell it, the company's lumberjacks had to fell the trees and pulp them and roll the pulp into paper of the highest quality, while the company's vast network of scholars and experts sifted through all the cumulative knowledge in the world to keep each nugget of vital information as up-to-date as possible, all of which was then painstakingly crafted into easy-to-read paragraphs surrounded by attractive graphs and photos, then printed by artisans in a secret monastery somewhere in Tennessee and bound in exquisite faux leather using book-binding techniques pioneered by blind monks who toiled away with joy in their hearts as they glued each page into place according to specifications handed down from Our Creator himself, who included these sacred instructions in a little-known extra tablet that Moses neglected to mention when he descended from Mount Sinai to deliver the Ten Commandments to the Israelites.

So yeah, it's going to take a while.

Then there was the money. The goal was to get them to pay up front, in full, and only settle for half if you absolutely had to. But people are understandably reluctant to part with eighty dollars for nothing more than a receipt and a promise, and they don't much like forking over forty dollars, or even twenty. As independent businesspeople, we were allowed to make judgment calls—to sell a book for 25 percent down, or even nothing—but the risk at that point was all ours. The less a customer puts down up front, we were told, the less likely they were to pay the balance when it came time to deliver the book. If, upon delivery, they decided they didn't want the book, there wasn't much we could do about it. The company did not have a team of lawyers to deploy on our behalf. If we couldn't convince them to pay the balance, we were stuck with an extra book. So "selling" a book for nothing down was potentially worse than selling no book at all, because you got no money up front and chances were they were going to stiff you in the end. Furthermore, a portion of that up-front cash was what we were supposed to live on throughout the summer, so there was an extra incentive to get as much cash as possible up front: survival. Selling a book wasn't enough; the measure of a good sale was how much money one was able to get up front. 100 percent and you were a sales god. 50 percent and you could still hold your head high. 25 percent tempted you to lie and say you got 50 percent. Below 25 percent was pathetic. Nothing down just meant you were a sad, desperate person who would do anything not to get rejected. Nothing down didn't even count.

Now, you might think that after getting in the door, delivering a presentation, making a sale and collecting a check, your business would be concluded. But no. Having gained Mrs. Jones's trust so much that she bought a book from me, my job on the way out the door was to leverage that trust and pump her for as much information about her neighbors as possible. Who lived where? What were their names? What did they do for a living? How many kids did they have? How old were the kids? Did they go to public or private school? Did they play any sports? Were they home or on vacation?

You might think people would be reluctant to divulge to a relative stranger all kinds of personal information about their neighbors. But you would be wrong. People love to gossip, they love to be helpful, and they love to show off how much they know. This makes it possible to glean a frightening amount of information about a neighborhood from just one or two people—information that the savvy book-person uses to their advantage. One must be careful, though: People tend to get a little creeped out when you knock on their door and already know their name, their husband's name, their kids' names, where they go to school, and how well their twelve-year-old, Freddie, is doing in math.

The point of squeezing people for information about their neighbors was to determine which houses on the block to hit. Houses with no kids were a waste of time unless you felt like taking a flyer on selling to grandparents. Knowing there were younger kids in a house was helpful, too, because an additional part of our sales arsenal was a set of children's books, the hook for which was that the books came with a record of a man with a sonorous voice narrating the stories. So, if you were a tired parent who didn't want to read the same book to your kid fifty times, you could simply let the record do the work for you. It was just like reading to your kid, only not.

The children's books cost only about thirty dollars, and were considered an up-sell to people who bit on the *Volume Library* but also had young-uns in the house whose joy of having a guy on a record read to them had yet to be nurtured. The children's books could be sold separately, but it was considered a waste of time because they were so comparatively cheap. There wasn't even much of a sales pitch for them: you just showed them one of the books, told them about the record, and asked them one or two of the canned and oh-so-awkwardly-leading questions we were trained to use. Such as: "Can you see how these books might help Sally discover the joy of reading?" or, "Wouldn't it be great if you didn't have to put Sally in front of the TV every time you wanted to get something done?" Or, if the husband wasn't home and she was claiming she couldn't make the decision to buy on her own: "Wouldn't your husband be proud to learn that you made an investment in your child's future all on your own?"

Practicing the "perfect pitch" was what our training was all about. We spent hours each day going from door to door to door in that crappy hotel, trying to perfect our pitches. In return, we got doors slammed in our faces, we got yelled at, we got accused of selling Bibles (or worse, insurance), we got rejected, time and time again, with every excuse in the book. Every once in a while we'd stumble through our opening well enough to be allowed inside, where the tantalizing possibility of a sale always lurked, hiding, just out of reach. Our managers were cruel taskmasters who scolded us for straying off script, and delighted in throwing us off with absurd questions or odd behavior. Once, while delivering my stock *Volume Library* presentation, one of the trainers kept making strange gesticulations and looking at me quizzically, as if he didn't understand what I was saying. He was pretending to be deaf, it turned out, and wanted to see how I'd handle the situation.

"You run into all kinds of people out there, so you have to be ready for anything," he warned, as if I was headed into the jungles of Vietnam. Stay sharp and respond to the situation naturally, was his advice—just don't deviate from the pre-approved sales script. How one was supposed to respond "naturally" while reciting the company's awkward sales script, he didn't say—only that the script would feel more natural over time.

That was a lie. The script never felt natural to me. Even after reciting it hundreds of times, it still felt like lines written for a 1940s play about aliens who landed here from a planet where the use of correct grammar and sentence structure was considered a capital crime.

Other peculiarities of superior salesmanship didn't sit right with me, either.

For instance, the bromides: "A good salesman never hears the word 'no,'" and "Every 'no' is just a stepping stone to 'yes.'" These were popular aphorisms in the book-selling business, because they put a positive spin on the reality of selling, which is that you hear a lot more 'no's than 'yes's.

In other contexts, of course, ignoring the word 'no' can land a man in jail. But in the sales game, fending off excuses and objections is part of the job. In the salesperson's psyche, what stands between them and closing the sale is the customer's stubborn resistance to open their wallet. That resistance must be broken down. People always say no a few times before they say yes—or they hem and haw and ask questions and make up excuses—so dedicated salespeople see it as their duty to guide customers through their own forest of doubts until they see the glittering "sale" light in the clearing ahead. There is no upside to accepting a 'no,' so sales people are taught to ignore any hint that the sale may not be imminent, in the hope that, eventually, the customer will run out of objections and excuses and finally say yes.

If, however, one has been taught to respect other people's opinions, and isn't inclined to dismiss what people say out of hand, pushing past that first 'no' isn't easy. It certainly went against my nature. When someone tells you no, they don't want to hear what you have to say, and no, they aren't interested in buying anything, and no, they don't have time to talk to you, and no, they aren't kidding, it's hard to ignore all those no's. The only way to do it is to convince yourself that the no-sayer doesn't know what they're talking about—that they don't really mean what they're saying. You have to tell yourself that these people secretly want to say yes, they just don't know it yet. In other words, you have to be *rude*. And presumptuous. And arrogant. You have to assume that you know what's best for the customer, and to believe that you are *doing them a huge favor* by refusing to listen to their objections, based as they are on ignorance and fear: ignorance of what you're selling and how it meets their needs; fear that they might actually want to buy it after listening to you. Or, a much deeper fear: that they might not have the stomach to keep saying no forever. You have to tell yourself that deep down people want what you are selling, and in half an hour they will be thanking you for ignoring them.

In sales training, we were taught that the first three no's didn't count, period. The next three no's might count, but probably not. After six no's, it's a judgment call. Because, as it turns out, some people actually do mean 'no,' and miscalculating the number of times they are willing to have their objections ignored can be dangerous, especially in the Midwest, where people are fond of their guns. In any case, we were taught to make a person say 'no' in one form or another at least five or six times before closing up our sales kit. Any less than that and we weren't doing our job.

For me, however, getting into the proper mindset to sell books all day represented a sort of psychological trap. On one hand, it was clear that the job would be easier if I believed wholeheartedly and uncritically in the the *Volume Library*, and could knock on every door with the conviction that the people inside *needed* this book more than they needed me to go away. On the other hand, if I didn't have complete faith in the transformative power of the *Volume Library* (which I didn't), it was clear that I was going to have to lie to myself—to "fake it 'til I made it"—and pretend.

The problem is, if you believe in something, working on its behalf is easy. But if you don't—if you're just pretending in order to make a buck or avoid looking like you're not as committed as everyone else—it's very hard. It takes a great deal of psychic effort to override one's own engrained impulses and misgivings. It means second-guessing everything you say and do. It means not being able to trust your instincts or your conscience. It means abandoning who you are in favor of *who you need to be* in order to get the job done. And yes, it sucks.

Russ was never plagued by such doubts. He was a true believer from the very beginning, and he championed the *Volume Library* as if it were, well, the Bible. This made a certain amount of poetic sense, since the Southwestern Company was started by a Baptist minister, James Robinson Graves, who recruited young college-bound men to sell Bibles door-to-door after the Civil War. It also made practical sense, because selling the *Volume Library* was a lot easier if you did it with a certain amount of evangelical zeal.

In keeping with that tradition, Russ treated the *Volume Library* as if it were the gateway to a better world, a thing one simply had to have faith in and it would lead to a promised land of ever-lasting prosperity and happiness. He believed in the power of education to transform people's lives, and he believed the *Volume Library* could be a conduit for that kind of transformation. He also believed that the summer would go by a lot faster and easier if he didn't clutter his mind with doubts about what he was doing.

"You're over-thinking it," he told me on the last day of training. "You've got to set all that stuff aside and focus on what you're trying to accomplish. Even if it's not the greatest book ever written, it's still a helluva lot better than most books out there. Have you read the Astronomy section? It's actually pretty cool."

"Yeah, but the world history section is pretty lame," I countered. "World War I gets maybe two-thirds of a page, and there's nothing about Vietnam."

"So what? Look, all you're trying to do is get them to pay $79 for a book. What else are they doing to do with that money? Go to a restaurant? Buy a bicycle? See a football game? Subscribe to a bunch of tittie magazines? If they give us $79 for a half-way decent book, at least they're not wasting their money on something stupid."

"It's still a lot of money."

"Take the money out of it then," Russ countered. "Think of it as a numbers game. If you knock on a hundred doors a day, at least two of those doors are going to open up and buy a book from you, right? So don't focus on the selling, focus on the knocking."

Russ was a natural. Every misgiving I had about selling the *Volume Library* he countered with a reasonable-sounding alternative, a different way of thinking that took the moral sting out of it. He did the same thing with the *Volume Library* itself, and soon was being tapped by our trainers to demonstrate for all of us how it ought to be done. At the door, he projected just the right combination of charm and enthusiasm. His setup was masterful, gradually establishing both authority and trust as he surveyed the room for clues about his potential customer. Information gleaned from his mental sweep was seamlessly inserted into his pitch, which was performed with a subtle theatricality that made the book's content come alive, no matter how moribund it might have been on the page. He met every objection with flawless logic, neutralizing every doubt with calm precision and a guarantee of satisfaction that could not, in fact, be guaranteed. And his close was a model of perfection: firm but reassuring, efficient without being hasty.

After watching him in action, it was clear that Russ had mastered the fundamentals of book-selling in a way I and most of our compatriots had not. Once again, he had established himself as a leader and role model.

As our training came to a close, I felt lucky that Russ and I were going to be doing this thing together, and I hoped fervently that some of his skills would rub off on me.

CHAPTER 12

Apart from the brute mechanics of memorizing and delivering a prepared sales pitch, a portion of our training involved ways to battle the demons of self-doubt and despair that would inevitably haunt us in the field. Rumors abounded about kids who got so spooked that they up and quit, preferring the shame and humiliation of failure to another day knocking on doors in suburban America. We were going to be out there alone, after all, so when the demons descended upon us, we would have to summon the strength of our inner resources to vanquish them. Otherwise, we might decide to stop selling books and go enjoy the rest of our summer back home, in the warm embrace of parents and friends, all of whom would probably agree that abandoning the book business was a wise idea. Jesus was a good friend to have in such instances. He would never quit, no matter how hard things got, so a chummy relationship with Our Lord and Savior was a distinct advantage in the field. This made a certain amount of sense. Southwestern salespeople were the original "Bible thumpers," and vestiges of that history remained in the evangelical fervor of the company's upper executives. Quite often, their pep talks sounded more like sermons, as they touted the benefits of faith to the lone bookseller facing another day of heartless rejection. Speaking with the passion of a tent-revival preacher, they all but assured us that the faithless among us had no chance of overcoming the challenges that lay ahead. Only Jesus could provide the strength and fortitude needed to endure an entire summer of thankless (but profitable) drudgery. Book-selling was 98 percent failure, after all, so one needed an emotional buddy to lean on when the going got tough. If Jesus wasn't your buddy yet, they advised, it was time to get acquainted with him.

As an agnostic who leaned toward atheism, I only half-listened to this nonsense. My parents were scientists, and I was raised to value reason and logic over matters of mysticism and faith. God was a non-entity in our household. We did not attend church. Sleeping in was the sacred thing to do in our house on Sunday morning, and no one embraced the sanctity of slumber more enthusiastically than me.

Nevertheless, I was curious about the mechanics of religious faith. I didn't understand how anyone could "believe" something that couldn't be proven, or why it even mattered that Jesus died for the sins of mankind. Most people die for a lot less, I thought, and get no credit whatsoever. I also didn't understand how anyone could believe the whole Jesus-died-and-was-resurrected story. Any magician worth his salt could figure out a way to make it look as if Jesus's body disappeared. (I'm certain Penn and Teller could.) Just because a bunch of illiterate people got fooled and began telling a fantastical story to connect the logical dots doesn't mean that's what actually happened. The more probable chain of events was likely much more mundane, and didn't involve an invisible all-knowing entity who sent his "son" down from heaven to get slaughtered by a bunch of vindictive Jews hopped up on righteousness and bloodlust. I also didn't understand why it mattered to God whether people believed in him/it or not. Belief in something doesn't make it true, after all. Belief doesn't change the fabric of reality or the nature of truth. As far as I was concerned, all the idea of "belief" did was make it possible for people to deceive themselves about the true nature of things, which is that the Earth is nothing more than a small speck of dust in the vastness of the universe, and humanity itself is just an anomalous blip on the inter-galactic radar, here one second and gone the next. To think that any individual person rates special consideration because they choose not to accept the clear message of the universe—which is that we are alone, and no one cares—seemed delusional to me. I understood that people needed to believe in something (I myself was still trying to figure out what I believed.) But I didn't understand why God needed—and seemed to require—people to believe in Him. Punishing people for their lack of belief seemed kind of petty for an omniscient, omnipresent, infallible Being. I also didn't understand how so many millions of people all over the world could be duped by such an obviously bogus story, and why—given that there are several thousand different religions in the world—Christians (particularly Catholics) thought they had a special claim to the keys of the Almighty's kingdom? It seemed obvious to me that all religions were created by people to answer questions they did not understand, and that the word "God" was just a nonsense syllable that means "shit we don't know."

In short, I was a skeptic.

Besides faith in Jesus, the company recommended several other ways to ensure that our summer was a success. The best way to ensure success, of course, was to adopt the habits of highly successful people. Ben Franklin counseled "early to bed, early to rise," so the advice handed down to us was that we should be in bed by 10 p.m., and to set an alarm for 5:59 a.m. Hitting the "snooze" button was not allowed. No, when that alarm rang, we were instructed to immediately hop out of bed and rattle off twenty push-ups. Because, you know, that's what successful people do. The idea here was that by 6:01 a.m. we'd be wide awake, blood pumping, ready to greet the day. And it does work. But it also turns out that, with a little practice, it is possible to wake up, do twenty push-ups, and go right back to sleep.

At some point, however, one does have to face the coming day. In the world of book-selling, every morning is a gauntlet that must be run, because it takes a great deal of courage to knock on a stranger's door at 8 a.m., the hour our workday was supposed to start. (Midwesterners wake up early, we were assured, because they are farm people who rise with the sun, and therefore don't mind having their breakfast interrupted by a friendly traveling salesperson.) Decades of training young people to overcome their misgivings and knock on that first door at least two hours earlier than the average person's conscience would normally allow had inspired them to devise a formidable weapon in the fight against prevailing social norms and basic respect for other people's time. That weapon was a song— The Bookman Song—a ditty seared so deeply into my gray matter that I can sing it to this day.

The Bookman Song goes like this:

It's a great day to be a bookman
It's the best thing I know oh oh
It's a great day to be a bookman
Everywhere I go oh oh
Goodbye no never
Goodbye doubt and fear
It's a great day to be a bookman
And be of good cheer
I feel healthy!
I feel happy!
I feel terrific!

The key to the Bookman Song is to sing it while you are dancing around in circles, flapping your arms like duck. It's best done in a parking lot, in public, where the sheer ridiculousness of it can be witnessed by someone unfamiliar with book-selling protocols—someone who, upon seeing you, will immediately assume you have a mental disorder. It is without a doubt one of the stupidest songs ever written, and the dance that accompanies it is idiotic in the extreme.

The first line always rings false, because there is never a "great" day to be a bookman (or booklady), only days that are somewhat less shitty than others. The line "goodbye no never, goodbye doubt and fear" gets to the heart of the matter fairly succinctly, because doubt and fear are the bookman's constant companions. But when you get to that line "and be of good cheer," it's impossible not to cringe a little inside, because the whole phrase seems to come from another era, one of aw-shucks innocence and gee-whillickers gullibility. In 1979, being "of good cheer" meant you were a vacuously happy moron who wasn't paying attention to the world situation, which consisted of a clusterfuck of calamities—pollution, oil embargoes, Iranian hostages, high interest rates, stagflation—the only intelligent response to which was an attitude somewhere between ironic detachment and hopeless cynicism. Nobody was cheerful in 1979, because there was nothing to be cheerful about.

Nevertheless, the curious thing about the Bookman Song was how well it worked. Yes, the first couple of times I sang it, I felt like an idiot.

But after singing it a few more times, I noticed that I did in fact feel better. By the end of the Bookman Song, it's hard not to smile and laugh, precisely because it is so damn stupid. The genius of the song is that it forces you to set your self-consciousness aside and embrace the idiocy of the moment. It's hard to take yourself too seriously when you are making a fool of yourself. The power of the Bookman Song also grows exponentially with the number of people doing it. Twenty or thirty people in a parking lot singing the Bookman Song is, after thirty seconds, going to be a happy bunch. Singing the Bookman Song is like taking a quick hit of dopamine, because that's exactly what it is—a clever mechanism for juicing your brain just enough so that you don't feel so awful about what you're about to do: Spend twelve hours trying to sell a book that most people don't want or need.

Perhaps it is needless to say that no one embraced the absurdity of the Bookman Song and its accompanying dance more eagerly than Russ. He threw himself into it with astonishing gusto, and, at six-feet-six-inches tall, his flailing arms and limbs were a sight to behold. When, at the end, he yelled "I feel happy! I feel healthy!" he did look happy and healthy. But he always changed the last line. Instead of yelling "I feel terrific!" like everyone else, he always yelled "I feel *specific*!" just to let everyone know that he was performing the song ironically. This made Russ much cooler than everyone else, and endeared him to us even more.

Unfortunately, the salutary effects of the Bookman Song only last about ninety seconds, after which your brain chemistry returns to normal and those doubts and fears you just said goodbye to are back, front and center. The other downside to the Bookman Song is that it does not work if you are alone. Singing the Bookman Song solo is almost impossible. It doesn't work, and it feels worse if you try, because it just reminds you how sad you really are. To work, the silliness of the Bookman Song must be shared, in a group, with people who are trapped in the same strange predicament and gripped by the same peculiar uncertainties. Performed this way, it serves as a bonding exercise for people who would otherwise have nothing to bond over, and for whom public displays of foolishness are normally *verboten*. A more intelligently inane method of cracking the self-conscious narcissism of American college students has yet to be devised.

CHAPTER 13

One source of more-or-less constant anxiety was the mystery surrounding our eventual sales locale. Thus far in our adventure we had all simply been whisked off our respective college campuses and deposited in a third-rate hotel somewhere on the outskirts of Nashville. Precisely where we would be spending the rest of the summer was a closely guarded secret, one that would be revealed on the final day of training—a day that had, at last, arrived.

After dinner on our final day in Nashville, all the new recruits packed into a room occupied by one of the senior trainers. There weren't as many of us as there had been at the beginning of the week, because some students had elected to drop out. Still, about twenty of us had survived training, a feat that felt at the time like an extraordinary achievement. Our reward for spending a week memorizing hokey sales pitches and getting chastised and humiliated day after day for not knowing the scripts well enough, or for any one of a hundred other missteps, was to learn—finally, and at long last—where we'd be spending the rest of the summer. All we had been told was that we'd be working "somewhere in the Midwest," which only narrowed it down to a dozen possible states. A large map of the United States was tacked to the wall of the hotel room, and, while we waited for the big "reveal," there was nothing to do but look at the map and speculate where the winds of fate would eventually deposit us.

"Somewhere near Chicago would be good," one guy speculated. "At least there'd be something to do on the weekends."

"Indianapolis would be okay," another offered. "My grandparents used to live there."

"Kansas City has good barbecue."

"Omaha sucks. Just hope you don't get Omaha."

"Springfield would be nice. That's where Abraham Lincoln was born."

"I went to summer camp in Missouri, and it was pretty cool. Very hot, actually, but lots of trees."

Russ and I tried to be a little more analytical about it. North and South Dakota were out, we figured, because they were too sparsely populated. Minnesota and Michigan were a long way away, but not out of the question. It was unlikely that we'd end up in one of the bigger, better known cities, we figured, because our training had emphasized the habits and values of people in rural communities. Not once had we ever heard of anyone selling a book in Chicago, or in any other city recognizable to a couple of guys from Arizona. Poor people with aspirations were a definite target market, which suggested an urban area of some sort, but plenty of poor people live in the hinterlands as well. We'd seen the movie *Deliverance*, and our deepest fear was that we'd be sent somewhere in the American outback to try to sell books to the parents of an albino banjo player with a buzzcut and a lazy eye and strange ideas about which of his body parts should be stuck where.

Russ's conclusion: "They're sending us to Bumfuck, you know that, right?"

"Where's Bumfuck on the map?" I asked.

"In Bumfuckistan, where else?"

"I hear eastern Bumfuckistan is nice this time of year. But the girls are supposedly prettier in the west."

"It's all Bumfuck," Russ replied. "It doesn't matter which part you're in, you still have to bend over and take it."

"Well, if we end up in Bumfuck, at least we'll be there together," I offered.

"Don't get your hopes up."

"I don't have any hopes, just perverse, disgusting desires that will condemn me to hell for all eternity."

"Me too," Russ replied. "I keep having this dream. You and me are walking along, minding our own business, when I suddenly cut your dick off and feed it to a raccoon. It's messy, but I'll bet a raccoon chewing on your severed dick would be kind of cute."

Now, after all these years, I cannot say for certain that Russ said those exact words in that exact moment. But it is the kind of thing Russ *would* have said, in a moment *like* that, because he was a twenty-year-old kid who, at the time, loved to shock people by conjuring the most disgusting image possible and watching people squirm and huff and protest that he had gone too far—that he had broken some sort of unspoken social code of decorum by saying something so perverse and twisted that the only reasonable reaction to it was "eeeeeeewww-ww." The best response, however—the response that got Russ's attention, respect, and laughter—was to double-down on the darkness and come up with a retort that out-disgusted him. So, in that situation, I might say, "Not half as cute as a baby squirrel gnawing on your nutsack to slurp out your man milk."

To which he might say, "Fuck you."

To which I might respond, "Fuck you too."

To which he might say, "That would be difficult if you didn't have a dick and I didn't have any balls."

Then we'd laugh and get back to the business at hand.

Since we had no control of the outcome, Russ and I felt that hoping to get assigned to a certain city was a recipe for disappointment, so it made more sense to approach the whole city-assignment ceremony with a more-or-less zen-like detachment to the outcome. Sure, it'd be nice to trundle into KC for some barbecue, or be close enough to Chicago to hear some blues—but we'd take whatever they gave us and go from there.

It didn't take long to realize that the cities to which we were being assigned were not prioritized by name recognition or nightlife potential. In fact, I had never heard of most of them: St. Joseph, Missouri; Bloomington, Indiana; Elgin, Illinois; Taylor, Michigan; Waukesha, Wisconsin; Salina, Kansas. These names meant nothing to me, a guy who had grown up in California, went to school in Arizona, and whose idea of a big city in the east was . . . Las Vegas. Until I'd arrived in Nashville, the territory between Arizona and New York was basically a blank hole in my consciousness. I'd never been there. I didn't know anything about it. And now, by some bizarre twist of fate, I was going to be plopped somewhere in the middle of it and left to fend for myself, with a few books and a shakily memorized sales script as my only survival tools. That and a tattered copy of Og Mandino's *The Greatest Salesman in the World*, which Scott loaned me, insisting that it was "inspirational."

Teams of two or three people were assigned to each city, and, as each city and team was announced, our man Scott stuck a red pin on the map to show us where, in fact, the city was located. Nowadays, we'd have whipped out our phones and looked up the city in question to appease our curiosity. But in 1979, personal computers and smartphones and the Internet did not exist, so there was no way to get any information on the cities to which we had been dispatched. For most of us, the only data we had about the place we'd be spending our summer was contained on that map of America, in that red pin. Once the pins were stuck on the map, they became tiny beacons of hope and possibility and dread, little red dots pulsing with all the uncertainties and mysteries of an adventure that hasn't been planned particularly well.

When our turn came, there was no drum roll, just a slight pause for dramatic effect, then the announcement: "Russ and Tad, you're going to . . . Davenport, Iowa!"

I'd never heard of it.

According to the pin on the board, it was near the Mississippi River, in a region known as the Quad Cities, because they'd somehow crammed four cities in the same general area: Davenport and Bettendorf on the Iowa side of the river, and Rock Island and Moline on the Illinois side. The only one of the four I'd ever heard of was Rock Island, and only then because of the Johnny Cash song "Rock Island Line," which isn't even about *that* Rock Island, it's about some train in Louisiana.

"What'd I tell you: Bumfuck," Russ said when our destination was announced.

"Could be worse," I said. "It could be Des Moines. At least I think Des Moines would be worse."

"It's in Iowa," Russ said. "Iowa is Bumfuck by definition. There is nowhere in Iowa that is not Bumfuck, so I rest my case."

A third guy, whose name I can't remember (let's call him Greg) was assigned to sell with us in Davenport as well. The good thing about Greg was that he had money—$300, to be exact—and generously offered to float all three of us until the cash from our book sales came rolling in. This was fortuitous, because Russ and I had less than $100 between us, and had been counting on strong sales our first week out to get us over the hump. The bad thing about Greg was that he couldn't be trusted. But we didn't know that yet. All we knew about him was that he was just like us: a college guy who had been sucked into the same strange vortex of ambition and apprehension as us. Also, none of us knew anything about Davenport, Iowa, and none of us had the remotest idea what we were getting ourselves into.

CHAPTER 14

The following morning, the three of us piled into the car of our "district manager," a fellow named Mike, for the eight-hour drive to Davenport. Mike had spent five years in "the field" and now oversaw the entire Midwest sales force, a group of about 250 kids stationed mainly in four states: Iowa, Illinois, Missouri, and Kansas. He was going to drive us to Davenport, he said, and help us get established.

Mike was strange fellow. He must have have been twenty-four or twenty-five at the time, a few years older than us and a whole lot cagier. Mike was a little guy, about five-foot-six, and he had one of those pseudo-mustaches that guys who can't grow a real mustache won't shave because they're hoping it will eventually fill out. He was a twitchy, nervous sort who talked fast and jerked his head around like a bird, as if he had six different thoughts going through his head at the same time. If he were in grade school today, he'd be the kid with a prescription for Ritalin and notes on his report card saying he was "disruptive."

Had any of us met Mike on a college campus, we would have immediately dismissed him as the sort of nerdy little weasel who spends too much time playing Dungeons and Dragons and not enough time thinking about girls and sex and all the "normal" stuff young men are supposed to think about. But, because he was now our manager—our boss—and he had spent five years knocking on doors and selling books, he had the power of experience on his side. And he knew it. I'm fairly certain he thought none of us would last more than a week or two. But he professed to have high hopes for us, which was why, he said, *he* was driving us to Davenport and not someone else.

"I need you guys to be leaders," he told us as we cut across the southwest corner of Kentucky and eased into Illinois. "You guys are going to be out there alone, but teamwork is what is going to get you through the summer. Every team needs leaders, so I'm counting on you guys to show the way, especially for the other rookies."

Selling books was a full-time, seven-day-a-week job, he told us. Six days of selling—then, on Sunday, all the kids in our region would get together at some central location to share stories, get to know each other, and "have a little fun." Those were the days he expected us to demonstrate our leadership, he said. Because, among other things, we'd be sharing with the group how many books we sold that week—how "successful" we'd been, in other words—and we needed to sell a lot, not only to enrich ourselves but to inspire everyone else to "dig deep" and do better each and every week.

"People are going to come up with all kinds of excuses why they couldn't sell more books," he told us. "Their aunt died. Their territory's bad. The people are mean. Nobody's home during the day. Nobody has any money. They're homesick. Whatever. Your job is to show them that it doesn't matter. What matters is getting out there and knocking on a hundred doors a day."

The thing about Mike was that he was relentlessly positive, sometimes annoyingly so. To him, there was no such thing as a bad neighborhood for book-selling; any person with eyeballs was a potential prospect. He lived by the dictum that every "no" was a stepping stone to the next "yes," that every lemon was a potential glass of lemonade. He didn't believe in excuses; he believed that if you couldn't sell books it was because you weren't actually knocking on doors, you were probably sitting around feeling sorry for yourself. He had internalized the mantras of success to such a degree that it was seemingly impossible to present him with a negative proposition that he couldn't pretzelize into a positive.

"When you don't feel like knocking on doors, the best thing to do is go knock on a door," he'd say.

"The best houses to hit are ones with a 'no soliciting' sign," he'd insist. Why? "Because those people can't say no. They hope their sign will do their no-ing for them."

"Poor neighborhoods are best for book-selling," he'd say. "People with money think they already know everything."

"The best time to sell a book is eight-o'clock in the morning," he'd proclaim, knowing full well that, even though the company insisted on it, none of us wanted to knock on someone's door that early the morning. His reasoning: "The coffee is hot and people will invite you in just to be polite."

Mike was equally sanguine about our concerns regarding where we might live during the summer and how we were going to pay for it.

The company did not give its hires any start-up money or anything like a housing stipend, nor was shelter of any kind arranged beforehand. When we were recruited, we were assured that the company was so beloved that there was an entire network of families out there who were more than happy to welcome a young book-seller into their home as a lodger. This arrangement might include a small rental fee, but more often than not, we were told, these fine people embraced book-sellers as "one of the family," so we'd probably end up living in an extra bedroom and getting fed by a kind mother-of-the-Earth type who wouldn't think of charging us rent. Mike himself had given us a list of half-a-dozen names and addresses of people with whom, he said, the company had "prior arrangements," and could be counted upon to shower us with kindness. All we had to do was ask. Some sort of arrangement would fall into place, he assured us. He himself had never paid a dime of rent in his five years of selling, he said, and he didn't expect we would have to either. The families in this extended network of generosity understood that we were trying to earn money for college, so charging us for rent and food would be rather inconsiderate, not to mention un-Christian.

All of this sounded promising. But a promise is not a guarantee. The closer we got to Davenport, the more doubts I had. The chances that we would find someone willing and able to give three tall college guys free room and board were slim to none, I figured. One of us might be able to find someone who had an extra room, but all three of us? Not likely. More probably, we'd end up having to find separate living arrangements, which, until that point, wasn't something I had considered. I had just assumed Russ and I would be living together somewhere, but it was starting to look like that might not be the case. And if we all lived separately, how were we supposed to coordinate activities like our weekly Sunday get-together, especially since none of us had a car?

Not to worry, Mike insisted. Everything would work out. It always did. All we had to do was have "faith," and work the plan he'd laid out for us. "Plan the work, and work the plan" was one of Mike's favorite mottos. The helpfulness of this motto depends a great deal on the quality and viability of the plan itself, however, and Mike's plan for us wasn't exactly thorough. Having given us the list of names, he was going to drop us off at a central location in Davenport and let us "get to work." It was Saturday, so all the prospects on our list would likely be home, he said. All we had to do was go down the list until we found someone who would take us in. Along the way we could also knock on some doors and sell some books, which would put some money in our pockets. By the end of the day, he assured us, all the rookie worries that were chipping away at our positivity now would be distant memories, and the work we had been sent to do could begin in earnest.

CHAPTER 15

Davenport is located on the eastern border of Iowa, on the Mississippi River, half-way between Chicago and Des Moines. It's the largest of the Quad Cities, but not nearly the nicest, or the cleanest, or the safest. Those distinctions go to Bettendorf, its sister community to the north. People with money and taste live in Bettendorf. People who cannot afford Bettendorf live in Davenport. It's as simple as that, though it would take us a while to learn this for ourselves. When we arrived in Davenport, the demographics of the area were a mystery to us, along with everything else about the city. We did not know, for instance, that the largest employer in the area was John Deere, the makers of conspicuously green tractors, combines, lawnmowers, and other machines used to tame the unruly sprawl of nature. We did not know that the most iconic building in the city was the Wonder Bread factory on River Drive, which everyone called "Twinkie Boulevard," even though Twinkies were never made there. We did not know how popular Harley Davidson motorcycles are among its residents, or why. We did not know that air could feel like a mixture of water and glue. We did not know that downtown Davenport wasn't safe at night for anyone except the sort of people who make it unsafe. We did not know anything about Davenport, in other words, except that it was there, in the middle of the country, waiting for us.

"By the end of the summer, you guys will know Davenport better than anybody," Mike chortled as we drove along River Drive past the Wonder Bread factory toward downtown. "You'll know everybody, and everybody will know you. If you do your job right, that is."

With startlingly little ceremony, Mike dropped us off at the edge of a small park in downtown Davenport and wished us "good luck." He gave us a phone number where we could reach him, and told us to check in with him at 7 p.m that evening to give him a progress report. Our job now, he said, was to "figure things out," which he expected would take us about six to eight hours.

Then he drove off.

So there we were, three college guys standing on a corner in the middle of Davenport wondering what to do next. Each of us had a backpack with all our belongings in it, a sleeping bag, and a bright red sales case that, turned on its side, doubled as a place to sit. None of us had taken a shower that morning, either, so we looked vaguely homeless. Which we were, technically, since we had no place yet to call home.

Russ was the first one to notice the smell.

It was not the smell of baking Wonder bread, which Davenport's Chamber of Commerce used to claim was the official odor of Davenport, a smell often described in the city's newspaper as "wondrous" (pun completely, totally, and unfortunately intended). No, it was the sort of smell that's more properly called a "stench," for it was a combination of all the foulest odors in the world—shit, piss, decay, disease, decomposition and death—mixed into a noxious, eye-watering cloud of awfulness, the sort of smell that makes your nose hairs curl and shoots an involuntary spurt of bile into the back of your throat.

"Oh my god," Greg choked.

"Sorry, I've been holding that one in since Springfield," Russ joked.

Then the source of the smell drove by: a semi-truck full of dirty, squealing pigs packed so tightly that their ears, noses, feet, and tails poked out slats in the side of the truck. There were three decks of them, one on top of the other, in a kind of hellish box of agricultural commerce. The pigs squirmed and jostled each other in a frenzy of fear and confusion. The fear itself was part of the smell, the acrid sting of impending doom. As the truck rolled by, one of the pigs looked at me through the slats. The look in its big black eye was one of resignation and disgust, as if it knew the end was near but no longer cared.

The truck rolled by and the stench slowly dissipated. Still, it seemed to stick in my nostrils and on my clothes for hours. Little did I know that it would stick in my head for decades.

"Let's go grab a cup of coffee and go figure this out," Russ suggested.

And just like that, we had a way forward.

The park where Mike had dropped us off was connected to the city's main drag, which was of course named Main Street, as Midwestern tradition demands. We walked down Main St. toward the river for several blocks until we came to a diner, the kind of eating establishment that tradition also demands: black-and-white linoleum with red vinyl booths, Formica tables yellowing at the edges, manually typed menus sheathed in a plastic sleeve, red plastic water glasses, an assortment of pies under cover of glass on the counter, coffee so thin you can see through it, and a lone waitress named "Madge," dressed in white nursing shoes and a powder blue smock who says, "What'll you have, boys," the way your favorite aunt might if she worked for minimum wage plus tips and had to smile all day to keep from crying.

This place, we decided, would be our home base. We'd split up the names on our list—two apiece—and go talk to these "friends of the company" about allowing one, two, or all three of us to invade their home, eat their food, use their bathrooms, and generally brighten their lives with our presence. For free, if possible. In between discussing living arrangements with these folks, we agreed it was a good idea to go sell some books in order to put some cash in our pockets. Meanwhile, Greg agreed to float us all for a few days with his $300, even if it meant staying at a motel for a night or two until we got our bearings. We'd meet back at the restaurant at 6 p.m, and check in with Mike, our mustachioed district manager, at 7 p.m., and go from there. After coffee and some pie (we'd had breakfast, but felt we had to eat something else for Madge's sake), we fist-bumped and parted ways for the day.

The first family on my list was located in a neighborhood so diametrically opposed to the neighborhood in which I grew up that I immediately feared for my life. It was full of black people, to begin with. Where I grew up, the African American population was pretty much zero. For good or ill, that's just the way it was. In fact, until that point in my life the only black person I'd ever met was Olympic long-jump champion and world-record-holder Bob Beamon, who shattered the world long-jump record by almost two feet in the 1968 Olympics and held the title for twenty-three years until Mike Powell bested him in 1991 by one-and-three-quarter inches. Beamon also happened to be our high-school track coach. (I went to a rich, all-white high-school in Southern California—the sort of school that hires Olympic champions to coach its track team.) So now, walking around this neighborhood, in this strange city, in a part of the country I had never visited and of which I was completely ignorant—this was perhaps the first time in my life I'd felt completely out of place. I'm not a racist, but I'm not an idiot, either. I knew instinctively that I didn't belong there, that I wasn't welcome, and that there was no place to hide. I didn't blame them. If I were black, and all my neighbors were black, and suddenly I saw a tall white guy in shorts and a Polo shirt carrying a red sales case and strolling through my neighborhood, I'd be suspicious of me too. Nobody actually did anything threatening; they just eyed me warily, as if I were some sort of wild animal that could be dangerous, but probably wasn't, if you just left it alone. I felt the same way about them, of course. If I caught someone's eye, I just smiled to let them know that I was harmless. If they smiled back, everything was cool. If not, I just kept walking, head down, in the hope that I would eventually become invisible.

After a few blocks, a kid about ten years old rolled up to me on a bicycle and said, "You ain't from 'round here, are ya?"

"How'd you guess?"

"Just a hunch," he said. Then he leaned closer and whispered, "You should probably get out of here. There's no tellin' what might happen." Then he smiled and sped off.

It was terrifying.

If the family I was supposed to approach was in this neighborhood, there had obviously been an enormous mistake. Even if someone were kind enough to offer me a room, there was no way I could live in that neighborhood. In fact, my desire to find a place to live was quickly replaced by a desire to live somewhere else, somewhere with rich, non-threatening white people who thought my college aspirations were admirable and who'd take pity on me and my friends because it was the nice, decent, friendly thing to do. Where were *those* people?, I wondered. Did they even exist in a place like Davenport?

The next address on my list was several miles away in a suburb on the outer edge of the city. I took a bus to the general area, which I'd circled on a map, the way we used to do back when our phones couldn't tell us where to go. I'd identified the street, but didn't know how the houses were numbered. The best I could do was find the street and walk along it until I hit the right number.

As I strolled and the blocks rolled by, it was impossible not to notice the difference between this neighborhood and the one I had just left. Tidy, upper-middle-class houses with manicured lawns and weed-free flower beds; cars that didn't have to be propped up on cinder blocks; dogs that were shampooed and groomed and belonged to a specific breed; mailboxes that weren't dented; street signs that didn't have bullet holes in them; streets paved with smooth, crack-free asphalt; roomy, two-car garages; sidewalks shaded by large trees that rustled in the breeze; a faint whiff of barbecue in the air; kids playing whiffle ball in the street; the busy hum of lawnmowers pushed by proud homeowners who devoted their weekends to landscape maintenance. This is more like it, I thought. This was the sort of neighborhood I was looking for, a neighborhood full of large houses with lots of empty rooms owned by nice people who might not think letting a college student live with them was such a bad idea.

After some hiking around, I found the address on my list. The house was a two-story brick Colonial, the kind with white, Romanesque columns on the porch that are intended to make the house look a wee bit grander than it really is—more like the Parthenon, say, than a three-bedroom house on the outskirts of Iowa's third-largest city. On the sidewalk out front I paused to think about the best way to introduce myself. Then the hard part, of course—how to segue smoothly into the subject of free food and lodging for the rest of the summer, starting today if possible.

After all, how does one ask a stranger, "Can I live with you?" without sounding desperate or pathetic? The company's advice on this matter was to lead with the fact that you were selling books for the Southwestern Company all summer. To hear them tell it, mention of the company's name would immediately elicit smiles and hugs, and any resistance to the idea of letting a strange kid live in the house would melt away like a pat of butter on hot skillet that's about to fry up a hardy Midwestern breakfast made by a woman who wants to be your summer "mom," because she knows how much you miss your own mother and doesn't want you to think you're not loved. Because you are—loved, that is. After all, you're a bookman who is dedicating his summer to the spread of knowledge and cheer throughout the region. So of course they're going to want to help you. Who wouldn't?

At the time, the proposition didn't sound quite so ridiculous. The good folks at the Southwestern Company had assured us that the country was teeming with friendly people who would jump at the chance to host one of their own for the summer. And I believed it, because I had to—because not believing it meant cutting the gossamer thread of hope that tied my precarious present to my allegedly awesome future.

After a few deep breaths, I worked up the courage to knock on the door. Book men don't knock on doors any old way, of course. In training, we were instructed to knock with three hard, confident raps at a metronome rate of about 120—quick enough to convey a sense of urgency, but slow enough to let the people inside know there was nothing to be afraid of. You were just a friendly bookman knocking on their door slightly slower than a normal person might, because, unlike normal people, you have been taught to pay attention to the force and pace of your knock in order to avoid sending "the wrong message."

A girl of about thirteen answered the door. She looked at me with casual indifference, utterly incurious about why I might be there. I asked if her parents were home. "Nope," she said. "They're at the country club," she said. "My mom is in a tennis tournament."

Tennis tournament? I could not believe my luck.

"Which country club might that be?" I asked.

She looked at me like I was an idiot. "Duh, there's only one."

"Of course," I said. "It's just that I'm new to the area and . . ."

"Anything else?" she interrupted. Clearly, I had worn out her patience.

"No. Thank you," I said as she closed the door. Then the scrape and thwunk of a deadbolt sliding into place. The feeling that the girl did not trust me. The depressing realization that even if I did succeed in convincing her parents to let me live there, I'd be living in the same house as that kid, who reminded me of my own younger sister, who, in her early teens, seemed perpetually annoyed by the fact that I was allowed to exist on the same planet as her. Scientific studies have of course determined that teenage girls are the worst—the most selfish, ungrateful, conceited beings on Earth—and that living with them is an utter nightmare. Then again, that kid was the perfect age for the *Volume Library*, so even if the whole housing-me-for-free-all-summer thing didn't pan out, maybe I could sell them a book, I thought. (Already, without even realizing it, my mind was starting to operate like a bookman, scanning the horizon for opportunities, trying to make a lousy situation seem better than it really was.)

I didn't know it at the time, but the Davenport Country Club is not in Davenport; it's in Bettendorf, the upscale quadrant of the Quad Cities. Somewhere along the way I had crossed over into this exclusive enclave of money and privilege, and felt right at home. I grew up in a similar area. In my youth, I spent an ungodly number of hours whacking a tennis ball to and fro at swanky country clubs where women played doubles with their friends and drank mimosas in between sets while their husbands played golf and smoked the fat, smelly cigars their wives wouldn't let them smoke at home. I knew these people. I grew up with them. And so, before I even met the couple on my list (let's call them the Hendersons), I felt we already had a rapport of sorts, a shared set of values, a mutual understanding that Saturday afternoons are for enjoying the finer things in life, the things that only successful people who have paid their membership dues are allowed to enjoy.

It didn't take long to locate them. The Hendersons were part of a group of about thirty people drinking and chatting on a patio near the pool. If there was a tennis tournament going on, it either hadn't begun or was already over. No matter. I found the table where Mrs. Henderson was sitting (which was not the table where Mr. Henderson was sitting) and approached her with what I hoped was a confident, charming smile. I introduced myself, and told to her that the Southwestern Company had given me her name, with the understanding that she and her husband might be amenable to hosting a student who was trying to pay his way through college by selling books door-to-door in the area. Fate had delivered me to Davenport, I explained, and now my friends and I were looking for a place to stay. A home base of sorts. An arrangement that would allow us to use a spare bedroom, say, and maybe a portion of the garage when it came time to distribute the books we sold at the end of the summer and our inventory needed to be stored temporarily prior to delivery. But before that, we'd be out early in the morning, before 8 a.m., and wouldn't be back until 9 or 10 p.m. at night. So we'd hardly ever be there, really. And yes, all of this might seem like a strange request, out of the blue and all of a sudden, with no warning whatsoever, but what she had to remember was that my cohorts and I didn't even know we'd be selling books in Davenport until yesterday, so there was really no way of arranging matters ahead of time. Instead, the company had given us a list of prospects to contact—people like her who had volunteered to sponsor a young book person at some point in the future, that point being right about now.

As I recall, Mrs. Henderson was a slender, blonde woman who did not appear to have a sense of humor or much capacity for dealing with oddball requests that didn't make any sense to her.

"What?" she said, puckering her nose as if she had just sniffed a carton of sour milk.

I showed her the list with her name on it. I explained that I had been instructed, by the company, to contact her and see if we could work out an arrangement.

She looked at the list, then at me, and said, "I have no idea what you're talking about, young man."

"Well, all I know is that you are on the list," I replied.

"And you're looking for a place to live?"

"Yes."

"So you're homeless?"

I laughed at that one. No, I'm not homeless, I explained—I'm in Davenport because this is my assigned territory. I don't yet have a place to live, I admitted, but hoped she might be able to help out on that front.

Annoyed and still uncomprehending, she said, "Let me get my husband."

"Frank!" she yelled. "Get over here!"

A tallish, semi-handsome man with middle-management hair walked over, and he too looked annoyed. At her.

"Do you know anything about, what was it, the Southern company?" she asked him. "Did you sign up for something. They appear to have put us on a list."

I went through the whole spiel again with Mr. Henderson. When I finished, he too looked like he'd smelled something bad.

"Nope. Doesn't ring a bell," he said.

Well, the two of them had to have some sort of connection with the Southwestern Company, I explained, because otherwise why would their name just randomly appear on a list?

"Hey, a couple of years ago, didn't we buy a book from some gal that showed up at the door?" Mr. Henderson said to his wife.

"Oh yes, I remember."

"Awful mess," Mr. Henderson said. "We paid her, but she never brought the book. Said she was going to, but didn't. Had to call them and raise some hell. They finally mailed the book, I think. Which was fine. But then it turned out the book itself wasn't very good. Lots of outdated information. The maps looked like they hadn't been updated in twenty years. And after about six months the pages started falling out. So, not a great purchase."

"I see," I said. "So you never volunteered to maybe someday host a young book person in your home?"

"What? No!"

"And the only contact you've had with the company is that you bought a book some time ago?"

"That's probably how they got our address," Mr. Henderson deduced. "I had to give it to them so they could mail the damn thing to us."

I could see where this was headed. I apologized for bothering them, and reiterated that I had been led to believe that they might be willing to put me up in a spare room for the summer, based on some previous communication between them and the company that obviously never happened.

"Sorry, son," Mr. Henderson said, chuckling at the absurdity of it. "Looks like they sent you on a wild goose chase."

"Yes, it appears that way," I agreed, and thanked them for their time.

As I was walking away, Mrs. Henderson chimed in, "And you can tell them to take our name off that list, thank you very much."

CHAPTER 16

Rather than take the bus back to downtown Davenport, I decided to walk back and try to sell a few books along the way. Other than the Henderson house, I had yet to knock on an actual prospect's door or sell a book, but I knew I had to start sometime, and now was as good a time as any. The neighborhood looked promising. Nice houses. Evidence of children (balls in the yard, plastic tricycles in the driveway, hop-scotch boards scrawled in colored chalk on the sidewalk, half-filled kiddie pools, basketball hoops over the garage). I scanned the neighborhood looking for clues as to which house might harbor someone in need of a *Volume Library*. The first house was important, I thought, because if I could get one sale out of the way, get over that first hump, the one everyone said was so difficult, I'd be on my way to a successful summer. Besides, I needed money. I had enough to get me through the day, and maybe the day after, but that was about it. I was counting on a strong first week to establish some economic footing, so that I could open a bank account and start building my little business. Because that's what I was—an independent businessman, an entrepreneur, a go-getter—and there is nothing more important for a go-getter than to get going.

The thing is, knocking on a stranger's door is scary. It's even scarier when you know people don't really want to talk to you. And it's even scarier when you know that your livelihood depends on overcoming their resistance. Still, I had spent the past week training for this moment, practicing my approach and my pitch and my close, so I felt prepared. Sort of. It'd been a couple of days since I'd gone through my sales presentation, and I was still a little shaky on my "answers to objections." And even though I couldn't quite locate all the words in my head that very second, I was reasonably sure they'd come to me in the moment, as I delivered my presentation.

Still, I had to knock on a door.

But I couldn't. Try as I might, I could not make myself walk up to someone's front door and confidently rap on it three times. The thought of encountering another pouty teenager was stuck in my head, and my failure to persuade the Hendersons to provide me free food and lodging for the summer had shaken my confidence. Things were not going as planned, and I feared that if I started knocking on doors and getting rejected, my plans, such as they were, would continue to unravel. There was also a bit of stage fright involved. Selling books is a kind of performance, the applause for which is someone handing you a check. In training, they try to prepare you for the fact that ninety-eight out of a hundred times, you are not going to get the applause you seek, or the check you want. They remind you that many of the most successful people in the world were also monumental failures: that for every home run Babe Ruth hit, he struck out three times; that Thomas Edison failed thousands of times before he invented a light bulb that worked; how Agatha Christie spent five years submitting her first novel to publishers before it was finally accepted. All of these people persisted, despite the odds against them, and overcame almost inconceivable obstacles to eventually succeed. And that was supposed to inspire us to do the same.

What all these stories also have in common, of course, is someone who endured a shitload of heartache and frustration. What about the thousands who have endured all those very same adversities and NOT succeeded beyond their wildest dreams? One does not hear about such people in sales training classes, because people who fail time after time and never succeed are, in fact, the embodiment of everyone's deepest, darkest fears. No one wants to be that person—the person who tried as hard as they possibly could, for as long as they could, and *still* failed. Those people are losers. You are a winner. Or at least you will be, the pep talk went, once you start *thinking positively* about how shitty you will feel when you get rejected over and over and over again in your pursuit of that all-important first sale.

The best way to avoid rejection is of course to avoid putting yourself in a situation where you can be rejected. Trying to sell someone a book is what a business consultant might call a "rejection-rich" situation, so if your objective is to avoid the pain and humiliation of hearing the word "no," the last thing you want to do is go bang your knuckles on a stranger's door. And yet, it is impossible to sell a book *without* knocking on someone's door, so you must find a way to overcome your fear of rejection in order to allow the possibility of success to materialize. This war of wills is the reason most people detest the idea of door-to-door selling, why the people who try it usually fail, and why so few people in the world are actually good at it. While your head is telling you that you must confront your fear in order to overcome it, your gut is telling you to flee, or at the very least to keep walking until you find a house that "speaks" to you—one that seems friendly and inviting and appears to offer a high chance of success. No such house exists, of course. Just because someone lives in an eight-room McMansion and drives a Mercedes does not mean they will buy a book, and just because someone lives in a rusted-out trailer doesn't mean they won't. I know this now; I didn't then.

Finally, at some point, I knew I had to suck it up and go knock on someone's door. I chose a nice-looking, two-story Tudor with a wood-paneled station wagon in the driveway. In the 1970s, station wagons—eminently practical cars with a large back seat and an even larger cargo area—were the mini-vans of the day. They were the family car that said to the world: I have abandoned style for practicality in all matters and now operate a shuttle service for children and groceries. The strip of wood-grained plastic running along the side of many station wagons was supposed to hearken back to the days of the "woodies" of the 1930s and 1940s, cars that had actual wood side panels. As with so many things in American commerce, the real thing was replaced by something fake, and the fakery itself served to cheapen the product—even though, ironically, the fake wooden panel along the side of a station wagon was supposed to be a nod to luxury and style.

In the eyes of a bookman, however, the presence of a station wagon meant parents with children. Parents with children meant potential customers. And so, after a few deep breaths, I set my sales case down and prepared to knock.

I was so nervous it felt like my blood was simmering. I stood on the porch for a while, trying to gather my courage. Then, finally, I opened the screen door and rapped on the door three times, tentatively, harboring the secret hope that no one would answer.

Nothing.

I knocked on the door again, this time with a bit more authority.

Still nothing.

Satisfied that I had done everything I could, and secretly relieved that no one had answered, I picked up my sales case and turned away from the door. Half-way down the porch steps, a voice behind me said, "Hello. Can I help you?"

It was a woman—the mother, I guessed. Simultaneously terrified and thrilled, I turned toward her and discovered, the moment I tried to open my mouth, that I could not remember what I was supposed to say. My mind went blank. The search for words turned to panic as the synapses in my brain fritzed and sputtered in a futile attempt to recall my "training." The trouble was, in training the person inside opened the door immediately. At no point did we ever practice a situation where the customer came to the door *as we were leaving*. Consequently, the rhythm of everything I had learned and practiced was thrown off. I couldn't remember what I was supposed to say in order to explain my presence on her porch, much less what I was supposed to say after that, if by some miracle she were to allow me into her home. And so I stood there, saying nothing, searching in vain for the magic words that would persuade her to invite me in.

After a few seconds, she broke the silence. "Are you selling something?" she asked.

I barely had a chance to process her question before she added, "No thank you," and shut the door.

Part of me was relieved that our interaction was so abruptly cut short. It meant that I didn't have to endure the embarrassment of stumbling through a sales presentation I couldn't remember. I had also accomplished three important objectives: 1) I had overcome my fear to do what needed to be done—knock on a stranger's door; 2) I had collected my first rejection—one of 98 to come, so I needed to get used to that feeling; and 3) I had survived the ordeal without suffering too much damage to my psyche.

Still, in the aggregate, the day had thus far been full of nothing but failure and rejection. No forward progress had been made on any front. More important—and more devastating—the goals I had set out to accomplish at the beginning of the day (secure a place to live and sell a couple of books to make some quick cash) seemed farther away than ever. The more I thought about it, the idea of convincing some random family to let three college guys live with them for the entire summer seemed ludicrous. Who would do that? No one, I concluded. I could imagine some goodhearted person taking in one of us, but not two, and certainly not three. It was an absurd request, and when I approached the Hendersons, they were right to balk.

My hope was that Russ and Greg were having better luck than I was. Russ could be very charming and persuasive. He might be capable of pulling off a miracle. For all I knew, when we all returned to the diner that evening, Russ would have everything wired up with some benevolent Midwestern family, his pockets full of cash from a successful day of selling. I didn't know Greg well enough to put much faith in him, but he seemed like a competent guy. Maybe he too would surprise us.

One thing was certain: I would not be saving the day. Not that I didn't want to be a hero; just that I couldn't see how it was possible. Without any more leads to check out, there were no more housing prospects to pursue. And before knocking on anyone else's door, I felt that I needed to go sit on a park bench somewhere and go over my sales presentation a few times. Freezing up on that woman's porch had shaken my confidence. I needed to regain it again before subjecting myself to another potential humiliation. Selling a book was actually the farthest thing from my mind. My goal now was much more humble: I just wanted an opportunity to get a few sentences out of my mouth before someone shut the door in my face. At that point, persuading them to open the door, let me in, listen to my spiel, and buy a book—well, it all seemed like an impossible pipe dream. Who would do that?, I wondered.

No one, that's who.

And that, it seemed, was the theme of my day.

I had every intention of getting back to it that afternoon. But I hadn't eaten lunch yet, and it was starting to heat up. I'd seen a McDonald's on the bus ride to Bettendorf. Finding it suddenly became my mission in life, and I pursued it with great passion. Because as long as I was headed to McDonald's, I did not need to worry about anything else. Finding a place to live and selling books could wait. Besides, I reasoned, if I didn't get something to eat or drink soon, I might experience some sort of low-sugar episode (which had happened to me before), or worse, I might faint from dehydration. In fact, if I didn't find that McDonald's, and fast, *I could die*, I thought.

So, for the sake of my friends Russ and Greg, and for the greater good of the Southwestern Company itself, it was suddenly imperative that I get a Big Mac with extra fries and one of those vanilla frosty shakes with the weirdly creamy texture that doesn't feel so much like cream on your tongue as it does some lab scientist's idea of the word "creamy." A McDonald's shake never tastes quite right, but it doesn't taste wrong, either—and it was a wholly synthetic mouth sensation for which I suddenly had an intense and undeniable craving.

By the time I found McDonald's, an hour or so later, I was a sweaty mess. Walking into that Mickey D's was like diving into a frigid pool. The air-conditioning was cranked up so high that the hair on my arms tingled. The air inside seemed lighter, too. Outside, the air was thick and humid; it had texture and weight. But inside this McDonald's—this blessed sanctuary of civilization, as I had come to think of it—the air was clean and cool. Just feeling it on my skin was another affirmation that I had made the right decision.

I ate slowly, deliberately, savoring every bite. One can, it turns out, chew a French fry quite a long time before it disintegrates in your mouth and disappears. And while one is chewing a French fry that long—especially a McDonald's French fry—one gets an appreciation for how much it differs from the taste of, say, an actual potato. These days, McDonald's fries are bubbled in vegetable oil. But in 1979 they were fried in beef tallow, which is fat rendered from a cow; fat that is solid at room temperature and does not need to be refrigerated, which makes it easy to ship and store. The flavor, too, is important, which is why McDonald's still formulates its vegetable oil to mimic the properties of beef tallow, even adding beef flavoring to the mix. McDonald's fries are also dipped in a sugar solution to sweeten them up, and salted so thoroughly that a generation of cardiologists has been employed to counteract their cumulative effect on the human heart.

Like so many other frankenfoods, the McDonald's French fry is little more than a delivery system for fat, sugar, and salt, the taste triad that food engineers have learned to manipulate in various way to deliver what is now referred to as a "bliss point," the point at which your mouth overrides your mind and you shove another Dorito, Cheetoh, Funyun, or Frito down your throat and experience, once again, the deadly deliciousness of science. I didn't know any of that at the time, of course. Back then, the general public didn't have access to much information about the food we were eating. We trusted the government to keep restaurants from feeding us anything deadly, and no one could imagine the lengths to which a corporate entity would go in order to develop something as strange as a scientifically optimized French fry.

Unfortunately, one can only sit in a McDonald's for so long before it starts to feel creepy. Or rather, before the people who work there start thinking you're a creep. I left my air-conditioned sanctuary at around three o'clock, several hours before I was scheduled to meet Russ and Greg at the diner. I knew what I should be doing: I should be systematically knocking on doors, gathering rejections, and telling myself that I was "doing my job." I'd just spent what amounted to 25 percent of my life savings on lunch, and rather desperately needed an infusion of cash. Still, I could not bring myself to knock on another door. Instead, I wandered around until I found a park where I could sit and go over my sales script. I knew I hadn't memorized it yet, and the company's insistence that we follow the script, to the word, made it seem important. The problem needed to be addressed. Immediately. After all, I reasoned, why jeopardize the possibility of a sale—and burn through an entire neighborhood—by delivering a bunch of inept sales presentations? At that moment in time it made much more sense to sit in that park and study my script until I knew it cold. It was also a handy excuse not to sell, and any excuse not to be selling books was a welcome one.

Instead of learning my script, however, I ended up lying down under a tree and taking a nap. As I discovered time and time again throughout the summer, not selling books is exhausting. It takes a great deal of energy to avoid doing what you're supposed to be doing. You have to keep coming up with rationalizations, justifications, and excuses for why—even though you're not doing what you're supposed to—you're still a good, hard-working person who is doing their level best to succeed. As I nodded off, the stream of my fading consciousness ran something like this:

"How the fuck did I get here? I should be at the beach right now, playing volleyball in the sun and looking at pretty girls in bikinis so skimpy they make your teeth ache. I should be washing the sand and sweat off my body in the brisk, churning waters of the Pacific Ocean, diving beneath the froth on my way out to the edge of the surf line, where a large, perfect curl of blue inevitably rises out of the ocean and carries me back to shore, exhilarated and refreshed. This evening, I should be sitting around a campfire on the beach, drinking beer and watching the flames dance on the sunburned cheeks of a dozen teenage girls, any one of whom could be a swimsuit model. A few of them might even be willing to take a nighttime stroll down the beach under the shimmer of a gibbous moon, the rumble music of water from hundreds of miles away ending in a trickle of water over our toes, followed by a tender, innocent—and then perhaps not-so-innocent—kiss. But no. For reasons that are not at all clear to me now, I am stuck in Iowa—Iowa!—a state I can honestly say I have never given a scintilla of thought to in my entire life. I never had to, because I lived in California, where states like Iowa, Illinois, Missouri, Wisconsin, Minnesota, and Kansas simply do not matter. And by "not matter," I mean they basically don't exist, at least not in the consciousness of Californians. People call it "flyover country," but that term at least gives this part of the country some physical substance. To most Californians, there is nothing but a blank space between the Rocky Mountains and New York City, a black hole of cultural and existential nothingness that cannot even be imagined, and isn't, because there are so many more pleasant things to imagine in California than what life is like in a place like Iowa—a place, Californians assume, where no one would actually *choose* to live. Or visit. Or anything else. Yet here I am, lying beneath a kind of tree I do not recognize—an elm, maybe? Or an oak?—and it is not altogether unpleasant. Except for the gnawing sense of dread in the pit of my stomach, the simmering juices of anxiety and foreboding that tell me I may have made a horrible mistake. What am I doing here, anyway? What am I trying to prove? Am I just trying to impress Russ that I, too, can sell books? That I, too, burn with the ambition of a thousand suns, and am willing to suffer any form of humiliation to prove it? Hell Week wasn't bad enough? I had to sign up for more? What is wrong with me? Why am I doing this to myself?"

And on and on.

The one thing I would not allow myself to think about was giving up. Russ and I had made a promise to each other—that we'd stick it out, no matter what—and the thought of reneging on that promise was too painful to bear. That and the thought of returning home, having to explain to my parents and friends how I had failed, was enough to keep me going. One of the core messages hammered relentlessly home during our training was that quitting was the ultimate act of cowardice. "Think about how disappointed your parents will be when they learn that they've raised a quitter," one of the company's pin-striped guilt-slingers had admonished. "And you wouldn't just be quitting on yourself—you'd be quitting on everyone who loves you, trusts you, and respects you. Even worse, you'd be establishing a pattern of failure for the rest of your life. Do you want to be the sort of person who quits when the going gets tough? Do you want to be the sort of person who responds to life's challenges by throwing in the towel? I've got a secret for you: Winners never quit, and quitters never win. Do you want to win? Then you cannot quit. And always remember, God is watching you. He knows what's in your heart. If there's an ounce of quit in your heart, He knows it. And if you let that ounce grow into a pound of quit, He'll know that too. And if you do quit, you can make up all the excuses you want, and you can lie to yourself about why you did it, why you couldn't keep going, why you chose the easy path. But God will know, and deep down *you* will know, that you quit because you lost faith, in both God and yourself, and you let that loss of faith consume you. Is that what you want? Of course not. But that's what's at stake here, folks. Selling books for the Southwestern Company isn't just a job. It's a fork in the road, an opportunity for you to develop the habits and mindset of success, which will put you on the path to happiness and prosperity. There is another path, the one that leads to failure and regret, loneliness and despair. And you can take that path. But if you do, remember there will always be a part of you that knew there was another way, a path you chose not to take. And you will always wonder: What if? What if I hadn't quit? What if I had kept going? What if I hadn't listened to that cowardly little voice inside me? What might have happened? How might things have turned out differently? Unfortunately, you will never know—because you chose the path of a quitter."

So quitting was not an option. But by the time my nap was over, neither was the prospect of selling any more books. I had to meet Russ and Greg back at the diner, which was several miles away. I didn't want to spend any more money on a bus, so I picked up my sales case and started walking. As I walked, I formulated the story I would tell to Russ and Greg about my heroic attempts to find us a place to live, and my courageous—but sadly disappointing—attempts to sell the *Volume Library* to the good people of Bettendorf. The parts about camping out in McDonald's and snoozing in the park didn't need to be mentioned, I decided. Those diversions did not align with the narrative about myself that I wanted people to believe—the one that proved I was a winner, not a napper.

To this day, however, whenever I am faced with a stressful situation for which there is no easy resolution, I feel a powerful urge to lie down and close my eyes. These days, anytime I can sneak in an afternoon snooze—well that, to me, is winning.

CHAPTER 17

I arrived at the diner a little after 6 p.m. and ordered a Coke. I was dripping with sweat from the long walk back, and the look of distress on my face was easy to read.

"Long day, hun?" Madge asked as she set the Coke down in front of me.

"You might say that," I said, smiling weakly.

"Well don't you worry," she said, "Madge'll take care o' you." Her tone was maternal and comforting, which was exactly what I needed at that moment.

Before Russ and Greg arrived, I needed to get my story of struggle and failure straight, so I began rehearsing in my head what I was going to say to them. What I hoped was for Russ and Greg to walk through the door with an entirely different story, one of challenges conquered and problems solved. That way, my story would seem more valiant than pathetic, and my lack of success wouldn't matter in the grand scheme of things, because Russ and Greg had come through in the clutch. If on the other hand Russ and Greg had a day more like mine, we'd all be instantly initiated into a three-person fraternity of failure. We'd bond over our mutual miseries and buck each other up with pledges to do better tomorrow. If neither of them came through, however, we were going to have to figure out where to sleep. Any place with a shower and a bed was fine with me, because I planned to crawl under the covers and remain unconscious for as long as possible.

Forty-five minutes later, neither Greg nor Russ had shown up. I took this as a good sign. Perhaps it meant that one of them had found a place for us to live. Or, maybe they'd each sold a ton of books and were on a roll. Russ had more fortitude than me, I was sure, and was probably out there using every last second of daylight to make sure he returned a hero. Saving the day was the kind of thing he was good at, I told myself, and nothing would give him greater pleasure than to walk through the door bearing the news that he, and he alone, had been successful in locating that elusive mythical family with three extra rooms in their house and an intense desire to shelter and feed a trio of college kids whose average height was about six-foot-three. If anyone could do it, Russ could, I thought—and for all of our sake's, I hoped I was right.

But when Russ finally did walk through the door, I could see immediately that he had not saved anyone's day, least of all his own. His shirt was soaked with sweat. His hair was a wet, matted mess, and he had none of his usual swagger. He looked the way I felt—tired, beaten, defeated.

"How'd it go?" I ventured as he slid into the booth across from me.

"Got my ass kicked. How about you?"

"Same."

"How about Greg?"

"Haven't seen him."

"A good sign, maybe?"

"Maybe. Maybe not."

Russ checked his wristwatch. It was 7:00 p.m., time to call our district manager, Mike, and report in. Neither of us wanted to make that call. Admitting defeat did not come easily to either of us. We knew Mike was going to give us a ration of shit for failing our first assignment. Worst of all, we deserved it.

We decided to wait until Greg arrived before making the call, in the blind hope that maybe, just maybe, he'd come through and save the day.

At 7:20 p.m. Greg still hadn't arrived, and Russ could take it no longer. "Let's get this over with," he muttered, resigned to the fate that had befallen us. He even agreed to make the call.

Due to a general lack of portable communication devices in those days, the nearest phone was in a booth outside the restaurant. Russ dialed the number Mike had given us, and spoke to him while I waited on the sidewalk. After Russ explained our situation, there was a long pause during which Russ said nothing. I hoped that Mike was giving us some sage advice gleaned from his many years in the field. But after a couple of minutes, Russ leaned out of the phone booth and said, "Greg isn't coming. He bailed on us."

I didn't quite know what "bailed" meant in that context. But I did know that if Greg wasn't going to show up, it meant Russ and I had less than forty dollars between us—enough for a day or two of food, maybe, but not enough to rent a motel room, and certainly not enough to get us through the week. I paced up and down the sidewalk while Russ continued to talk to Mike. Perhaps he'd be willing to front us some money until we got on our feet, I thought. Or maybe he knew of some people in Davenport we could call, people who were available in case of an emergency. A company as large as Southwestern had to have a larger network than the few names we had been given, I reasoned. Besides, we couldn't possibly be the only people in this position. Hundreds of college kids around the Midwest were attempting to do the same thing we were, and not all of them could have succeeded. What did the company do in such situations? It was simply irresponsible—and probably illegal—to abandon young people in strange towns knowing that they had no money or resources at their disposal. There had to be a backup plan, I thought. During our fraternity hazing, for instance, when pledges were left in the desert with nothing but their underwear and orders to find their way back, they may have felt alone—but they were not. Unbeknownst to them, a senior fraternity member had been assigned to each one, and was responsible for making sure that the pledge made it back alive, one way or another. These observers were out there, in the dark, hiding out of sight, providing a safety net that the pledges themselves were not aware of, but existed nonetheless, by design. Cruel as the episode might be, those who invented it were not so cruel that they'd just leave someone in the desert to fend for themselves. Many students in a fraternity are pre-law, and even pre-law students know that if something bad happens to a pledge in the desert, the fraternity could get sued or expelled. No matter how sadistic the hazing ritual, measures were always taken to prevent a catastrophe. That's what I hoped was going on here. I hoped that the situation we were in wasn't as dire as it seemed, because people like Mike were responsible for making sure that we succeeded. If we didn't succeed, the company didn't make any money. So, I reasoned, while it may serve the company's interests to frighten us into action, to motivate us by putting us in a situation that required the selling of some books to escape from, it was not in the company's best interests to break our spirits and send us running home to our parents—which, it turned out, is what Greg had done. He'd used his $300 to buy a plane ticket home. That had to be as unforeseen a development to management as it was to us, so I assumed the company would course-correct accordingly and step in to help us through what we all hoped was just a temporary setback.

And they did, sort of. It's just that the company's response to our predicament—and many predicaments to come—was not quite what we expected.

After talking to Mike for a couple of minutes, Russ leaned out of the phone booth and put the receiver to his chest (which is how, back in the day, one "muted" a phone call).

"What's he say?" I asked.

"He wants us to sing the Bookman Song," Russ replied.

"Right now?"

"Yes."

"Let's not and say we did."

"He wants to hear it."

"What do you mean?"

"He wants us to do it right here, right now, while he's on the phone."

"You're kidding."

"No."

One of the great—and sometimes grating—things about Russ was that requests like this did not throw him. He was more than willing to make a fool of himself in public. And if you dared him to do something, he could usually figure out a way to do it in a way that humiliated the darer, not him.

He did not miss a beat. Russ stepped out of the phone booth and motioned for me to join him. "Okay Mike, this is for you!" he yelled.

Then he began.

"It's a great day to be a bookman, it's the best thing I know," he shout-sang. As he sang, he bounced around on one foot and did a kind of helicopter pirouette, twirling his arms as if he were a hummingbird trying to fly for the first time. He gave me a look that said, "You better start making an idiot of yourself too or I'm going to kill you," and suddenly my feet began to shuffle and my arms began to swing, and I too was belting out the next line, "It's a great day to be a bookman, everywhere I go-oh-oh," (a line that the day's events had proven to be, at best, an ironic in-joke). With each line we sang louder and danced crazier, whirling around in circles and attracting the attention—and dismay—of passers-by. By the end, we weren't singing anymore, we were shouting. We screamed the line "and be of good cheer!," in a tone that let Mike know we were not feeling very cheerful, not cheerful at all. Then, in unison, we shouted, "I feel happy! I feel healthy! I feel SPECIFIC!" Russ then started slapping the backs of his hands together and barking like a seal. This was for my benefit, since Mike couldn't see it. In the faraway world of fraternity life, barking like a seal at someone was a short-handed way of saying, "I just did what you asked, but fuck you for making me do it." It fit the situation perfectly. Then we started laughing, in that hysterical, convulsive, "I can't believe we just did that" way, the sort of laughter that cleanses the soul and puts everything in perspective.

Then again, maybe our manager Mike had encountered derisive seal-barking before. Other than the Bookman Song, he had nothing to offer us in the way of help. "There, don't you feel better?" he told Russ on the phone. "You'll have better luck tomorrow, I'm sure of it," he assured us. Then he hung up.

And it was true, we did feel better. For about thirty seconds.

The unfortunate thing about cathartic, perspective-altering laughter is that once the mirth subsides, your old perspective starts to reassert itself. Our situation had not changed, and Mike had given us no guidance or help whatsoever. Greg had abandoned us, which meant that after dinner and paying for the cheapest of all possible hotel rooms, we would likely run out of money by about noon the next day. The gravity of the situation had made us both hungry, so we headed back into the diner to formulate a plan.

"That was quite a show you boys put on out there," Madge remarked as she set two water glasses down in front of us. The tone in her voice was one part amusement, one part concern.

"It's our Vegas act, what do you think?" Russ quipped.

"I think you boys are a crazy," she said, only half smiling.

We ordered hamburgers and fries, then sat in stunned silence for a minute or two.

"What now?" I offered.

The priorities, we agreed, were to eat and find a place to sleep. After that, things got a bit more complicated. We still had to find a place to live, and if we wanted to eat again anytime soon and not sleep on the street, we had to sell a few books in order to make some money. It was depressing to think about, but it would go on and on like that in a vicious circle until we found that mythical family that would take us in and love us and support us for free, either out of the goodness of their hearts or because they felt sorry for us, we didn't care which. Our backs were up against the wall. It was do or die. The only other thing we agreed upon was that we would not break down and call our parents for money. That was too easy. Both of us had a deep, almost primal need to figure this thing out for ourselves. As the Southwestern executives had warned us, and we firmly believed, calling our parents would be an admission of failure, of weakness. My parents had questioned my judgment about selling books in the first place (Are you sure that's what you want to do with your summer? Aren't there other jobs you can do? Maybe you could get an internship instead?), and crying 'help' from half-way across the country would only confirm their suspicions and give them one more reason to say they told me so. Russ's father was a top-rated lawyer, a legal success machine who had insanely high expectations for his eldest son. Russ would dine on sewer rats and sleep in a cave before calling his dad. So no, calling the 'rents wasn't an option. Unless things got really, really bad, in which case we could of course call them. Just not now, before we'd even gotten started, before we'd had a chance to fail a little more spectacularly and suffer a bit more legitimately. So we'd had a rough day. So what? Tomorrow would be a better day, just like Mike said. It had to be. Because another day like today was going to seriously test our resolve, and suck extremely hard to boot.

"This whole finding a family to live with thing is bullshit," I said. "The people I talked to hadn't even heard of the Southwestern Company. Or if they did, they didn't have anything good to say about it."

"I'm pretty sure it's a test," Russ replied. "Yes, it's bullshit. That's what I think we were supposed to figure out today, and now I think we're supposed to figure how to deal with it. How to adapt, change our game plan, and move forward."

"So you think Greg was a plant? Some kind of corporate shill who did his job and left us out here holding our nuts and running for cover?"

"I don't think that part was planned," Russ said. "But it doesn't matter. We still have to deal with the situation in front of us."

Mid-way through our discussion, a man the likes of which I'd never seen before approached our booth. He wore purple bell-bottom pants with white, patent-leather shoes so shiny they looked like they were made of glass. Holding the pants up was a fat, white belt studded with sequins, which wrapped around his slim waist and came together in a brass buckle shaped like a large heart. Tucked into those pants was a sheer lavender shirt with puffy sleeves, the kind you try not to get stuck wearing to your high-school prom. Several gold chains hung around his neck, and on his head he wore a large lavender hat with a white feather stuck in the brim, the kind of hat you might wear if you were a gay musketeer or a splendidly dressed pirate. Each finger on his hand sported at least one ring, and he leaned on a white cane, the top of which was crowned with a huge, fat heart made of brass. Encrusted in the middle of the brass heart was a red ruby, also shaped like a heart, except if you looked closely, the heart was cracked.

In other words, he looked like a pimp. It is of course unfair to judge a person by their wardrobe, but just because you do it doesn't mean you're wrong.

"I gather you boys are new in town?" the man said in a low, smooth baritone.

"We are," Russ said.

"Welcome then," he said. "May I sit?" he asked, pointing to the seat next to me.

"Uh, sure," I said, and scooted over. The man slid into the booth next to me, and a dense cloud of spicy cologne suddenly invaded my nostrils. We introduced ourselves, but he did not shake our hands. Nor did he tell us who he was.

"You college boys?"

We nodded.

"Where from?"

We told him.

"Arizona?" he laughed. "You come all the way from Arizona? To be here? What, you tryin' to beat the heat?"

We laughed nervously, and explained that no, we were in Davenport for work

"What kinda work?" he asked.

When we told him, he eyed us for a few seconds to see if we were bullshitting him. When he saw that we weren't, he leaned his head back and laughed, long and loud, as if it was the funniest thing he'd ever heard. Then he confirmed it.

"That's the funniest thing I ever heard," he said, catching his breath. "So let me see if I understand," he mused. "You got hired by a company to come here and sell books to poor people so you can go to college? But you ain't gettin' paid yet, so you're shit out of luck."

"Not just poor people," I corrected. "Anyone."

"Other than that, you understand our situation perfectly," Russ interjected.

"Uh huh," he nodded. "So, how do plan to sell these books of yours? You gonna just walk up and knock on people's doors and ask 'em, 'Hey, wanna buy a book so I can go to college and not have to live in a motherfuckin' shithole like this?'"

"Sort of," I said, "though in our line of work, swearing is discouraged."

He paused for a moment and took our measure. "You ain't sellin' Bibles are you? 'Cause if you're sellin' Bibles, this conversation is *over*. I already got a Bible."

We laughed and assured him that no, we were not Bible-thumpers, we were sellers of a mini-encyclopedia of sorts, a reference book for people who don't want to spend hundreds of dollars on an actual set of encyclopedias, but who still might want to edify themselves or occasionally look something up.

"So you're knowledge thumpers?" he said with a wry smile.

"Something like that."

"Okay, so sell me a book," he said.

"What do you mean?"

"Let's see whatcha got," he said. "Maybe I wanna buy one o' your books."

Russ and I made eye contact and agreed, via eye language, that this conversation needed to end.

"Look man, we're just trying to finish our meal and get on our way," I said.

He looked disappointed. "You want me to go, is that it?"

"No offense," I said, "We're just . . ."

"You're just lost in a city you know nothin' about, in a part o' town you know nothin' about," he said. "Have I got that about right?"

Neither of us dared to respond.

"So what's the plan?"

We didn't answer.

"Who knows, maybe I can help," he offered. "I got kids. Lots of 'em. Maybe I wanna buy a book for them."

At this, Russ reached to his right, unbuckled his case and brought out the *Volume Library* Sample book, the trimmed-down version that we used for demonstrations. He opened it to the astronomy section and immediately dove into his pitch. The man's eyes lit up. He shifted in his seat and rubbed his hands together. "Space. I fuckin' love space," he said.

He wasn't so keen on the geometry section. Or world history. But he did like the geology section. "Rocks. I fuckin' love rocks."

After getting three "cues" like this, indicating that a customer likes what they are seeing, we were trained to try to close the sale then and there. When sales people talk about the "ABCs" of selling, it stands for Always Be Closing, meaning that you should always be moving things in the direction of a sale. Anything else is a waste of time. Russ paused after the geology section and asked the first "closing" question we'd been taught: "Can you see how a book like this might be helpful to your kids?"

"Shit no!" the man laughed. "Not *my* kids."

"Can you see how having a book like this around the house could be helpful in general?"

The man leaned back and slapped his hand on the table. "Helpful? In my house? I don't think so," he chuckled.

"Suppose you needed to figure out the height of a tree and forgot how to calculate the hypotenuse of a triangle?" I offered. "What would you do? How would you find that information?" (Remember folks, the internet did not exist in those days, so questions like these were actually relevant. To some people, that is.)

The purple musketeer looked at me as if I was crazy. "Look, I don't want no fuckin' book," he said. "Actually, I came over here to ask you what the fuck kind of dance you were doing out there on the sidewalk. That was some crazy shit."

Russ did not hesitate. "We were singing the Bookman Song."

"The Bookman Song?"

"Yes. We sing it when we're feeling low and need to improve our mood," Russ explained.

Russ then slid out of the booth and stood up. "Do you want to hear it?"

The man looked skeptical, but indicated with a flourish of his many-ringed hand that Russ had the floor. Russ then began singing the song and dancing as preposterously as he possibly could. He bowed his legs, twirled his arms, rolled his head, bounced on his toes like a cheerleader, and threw in a little soft-shoe flourish at the end. He then bowed. There were only a dozen or so people in the diner at the time, but as soon as the man in purple began to clap, they all clapped along with him. The man leaned his head back and laughed again, even louder and longer this time. He was so amused by Russ's performance that it took him a minute or so to compose himself.

"Oh man, that is some seriously stupid shit!" he exclaimed. Then he leaned in toward both of us and spoke in a confidential whisper. "Lemme give you boys a piece of advice," he said. "Don't ever let anyone around here see you do that again, or you're going to get yourselves killed."

He seemed to mean it.

"But hey, good news: You're not gonna die today!" he said, laughing.

The reaction from us: terrified silence.

"In fact, this is your lucky day. Why? Because the Love Train just pulled into your station!" he exclaimed.

"Tell you what," he said. "Dinner is courtesy of Love Train tonight. How's that sound?"

Neither of us knew what to say. We were both waiting for the catch.

Then it came. "The catch is, you gotta come back here tomorrow night and tell me some stories," he said. "You guys are funny. I like funny. Come back tomorrow and tell me some funny stories. We could use a little more fuckin' funny around here."

Love Train (that was his name, it turned out, or at least his *nom-de-pimp*) stood up and straightened his slacks. Then he said, quite seriously, "You boys gotta be careful. There's some rough neighborhoods around here. You get into any trouble, tell 'em you a friend of the Love Train." Then he smiled and slapped the fat brass heart on top of his cane into his hand a few times. Under different circumstances, it was clear, Love Train's big-hearted cane could also double as a formidable weapon.

"Where you boys sleeping tonight?" he asked before he left. We told him we didn't know. He reached into his pocket and pulled out a business card. On the back he wrote down an address. "Here you go," he said, handing me the card. "Show 'em this, and tell 'em you want the Love Train special," he advised—advice I was fairly certain we shouldn't take.

True to his word, though, Love Train paid for our meal and wished us good luck. He left the restaurant before we did, and through the front window we watched him amble down the sidewalk as he twirled his cane and nodded at passers-by. Half-way down the block he stopped at a car, a pink Cadillac convertible, the kind of Cadillac only Mary Kay salespeople drive—and, apparently, Midwestern pimps with a flair for the absurd. He didn't get into the car; he just leaned on the passenger side and continued nodding at people and tipping his ridiculous hat as they walked by. Occasionally someone stopped to talk to him. The conversations never lasted long. It didn't take an MBA to figure out that the car wasn't just a car, it was Love Train's office. Whatever range of businesses he was involved in, we didn't really want to know. At that moment, we were just grateful to have a full stomach and at least a little bit of money left over. The fact that it was all courtesy of Davenport's most notorious pimp hardly mattered. What mattered was that we had survived the day, and with any luck might survive until breakfast. Things got a bit foggier after that, but we didn't care. Madge told us we could grab our backpacks from the back room, and if we needed to, we could store them there the next day, too.

"Anything else I can do to help, you just holler," she said. She had observed our conversation from afar, and had some advice for us as well: "Love Train's all right," she warned, "but whatever you do, don't get on his bad side."

CHAPTER 18

The address Love Train had given us was for a place where the term "fleabag motel" might be considered aspirational. The proprietor was a large, squash-faced lump of flesh who looked like he'd been chewing on the same cigar butt for about a year. He sat in a tiny room guarded by an iron cage. What combination of circumstances could reduce a person's life down to a 6 x 6 box in Davenport, Iowa?, I wondered. A small black-and-white television was propped up on a couple of books, and he was watching an episode of *Welcome Back, Kotter*, the show that launched John Travolta's acting career. In the show, Travolta plays a high-school delinquent named Vinnie Barbarino, a loveable dunce from Brooklyn whose idea of wit is shouting things like, "Up your nose with a rubber hose!" or "Off my case, toilet face!"—precisely the sort of things I imagined the man in the cage might say if he ever spoke. Which he didn't; he just pointed at the sign indicating that a room for the night was going to cost us ten dollars. We paid him and he slid us a key. He indicated with a nod of his head that we should go through the door on our left and up the stairs. We did not ask for the Love Train special, whatever that was, because we did not want to find out. Our fear was that it might involve hookers and blow and guns, three elements of inner-city life for which our suburban upbringings had not prepared us. Instead, we told ourselves that once we turned out the lights and went to sleep, it didn't matter where we were, because we'd be unconscious.

Since we expected the worst, we were pleasantly surprised to find that the room itself wasn't quite as skeezy as we had imagined, given the price and location. It wasn't exactly a Hilton, though. The only furniture in the room was a twin bed with a table and a lamp. The bulb in the lamp was only forty watts, which made the walls look like they were painted with mustard. The carpet was nubby and brown, with rust marks and cigarette burns in odd places here and there.

There was no TV, and the bathroom was down the hall, or what a creative brochure might call "European-style." The room wasn't what my mother would think of as clean, but there were no visible insects or vermin, so it could have been worse.

I elected to sleep on the floor, because I thought it'd be cleaner than the bed and better for my back. Russ took the bed, which sagged under his weight and was about a foot too short for his 6-6 frame, so his feet dangled off the end like the limbs of a corpse. Neither of us really cared, though. It had been a long, tough day, and, unless our luck changed, the following day was not going to be any easier. For the moment, sleep was the only way out of our current situation, and we craved it like a couple of hungry animals.

Moments later, it seemed, the alarm clock on Russ's wristwatch went off. He immediately leapt out of bed and fired off twenty push-ups. It was 7:00 a.m., and this, according to the Southwestern Company, was the best way to wake up and get your blood pumping so that you could greet the day with a clear head and a happy heart. I prefer a less athletic wakeup routine, personally, one that involves several gentle taps of the snooze button. But Russ insisted that we do it the "company way," so I rolled over, did three push-ups, and collapsed.

"You're pathetic," Russ huffed as he finished his requisite twenty.

"Says the man doing push-ups in his underwear."

"Big day today."

"Too big."

"It's now or never."

"I'm leaning toward never."

We only had twenty dollars between us, so breakfast that morning was an Egg McMuffin and a cup of coffee at McDonald's. In America, it seems, the less money you have, the more likely you are to end up eating at fast-food franchises. Which makes a crude sort of sense. In 1979, an Egg McMuffin cost less than a dollar. If I ate two of them, as I always did in those days, I was getting 600 calories, 36 grams of protein, and 26 grams of fat for two bucks. Granted, a Big Mac and fries is a much more cost-effective delivery mechanism for calories—1,120 calories, 48 grams of fat, and 26 grams of protein for $1.49—but only a savage eats hamburgers for breakfast. Which is one of the reasons Ray Kroc introduced the Egg McMuffin in the first place. In 1972, when the Egg McMuffin was introduced, hardly any fast-food franchises served breakfast. But by 1981, fully 18 percent of McDonald's profits came from breakfast, sparking a morning gold rush of broken yolks and griddle cakes across the land. By the late 1970s, you could get an egg-like-sorta-ham-and-cheese-like-substance sandwich before noon at pretty much any of the major fast-food franchises. The only hold-out—and it remains so to this day—was Kentucky Fried Chicken, now known as KFC. I don't know why KFC never got into the breakfast market. Perhaps they saw White Castle roll out the Breakfast Waffle Slider and simply concluded that therein lies madness.

Now, it is of course cheaper to fry eggs at home. In 1979, a dozen eggs cost 82 cents, which is enough eggs for twelve Egg McMuffins. But the relative cheapness of a dozen eggs presumes that you have a home, and that you have a stove and frying pan at your disposal, and that you have a refrigerator to store said eggs, and that you've paid the electric bill. If you have none of those things and are down to your last ten dollars, eating breakfast at McDonald's makes considerably more economic sense.

I knew none of this until I was down to my last twenty dollars and realized that I had *no choice* but to eat breakfast in a fast-food franchise. Alas, the previous night's accommodations did not include a mini-fridge, so buying some milk for cereal wasn't an option. There were no bowls or spoons, either, and no coffee maker or toaster. In truth, the average American breakfast requires a great deal of equipment, most of which needs to be plugged into an outlet in a structure that's plugged into the electrical grid. Without these infrastructure basics in place, managing something as simple as a morning meal becomes exponentially more difficult. When we accept these limitations voluntarily, we call it "camping." When they are imposed on us involuntarily, we call it something else: poor, homeless, destitute, indigent—take your pick.

Russ and I were somewhere in between. We had homes—back in California and Arizona—but we had no money. Neither of us had ever been completely broke, so we were flirting with circumstances that we'd never before encountered. We weren't technically on the brink of homelessness in the larger sense, because at any moment we could call our parents for salvation. In college, when I discovered that I'd blown my entire monthly food budget on cans of Dr. Pepper from the dormitory vending machine, my mother simply sent me more money and told me to drink water. But, as I've said, this whole book-selling/poverty thing was a problem of our own making, so we were determined to solve it ourselves. Also, we knew it was temporary, because it was only a matter of time before we started selling books hand over fist. In a strange way, the fact that we had no money and could not yet see the light at the end of the tunnel—well, it was all part of the adventure. We didn't know how it was all going to turn out, only that *something* had to happen, because we couldn't go on like this forever. We had also not lost faith in our ability to overcome adversity in all its forms, owing to a potent combination of youthful arrogance and total ignorance. We didn't know what we didn't know—namely, that things could get quite a lot worse before they got better—and the not knowing made it possible for us to forge ahead with confidence. Never mind that this confidence was manufactured out of thin air and based on nothing but a bizarre faith in our ability to endure hardship and misfortune. The only time either of us had to endure anything close to actual hardship was during our fraternity's Hell Week, and that didn't count, because it was done for fun. In short, we had no idea what we were getting into or how we were going to get out of it. Fortunately, that was precisely the mindset we needed at the time. Because if we knew—if someone told us beforehand what the next few days and weeks had in store for us—we would have begged our parents to save us.

CHAPTER 19

After breakfast, we debated doing the Bookman Song in the parking lot, but decided against it, lest we rob the tune of its mood-altering power by performing it too often. This went against company policy. The company recommended that we sing the Bookman Song *every* morning before heading out into the field, and anytime we felt the need to banish those demons of "doubt and fear," the ones that plague door-to-door salespeople all day long. We had discovered, however, that doing the Bookman Song too often was a mistake. The song only worked if you shared the humiliation with someone else. Doing it alone was like trying to tickle yourself; impossible, pointless, and, if someone sees you, embarrassing.

Today, our first priority was money. Rather than waste our time trying to find some magically generous family to live with, we agreed to focus our energies on selling books. What we needed to do, we knew, was persuade our customers to give us at least half of the money for their books in cash, up front. If we sold two Volume Libraries apiece that day and got half in cash up front, we'd each have forty dollars, enough to eat somewhere other than McDonald's, and pay for a room somewhere else. Anywhere else. If we did that every day for a week, we'd each have two-hundred dollars, enough for a down payment on an apartment. The more money we made, the better we could control our fate. So we made it our mission that day to trust our training and work has hard as possible. We had hit bottom, and now was the time to turn it all around.

In training, we were taught not to focus on sales per se, but to set an achievable goal—knock on one hundred doors a day—and let everything else fall into place. Sales would take care of themselves, we were assured; all we had to do was stay disciplined and follow our sales scripts. Selling books door-to-door (or anything, for that matter) is largely a matter of perseverance, we were taught, of overcoming our natural desire to quit when things get hard. Rejection comes with the territory, and as long as you can manage your own reactions to a seemingly infinite series of 'no's—not to personalize them or consider them a mark of failure—everything else is easy.

The thing is, rejection is hard *not* to take personally. Every time someone tells you they aren't interested in what you're selling—not even interested in hearing about it, in fact, and if you don't get off their property in thirty seconds they're going to call the cops—it stings. When a nice-looking lady comes to the door, looks you over for a few seconds, then shuts the door without saying a word, it hurts. When some bald, beer-bellied degenerate opens the door and says, "What're ya peddlin'?,"—then, when you tell him, he looks at you like you're the degenerate one—it smarts. When that happens over and over and over again in relentless succession, it tends to ground down one's resolve. You are trying to sell something, after all, and they are not buying, so your primary goal is not being achieved. And it is not being achieved because these people aren't even giving you a chance. They start judging you the moment they open the door: Your clothes, hair, shoes, height, gender, age, body language, facial expression, and sweat level are all instantly assessed and run through a complicated algorithm of prejudice based on their own personal experience and whatever they watched on television last night. In a matter of seconds they conclude that they do not want to talk to you. And they decide it so quickly, often without even hearing you speak, that it's hard to avoid concluding that the weak link in this process is . . . you. It certainly isn't the books. They haven't even seen the books!

You are the one they are rejecting. *You* are the person standing on their doorstep asking for a few minutes of their time. And *you* are the one who is being told to go away. Of course it's personal! The only way it could be *more* personal is if your mother was at the door and your father was behind her, aiming the shotgun at you.

In other words, if you are a nice person with a cheerful attitude and excellent intentions who believes in the overall goodness and generosity of humanity, an hour of door-to-door sales will change your outlook entirely.

That first full day of selling was devastating, for several reasons. Yes, I knocked on doors. No, I did not sell anything. In fact, I did not even get a chance to sell anything, because I never made it past the front door. Every time I knocked and someone came to the door, they declined my invitation to "find out what everyone in the neighborhood is so excited about," the company line with allegedly magical properties that broke down people's defenses and tweaked their natural curiosity. Unfortunately, no one I talked to that day seemed the least bit curious about anyone else's excitement. They declined with varying ranges of politeness, from the people who simply slammed the door to those who made up excuses to those who apologized profusely for being so poor that they couldn't even listen responsibly to what I had to say because their finances were so tight and what with another baby on the way, you understand, but thank you so much for stopping by. And, truth be told, even if someone were gracious enough to let me in to their home, it had been so long since I had practiced my entire presentation that I wasn't even sure I could remember it.

Slowly but surely, the mounting rejections sapped my confidence. By three o'clock in the afternoon, selling anything to anyone seemed like an impossible task. The distance between my knock on the door and someone handing me forty dollars in cash (the half-down payment on a *Volume Library*) felt like a vast, unnavigable sea of despair. The notion that someone would ever be interested enough in the book I was selling receded into the distance to a point somewhere between purgatory and infinity. I had started the day with the conviction that failure was not an option, and I was ending the day with the equally strong conviction that failure was my *only* option.

Sometime around four o'clock, I was getting ready to call it quits when a police car pulled up beside me and one of the officers inside asked me if I was me.

"Is your name Tad?" they asked.

I replied that it was, letting alone for the moment that it is rarely a good sign when police officers know your name.

"Do you have a license to solicit?" they asked.

A license to what? "No," I replied. "Do I need one?"

"In order to sell anything door to door in Davenport, you have to register with city hall and obtain a solicitor's license," they said.

"But I'm just selling books. Or rather, I'm trying to sell some books," I replied. "But I'm not having much luck, so technically speaking you could say I'm not actually selling anything at all, ha ha."

"We're going to need you to come with us," they said, and indicated that I should get into the back seat of their cruiser. I hesitated a moment, and the officer behind the wheel added, "Do you know someone named Russ?"

I nodded yes.

"Then get in."

At the police station, after a few questions about who I was and why I was in Davenport and showing the officers the sales materials in my little red case, I was ushered into a small room with a table and two chairs—an interrogation room, as it were. There, one of the officers who had picked me up informed me that he was not going to issue me a citation for my transgressions, but if I wanted to keep selling in Davenport I was going to have to obtain a solicitor's license. The fee for said license, he said, was $75, and could be paid at city hall across the street from the police station.

I gulped at the cost, and silently cursed our district manager, Mike, for not informing us that we needed such a license.

The office then informed me that, while I was being let go, my buddy Russ was in a bit more trouble. Russ, he said, was being held on misdemeanor and possible felony charges, and would likely need to post bail to get out. The officer would not tell me what Russ had done, only that his bail was $200 and investigators were currently reviewing his case.

"His case?" I asked. "What did he do?"

They weren't at liberty to tell me, he said, but Russ could go with me and tell me himself if I posted his bail. At that particular moment, however, $200 might as well have been $20,000. There was no way I could pay it.

"Can I make a phone call?" I asked.

"Make as many calls as you want," the officer said, and handed me the phone receiver on his desk.

I dialed Mike, our district manager, and he answered on the third ring. As calmly and coolly as I could, I explained the situation: that Russ and I were at the Davenport police station, Russ was in jail, and I had no money to bail him out. Oh and by the way, why hadn't he mentioned that we'd need a license to do the Southwestern Company's business in Davenport?

He listened, but did not respond in the manner I expected—with concern, advice, and some reassurance that everything was going to be alright.

Instead, he shouted, "That's fantastic!"

"Fantastic?," I cringed. "How is this fantastic?"

"It's the best news I've heard all day."

"Are you nuts?!" I yelled. "This is a nightmare!"

"No it's not," he replied. "It's great. If you guys got arrested, that means you've been out there hustling, doing your jobs. In fact, I'd be worried if you *didn't* get arrested."

"That makes no sense," I objected.

"Sure it does," he said. "You just have to learn how to turn a negative into a positive. It's all in how you look at things."

No matter how I looked at it, being in jail was not a good thing. And I told him so.

"Did you sell anything today?" he responded.

"No."

"How many doors would you say you knocked on? Fifty? Sixty?"

"Thereabouts," I said.

"Again, that's really great," he said. "That means you're sixty doors closer to a yes."

"I do not feel any closer to a yes," I said. "And the fact remains that Russ needs to be bailed out, and we need $150 for licenses."

After a few beats of silence he said, "When was the last time you sang the Bookman Song?"

I knew where this was heading. "I am not singing the Bookman Song in the lobby of the Davenport police department!" I fumed.

"You'll feel better if you do. Trust me."

"No, I'll feel better about everything when we get out of here!" I hissed, trying to control my anger.

"C'mon, lighten up," he said. "Let me talk to someone there."

"My district manager wants to talk to you," I said, handing the receiver back to the police officer who had loaned me his phone.

Fifteen minutes later, Russ and I walked out of the police station with instructions to obtain a solicitor's license at city hall. Mike had persuaded the police to drop Russ's bail, and agreed to loan us the money for the licenses, but only under one condition: that we sing the Bookman Song in the parking lot of the Davenport police department, preferably within sight of a few officers in blue.

We promised to do it, but didn't, a small but important rebellion on our part. Instead, we headed over to the diner to lick our wounds and beg Marge and/or Love Train for a free meal.

When we reported that we had just come from the police station after being arrested, Love Train did not disappoint. "Coupla burgers for my homies," he told Madge.

"You two are practically ex-cons now," he chortled as he scooted into our booth and sat next to Russ. "That almost makes you brothers. Now all you gotta do is kill someone," he whispered conspiratorially, then laughed at himself for being so damn funny.

"Seriously, what'd they gitchya for?" Love Train wanted to know.

"Soliciting without a license," I said. "Trying to boost the collective IQ of this city's populace is, evidently, a crime."

"You got that right," Love Train said. "I been tryin' to do the same thing my whole life. Cops don't care. They just as stupid as ever."

Technically speaking, I had only been detained; Russ was the one who had actually been arrested. But I still didn't know why. I assumed some sort of complaint had been lodged against him by some disgruntled citizen who thought buying any book other than the Bible was an affront to the Almighty, who of course only wants people to buy and read *His* book.

But according to Russ, it didn't go down like that at all:

"I was working a neighborhood when I came across this playground," Russ explained. "Lots of kids were playing, and a couple of mothers were watching. Well, not really watching, just basically talking to each other. Anyway, I'd been striking out everywhere and figured I needed to get some information about the neighborhood, like where people with kids in high school lived. So I approached this boy, about seven or eight, at the edge of the playground and asked him if he had any older brothers and sisters? He said he did, a sister who was eleven, so I asked him if any of the other kids on the playground had older siblings. He said a couple of them did, but mostly he didn't know. Then I asked him where he lived, and he told me: just up the street, in the brown house on the corner. Great information to have, and I thought to myself: If I could ask each of these kids whether they had older brothers and sisters, I'd have intel on the whole neighborhood. Then I got an idea. I went up to the mothers and told them I was a representative from the president's council on physical fitness, and could I borrow their kids for a couple of minutes? They said sure, so I gathered all the kids on the side of the playground and made them do push-ups and jumping jacks. Then I asked them to raise their hands if they had any older brothers or sisters. A few of them did, so I asked them where they lived. Then I thanked the moms and went on my way. Half an hour later, a police car pulls up and they take me in. Turns out, one of those kids went home and told their dad about the fun guy at the playground, and that kid's dad was a cop. End of story."

Once again, Love Train thought this was just about the funniest thing he'd ever heard. To him, the idea of a tall, lanky dude shaking down six-year-olds for information was just further evidence that we were both crazy. That Russ wasn't shot or shipped off to prison was simply evidence that we were white.

"You lucky," Love Train snickered. "Black man try that and he don't end up laughin' about it a coupla hours later. He end up dead. Or worse."

After dinner, Russ and I grabbed our backpacks and went to a nearby park to wrap our heads around the fact that we only had about five dollars between us—not enough for a room at the boarding house where we'd stayed the night before, and hardly enough to buy breakfast, even at McDonald's. We reviewed our options, which didn't take long, because we had none. Mike wasn't going to meet us until the following day to purchase our licenses, and we felt we'd exhausted the generosity of both Madge and Love Train, the only two people in Davenport who had been nice to us thus far. We both realized more or less simultaneously that we were going to have to "rough it" and sleep outside, at least for one night. In the park, there were plenty of low-lying shrubs under which a person could probably hide, and sleep, if one absolutely had to. And, unfortunately, we were at that point, the point where one has to decide what to do when the sun goes down and there is simply nowhere to go. We both had sleeping bags, so we reasoned that once it got dark, it would be almost impossible for anyone to see us if we hid amid the park's shrubs and bushes. Tucked beneath a hedge of juniper under the cover of darkness, we'd be invisible, and as long as we didn't cause any kind of ruckus, we figured we'd be safe until morning. There was of course the outside possibility that we weren't the only homeless people eyeing those bushes as a hiding place. But we scouted them and didn't see any sign of people—no cigarette butts or beer cans or anything else indicating that someone else might have taken up residence there. So it was free for the taking, in our estimation. All we had to do was wait until dark and sneak beneath the bushes when no one was looking. Once we were buried in our sleeping bags and fast asleep, what did it matter where we were? For the second night in a row, unconscious oblivion would be our refuge.

It was a decent plan. Until it started to rain.

Shortly after we unrolled our sleeping bags and crawled inside, the drops began to fall, a few puffs in the dust here and there at first then the steady pitter patter of a shower, followed by nature's early warning system for all living things in the vicinity: a flash of lightning, a pause, then a sharp blast of thunder. According to my high-school science teacher, the pause in between indicates how far away the storm actually is, the formula for which is five seconds for every mile. If lightning flashes and ten seconds go by, the storm is two miles away. In most cases, the onset of a thunderstorm is one of nature's more welcome dramas. Observed from the relative safety of a dwelling with its roof intact, an evening thunderstorm can be a source of tranquility. Apps to help people sleep always include a distant rumble of thunder and the soothing hiss of falling rain, because people are generally calmed by the liminal fluidity of a passing storm. Unless . . . they are outside, unprotected, and in danger of being barbecued by a bolt of electric outrage from above.

By the time we realized that the bushes we were hiding under were not going to protect us, there was almost no gap between the flashes of lightning and explosions of thunder. It was as if Zeus himself were hurling thunderbolts out of the sky, directly at us—flash-boom-crack—while simultaneously reaching into his pocket to toss fistfuls of hail at us.

As quickly as possible we scrambled out of our sleeping bags, stuffed them, grabbed our backpacks and ran. But there was nowhere to go. The park was on the outskirts of town. Every building was dark. Torrents of rain pelted us as we scurried from tree to tree trying to find shelter. Finally, we spied the entryway of a building. The doors were recessed, so there was a small space in front of the doors that was dry and protected from the rain. We huddled there for a time, wet but not particularly cold, as the night air, despite the storm, was still warm and humid. We had nowhere else to go, so we elected to stay put until the storm passed, at which point we would decide our next move. We unrolled our sleeping bags to provide at least some cushion from the concrete below, and attempted, insofar as possible, to get some much-needed shuteye.

Just as we were dozing off, two flashlights appeared out of the darkness and a voice inquired, "How are we doing tonight? Had a little too much to drink, have we?"

The officers were actually quite polite. We explained that no, we were not drunk, just caught in an unfortunate situation and trapped in this doorway with nowhere else to go.

"Well you can't sleep here," the officers told us after patiently listening to our tale. "If you don't have anywhere else to go, we're going to have to take you to a shelter."

A homeless shelter, to be precise.

Where I come from, there weren't any homeless people. Or if there were, the authorities did a fantastic job of hiding them. The mere idea that someone could entirely run out of money and options, as we had, was all but inconceivable where I grew up, because there was so much wealth in the area. And one thing extraordinary wealth tends to buy is insulation and distance from people whose misfortunes are too large to ignore. Davenport, Iowa, was not too different in this regard. It hadn't taken the authorities long to locate us, and local law demanded that we be removed from the streets and deposited somewhere out of sight, where the good citizens of Davenport did not have to think about us. Waking up with homeless people on your doorstep? No, thanks. That's for places like San Francisco and Portland, where mush-minded liberals take the whole "live and let live" philosophy all the way to the edge of insanity. Sure, homeless people are free to live, is the Midwestern philosophy—just not anywhere that violates any one of a million civic codes intended to reinforce a "community standard" that does not look kindly on people whose luck has entirely run out.

On the other hand, it was, at that moment, nice to know that there was somewhere for us to go. Just a few hours outside in the rain had convinced us that a roof overhead, any roof, was better than no roof at all.

So we tossed our backpacks into the trunk of the police car and crawled into the back seat.

Our first stop, the main shelter in town, was a bust. The place was full, and in any case the doors closed at 10 p.m. It was almost midnight, and that only left one option, according to the cops: the Salvation Army "drunk tank," where the most unrepentant alcoholics and drug addicts in town were kept. I didn't know it at the time, but when the Salvation Army was founded—in 1865, by a London minister named William Booth and his wife, Catherine—the organization's original "three S's" were "soup," "soap," and "salvation." Society's "down and outs" were the sort of people the Booths were trying to help. And indeed, according to one history of the organization, its first converts were "alcoholics, morphine addicts, prostitutes, and other 'undesirables' unwelcome in polite Christian society." The Christian thing to do, then, was to feed the undesirables, bathe them, then persuade them that their sense of hopelessness and despair was due primarily to their lack of faith in (or fear of) God. Committing mortal sins whenever the opportunity presents itself has always been a sure path to eternal damnation, as every polite Christian knows, but creating a society that allows the indignity of homelessness in the first place is, apparently, little more than an affront to everyday decorum and civility.

Not much has changed.

While one of the cops stayed in the squad car, the other one escorted Russ and me to the front door of the Salvation Army. It was close to midnight, our clothes were damp, and I had to take a leak something fierce. The place was entirely dark. Like a house on Halloween that does not want trick-or-treaters, it did not look very welcoming. The police officer punched the doorbell with his middle finger and we waited. Nothing. The officer punched the doorbell again four or five times in rapid succession. After a long pause, a porch light stabbed through the darkness and the door opened. A large, bald man with an incongruously thick beard stood in the doorway. He wore a leather vest over a dirty white undershirt, and he had a leather pouch around his neck, the kind medieval soldiers wore to store the teeth of enemies they'd killed in battle. He was not amused.

"Hey John, you got room for a couple more tonight?" asked the officer.

The man did not say anything. He frowned and looked at us as if we were in the wrong place at the wrong time for all the wrong reasons. I had to agree.

"C'mon John. I got nowhere else to take them."

"Full up," the large man mumbled.

"It's only for a night. Can't you squeeze them in somewhere?"

The large man sighed and motioned for us to enter.

"First sign of trouble, you're outta here," John told us as we entered. He led us through a small entryway into a dark room that smelled like urine and vomit. As my eyes adjusted, I could see that the floor was covered with bodies, men sleeping everywhere, curled up on the floor shoulder to shoulder with barely any space in between. Besides smelling bad, the air was hot and thick and moist, as if each and every occupant had, like us, been caught in the rain and was now molding and rotting on the floor. The rancid stench of unwashed man-sweat assaulted my sinuses as John led us around to the back of the room. We had to step over several bodies to get there, and on the way I stepped into something wet and slippery. Vomit was my guess, but I couldn't tell and didn't really want to know. John pointed to a couple of spots on the floor, spaces where we could squeeze between a couple of other bodies.

"My advice is to sleep on your backpacks and don't let them out of your sight," John warned. The implication was that we were sleeping amid a den of thieves and, if given the chance, they would rob us blind. Not exactly a thought conducive to sleep. But we laid down on the floor nevertheless, as we had no real choice in the matter. I tried to make myself as small as possible, to disappear in fact through the back door of my imagination, where tanned girls in bikinis lay on the beach glistening in the sun and the roar of the surf blocked out the cacophony of snoring and wretching and farting in that godforsaken room. I tried to will myself to sleep, to escape into unconsciousness once again, but I felt too sorry for myself and was too afraid to relax. Two thoughts kept circling in my brain like horses on a carousel: "How did I get here?" and "How am I going to get out?"

Sleep came at some point during the night, but it came to an abrupt end when a guy wearing army boots stepped on my ankle. My eyes flew open from the pain, but the physical pain was immediately replaced by the more acute and terrifying sensation that I could not breathe. The room had smelled horrible when we arrived, certainly, but now, in addition to smelling ten times worse, there seemed to be no oxygen in the room. I tried to breathe, but could only pull a thick and nasty gas into my lungs. I felt like I was drowning. A few other men in the room were also awakening to the same realization and were headed for the door. I felt like I had to get some fresh air in my lungs in the next sixty seconds or die, so I too scrambled over several bodies and followed them outside.

It was early, and the morning sun was rising through an orange haze. As soon as I got outside, I took a deep breath—and gagged. It didn't seem possible, but in some ways the smell was worse outside, as if a ton of raw sewage and rotting shellfish had been simmering in a pit of tar and set on fire.

"Oh my god, what is that smell?" I exclaimed to no one in particular.

A homeless guy in an Army jacket smoking a cigarette laughed and said, "That's the Oscar Mayer plant. You don't want to be downwind of the Oscar Mayer plant," he said, taking a long drag on his cigarette. "Yet here we are."

"Smells like the inside of my asshole," another guy commented.

"How do you know what your asshole smells like, Earl?"

"He ought to. His is head is up there most of the time."

"Everyone knows what Earl's ass smells like," said another. "All you have to do is stand next to him for five minutes."

Such was the tenor of the conversation outside the Salvation Army on this particular Iowa morning.

Turns out, the Salvation Army in Davenport, Iowa, was located only a few hundred yards away from the Oscar Mayer slaughterhouse, where hundreds of cows and pigs were at that moment being killed and eviscerated, their unusable body parts rendered in giant vats and dissolved into a putrid, protein-rich slurry that is sold off to make pet food. Whatever isn't boiled off is used to make various Oscar Mayer products—hot dogs, bologna, sausages—few of which, in 1979, looked remotely like meat. Indeed, it's hard to tell what you're smelling when you're downwind of a meat-processing plant, because the process for making hot dogs isn't much different from the process for making pet food. Most hot dogs are made from the trimmings left over after all the parts of a cow or pig that can be sold for a higher price (steaks, ribs, chops, hams, bacon, brisket, etc.) are cut away. Which leaves the snout, ears, brains, blood, intestines, gristle, sinew, and other delectable parts, all of which are ground together into a thick puree, flavored with salt and sugar, injected into a casing and cooked. In the 1970s, word also leaked out to the public that if the normal hot-dog production process wasn't gross enough for them, government regulations also allow for the inclusion of a certain number of insect parts, roach droppings, and other delicious flavor enhancers. (To be fair, the same regulations—and inadvertent ingredients—apply to chocolate, cereal, bread, or almost any food processed in a factory.) Oscar Mayer's claim that its hot dogs are "all beef" is technically almost true, since the word "beef" encompasses the entire cow. That said, calling them "bullshit" would also be technically true, since fecal matter is also in inescapable part of the recipe.

But you would never know any of this if you were a kid growing up in the 1970s. Back then, due to the hypnotic power of television advertising, what would have popped into your head at the mention of the words "Oscar Mayer" was the lyrics to "The Oscar Mayer Song," which pretty much anyone over fifty in this country can recite by heart.

It goes:

Oh, I wish I were an Oscar Mayer weiner.
That is what I'd truly like to be
'Cause if I were an Oscar Mayer weiner
Everyone would be in love with me

In advertising lore, "The Oscar Mayer Song" is regarded as one of the most successful and iconic jingles of all time. But it masks an awful truth. The pigs in the truck I had seen (and smelled) on our first day in town were scared precisely because they were on their way to becoming Oscar Mayer weiners. Love wasn't the first thing on their minds. Somewhere deep in their animal psyches they knew where they were going, and they knew they couldn't do anything to prevent it. I'd felt something similar the night before, ushered by the police into the place people go when they have no more choices and all their options have run out. The difference was that the Salvation Army wasn't the end of the line for me and Russ, it was only the beginning. That and I'm a person, not a pig.

After a night in the Salvation Army drunk tank, however, it's hard not to look like a sort of pig-person, somewhere half-way between a human being and an animal. You smell awful, your hair is stringy, your clothes and hands are filthy, and the mighty force of your superior human intellect is focused on two things: eating and shitting. Showering and shaving come later, after you've satisfied your baser animal drives. And selling books? For us, hitting the streets again was the reward for having survived the night. It was also the only way out of our predicament, and we both knew it.

Mike, our district manager, was supposed to meet us at city hall that morning at 9 a.m. to purchase our solicitor's licenses. Unfortunately, dealing with Mike was like playing a perpetual game of "opposite day." If you thought something was bad (like getting arrested), he thought it was good. If you thought something was good (like not getting arrested), he thought it was bad. And if he promised to do something for you (like lend you the money for a solicitor's license so that you wouldn't be arrested again), it meant that he was going to break that promise—which he of course did.

Russ and I waited on the steps of city hall for a couple of hours before coming to the mutual realization that Mike wasn't coming. We were fools for believing him, we concluded, and our best course of action was to forget about him and forge ahead, license be damned.

"It's probably one of his bullshit tests," Russ proclaimed.

"Probably," I agreed. "He seems to specialize in bullshit."

"Fact is, we're on our own."

"Seems that way."

"The question is: What are we going to do about it?"

"We have no choice," I replied. "We have to sell some books, even if it means getting arrested again."

"And if we get arrested again, we'll just blame it on Mike," Russ mused. "What can he say?"

"He'll say it's fantastic, and tell us to keep up the good work."

The plan we agreed upon was to dedicate the day to selling, but to do it in a way that did not attract too much public attention. "Yesterday was just bad luck," Russ rationalized. "Maybe we'll have better luck today."

Maybe.

CHAPTER 20

Alas, we did not.

I don't remember much about that day, except that it was a blur of continuous rejection. I knocked on doors all day long and sold absolutely nothing. My goal was to knock on at least one hundred doors, per the company's guidelines, in the hope that at least two of those doors would open up to a paying customer. I knocked until my knuckles were raw, hitting door after door after door on block after block after block of houses that looked from the outside like a bookman's dream: middle-class homes with plastic wading pools and Slip 'n' Slides in the backyard and basketball hoops in the front; garages full of bicycles and snow sleds and camping gear; cars built for hauling children and groceries. But no matter what I did, no matter how many approaches I tried, I couldn't get so much as a single person to invite me into their home, much less let me give them a demonstration.

Russ's luck was no better. At the end of the day, he too had failed to sell a single book. The only positive was that neither one of us had been picked up by the police—a happenstance that opposite-Mike would surely consider a failure, but for which we were extremely grateful. We'd had enough run-ins with the police already; we didn't need any more.

As darkness fell and the gravity of our situation weighed on us like a ton of unsold books, we knew we had no choice but to spend another night at the Salvation Army. There is nothing quite so dispiriting as trying your hardest to avoid a situation only to have that exact same situation come around and bite you in the ass again. Heading back to the Salvation Army was, for us, a brutal confirmation of our ineptitude, a complete repudiation of the idea that if you "try hard" and "do your best," everything will turn out okay. Things weren't turning out okay for us; they were getting shittier and more depressing with each passing hour.

When we arrived at the Salvation Army, Big John informed us that the place was already "full up," and that his hospitality the night before had been a courtesy to the cops, not us. We explained our situation to him and promised that this would be the last night he'd have to deal with us, but he wouldn't budge. He just stood in the door frame, huge and immovable, like a fat king protecting his fiefdom.

"Well where the fuck are we going to go then?" Russ blurted, having apparently decided that gentle diplomacy and persuasion were not going to work.

"Don't know. Don't care," was the big man's response.

"Here's what's going to happen if you don't let us in," Russ argued. "We're going to set up camp in the middle of the park, the police are going to pick us up again, and they're going to deliver us right back here. Then you'll have to let us in."

"Perhaps."

"How about we skip all that and you let us in now," Russ sneered.

I could see that this tack was going to get us nowhere. This was a man who needed to be pleaded with.

After several minutes of humiliation and prostration, followed by a healthy dose of groveling capped off by the threat of tears, the big man relented.

"Look, I don't have room here," he said. "Tonight you can stay across the street—but only for one night. After that, you're on your own."

By "across the street," John meant a kind of sister facility for "unwed mothers and runaways," as he put it—people whose circumstances made them too vulnerable to stay in the main house, where all the letches and perverts were kept. In reality, it was some kind of juvenile safe house, a place where kids in trouble could stay if they had no other options, or if their options at the moment put them in danger of being hurt or killed.

The place was much cleaner than the Salvation Army, even though John himself also seemed to be the proprietor. The occupants, too, were much less likely to throw up in their sleep.

One of them was a girl—let's call her Mary—who was there, she said, because she had informed her boyfriend, with whom she lived, that she was pregnant, and he had beat her black and blue. Mary told me her story over the course of an hour or two as we sat outside, underneath the stars on a dark, moonless night. She was a plain-looking girl, a little on the pudgy side, almost cute but not quite. She smoked while she talked, one cigarette after another, and her face was swelling purple proof that her story was true.

Her dad was in prison, she said. Her mother was a drug addict. She was only sixteen years old and had dropped out of school because she wasn't learning anything and thought school was "a waste of time." She too had a bit of a drug problem, she admitted, but now that the baby was coming she was going to clean up her act. She didn't have any other family. Her grandparents were dead, and so was her older sister, the victim of a drug overdose the year before. Her boyfriend was the only person who cared about her, and now he too had been heaped on the steaming pile of disappointment and regret that was her young life thus far. She'd probably end up going back to him, she reasoned, because that's what girls in her situation did, right? What other choice did she have? He just needed to cool off, to get his head around the idea of being a father. He'd come around, she figured. Aborting the baby did not seem like an option she had considered, or ever would consider, and I did not mention it. I just listened, because that's what she seemed to need the most.

As she talked, I thought about the differences between my life and hers. I also began to appreciate how lucky I was, all things considered. After all, I came from a loving, fairly functional family in an affluent suburb of San Diego. I was in college. I had aspirations and dreams, and the means and support to achieve them. She had none of these things. As she talked I began to feel ashamed, because the difference between real poverty and the pretend sort that Russ and I were playing at was suddenly so clear to me. In reality, she and I came from entirely different worlds. Russ and I both knew that no matter how bad things got, each of us could make a phone call and our parents would air-lift us out of our misery in a matter of hours. If I wanted to, I could be sitting on the beach tomorrow, and I knew it, which gave me a sense of security and a fund of courage that she had likely never known. In fact, her life was such a colossal clusterfuck of trailer-trash clichés that I wanted to buy her a plane ticket to San Diego so that she could take a break from her misery for a week or two, to just sit on the beach and stare out at the ocean for a while. That's what she needs, I thought—a week or two of the life I had abandoned to be here with her on a muggy night in Iowa, next to the Salvation Army, downwind from the Oscar Mayer plant, listening to her sad tale of abuse and dysfunction.

The following morning, Russ and I woke up to discover that we had missed breakfast. We had slept in somehow, and the home for unwed mothers and runaways did not have a kitchen. So we were on our own. Between us, Russ and I had maybe two dollars. Not even enough to eat at McDonald's. Still, we had to eat. Somewhere. Somehow.

That's when we discovered the glories of the Hostess Thrift Bake Shop. It turns out there are places in this world where one can buy food—or calories, at any rate—if an Egg McMuffin is beyond your budget. The Hostess Thrift Bake Shop was just such a place, a veritable goldmine of snack, shelves piled high with Twinkies, cupcakes, donuts, Suzy Qs, Ho-Hos, Ding-Dongs, Zingers, Honey Buns, you name it. There was an entire wall of Wonder Bread, its plastic polka-dot packaging arranged in neat rows that repeated the word "Wonder" over and over and over again like a mantra from some faraway corner of human consciousness where nutritional considerations are irrelevant and the only thing that matters is beautiful branding. The expression "the best thing since sliced bread" refers, obliquely, to Wonder bread, because it was the first brand of bread to come pre-sliced. Before Wonder bread came along, people had to use a bread knife to cut slices of bread. It took some skill to produce even, symmetrical slices. And let's not forget about the crumbs. Every time you take a loaf of bread out and dig into it with a knife, the damn thing produces crumbs, which have to be wiped up with a sponge and disposed of either in the sink or in a proper trash receptacle. If you were a housewife during World War II, making, slicing, and crumbing bread was an annoyance you had to deal with every day. Then along came Wonder bread, eliminating the need for all three, and *voila*, your life was transformed.

Apparently.

When I was a kid, the running joke about Wonder bread was always that one had to wonder what was in it, and who would buy it? There were plenty of other things to wonder about Wonder bread as well. The crust, for instance. Unlike normal bread, the crust on a slice of Wonder bread is exactly the same texture as the inside. This "crust" is a thin brown layer of sponge-bread on the outside that surrounds the impossibly puffy pillow stuff inside. This was not "bread" as humans have known it for millennia—it was a strange, loaf-shaped substance that mimicked certain properties of bread but really belonged in an entirely different food category.

Indeed, no simulated food product in the world was more "processed" than a loaf of Wonder bread. In fact, scientists had so perfected the extraction of all nutrients from a hull of wheat that Hostess had to *add* vitamins and minerals back into the mix, which it proudly advertised with the slogan, "Helps build strong bodies twelve ways"—twelve being the number of vitamins the company had replaced. Whole wheat helps build strong bodies in more than a hundred different ways, of course, and has fiber and protein to boot, so, technically speaking, Wonder bread is a scientific marvel of sorts. The strange thing is, people thought of it that way too—and liked it. Texturally, Wonder bread has more in common with asbestos than a baguette, but in the 1950s and 1960s, Wonder bread was thought of as the bread of the future: a scientifically formulated food-like substance that was produced in a modern factory, did not mold in the cupboard (making it impervious to disease) and that, miraculously, kids would actually eat. In fact, it's estimated that in 1960, Americans got 25 to 30 percent of their calories from white bread, a rather frightening statistic when combined with the fact that the average American in 1960 also got approximately twenty percent of their calories from alcohol. So if, say, you had somebody who enjoyed washing down their peanut-butter-and-jelly sandwiches with a case of Budweiser, you also had someone who would quite literally swallow anything, especially if it was advertised on television.

Russ and I did not buy a loaf of Wonder bread. Instead, we each bought a bag of powdered mini donuts for fifty cents—partly because, as empty calories go, powdered mini donuts are awesome, and partly because the bag itself fit neatly into our sales cases, making it possible to snack on them all day long. If by the end of the day I had not sold any books, I made a mental note to return to the Hostess Thrift Bake Shop later in the day to grab a couple of fruit pies for dinner. Cherry if they had them; apple if they didn't.

That morning I sold my first book. I could not believe it. Instead of shutting the door in my face, as I had come to expect, a pleasant young mother answered my knock, smiled when she saw me, invited me into her house, and seemed genuinely interested in what I was selling. It didn't seem to matter what. She had two young children—toddlers, really—so the *Volume Library* was a stretch, as it was geared for high-school students. But I did have the children's books, which sold for about half of what a *Volume Library* cost, and came with a record that narrated the copy. Asking someone to fire up their stereo system just to listen to the record was a hassle, though, so I dispensed with that step and just read a few pages of the books to her kids. That's when I discovered that if I read the stories with funny voices for each character, the kids would laugh, the mom would be delighted that her kids were laughing, and could not bring herself to say no when it came time to either purchase the books or send me on my way. I also discovered that, because the children's books cost less, people were more likely to pay me cash in full for the books rather than a third or half, as was usually the case with the *Volume Library*. When I asked this particular woman for thirty dollars, she reached into her purse and gave it to me like it was nothing.

To me, however, it was everything.

Selling this woman a set of children's books was so easy, in fact, that I began to wonder if it might be a setup of some sort. In order to boost my confidence, had the company hired someone to invite me into their house and buy a book? It made a certain kind of sense. After all, thus far I had proved incapable of selling a book on my own. Maybe the company thought I needed a "success," and had engineered one so that I wouldn't drown in a sea of despair. Maybe that's what they did with their worst salespeople, I thought, the ones who were clearly flaming out and headed for failure. But then I thought, no, I have thirty dollars in my hand, and if there's one thing I've learned about the Southwestern Company it's that they don't just give money away. They also were not known for doing anything to make Russ and me feel better, or to make our lives any easier. They didn't even keep the promises they actually made. Why, then, would they go out of their way to do something nice and uplifting for me? They wouldn't, I finally concluded. No, I had sold those books fair and square. Somehow, some way, I had persuaded another human being to give me money in exchange for a book—and it felt very good.

I sold two more sets of children's books that day, and ended up with close to eighty dollars in my pocket. Russ had finally succeeded in selling one or two Volume Libraries as well, so he too had some cash in hand. Between us, we had enough to treat ourselves to a burger at the diner and find some place else to stay, somewhere that didn't smell like pig entrails and vomit.

That place ended up being a boarding house that rented by the week. Russ and I bought one week of lodging, figuring that in a week's time we'd have earned at least enough rent for another week. And, if we were lucky—and got better at selling books—we'd eventually have enough money to upgrade our accommodations accordingly. We were aware, however, that the pre-summer promises about how much money we'd make selling books did not include shelling out for rent. In a parallel universe where everything goes according to plan, we were supposed to be living for free under the roof of a benevolent caretaker who thought charging college students rent and board was un-Christian. We were not supposed to be living in a rent-by-the-week flophouse for people who can't scrape enough cash together for an actual apartment. Still, we felt like we'd turned a corner. We'd sold a few books, after all, and had a roof over our heads.

Unfortunately, the new place wasn't much better than the flop house Love Train had recommended. There was only one twin-sized bed, which Russ and I rotated sleeping in while the other person slept on the floor. And, as with our previous flop-house experience, there were no amenities whatsoever. No kitchen, no stove, no refrigerator, no sink, no bathroom. No nothing. The toilet was at the end of the hall. There was a communal kitchenette on the first floor, but the only appliance in it was an old toaster.

Aside from the bed and a small end table with a lamp on it, the only other piece of furniture in the room was a ceramic, claw-foot bathtub. There was no shower attachment, or any other way to bathe, so the tub was the only place to wash other than the small sink at the end of the hall.

The thing about the tub was that it was impossible to fill with hot water. As we learned the first time we tried it, the hot water ran out after a few minutes, so the best we could get on any given morning was one lukewarm tub full of water. This presented a dilemma. If both of us wanted to bathe with clean water, it meant that the second person, after draining the tub, would have to fill it with cold water and pretend they were cleaning themselves in a brisk mountain stream. If we didn't want to freeze, it meant that we'd have to share the bathwater.

This meant that one of us had to go first, and the other had to follow. In practice, this meant that one of us got to scrub our sweaty self with soap in a bathtub full of warm but not unpleasant water, then the other had to use the same water, which by then was tepid and murky with the soap and scum of the previous fellow floating in a thin film on the surface. We also learned pretty quickly that the tub didn't drain very well, so it took a long time to drain and refill it. Considering the hassle involved, we quickly concluded that alternating communal bathing was our only real option.

So that's what we did. In the morning we filled up the tub and traded off the privilege of bathing first. It was disgusting and humiliating and repellant in all the ways you might expect. Going second meant immersing yourself in a milky soup of someone else's sweat and grime.

And, being young men with a certain sick sense of humor, rather than trying to make it more pleasant for the second person in the tub, we tried make it worse—chiefly by farting in the tub when it was our turn to go first.

That was the fun part of living there.

The not-so-fun part was the caliber of residents with whom we were sharing our little hellish Hilton. It's not hard to imagine the sort of people who end up living in the cheapest available accommodations in Davenport, Iowa. They, like us, were only one rung up from homelessness on the ladder of social undesirability: drug addicts, drug dealers, prostitutes, alcoholics, schizophrenics, psych-ward discharges, ex-felons, wife beaters, parolees, small-time criminals, skinheads. Our neighbors were the bottom-dwelling dregs of humanity, people who simply could not function in society at large and so sought shelter and community wherever they could. They terrified me. It was one thing to end up there as part of a personal quest for self-sufficiency that hadn't quite panned out yet. It was quite another to have exhausted all one's options and resources and to end up there, with little hope of advancing or improving your circumstances, having already traveled a long and tortuous road in this, your crummy life.

On our second or third night there, Russ and I were getting ready to go to sleep when there was a knock on our door.

Reluctantly, we answered—conditioned, I suppose, by a certain sympathy for people who knock on doors and are ignored.

Standing in the doorway was a skinny fellow with stringy hair who was wearing a green army shirt and smoking a cigarette. I did not invite him in, but—as if he had been trained by the Southwestern Company himself—he took the open door as an invitation and stepped inside. He didn't come very far into the room. Instead, he leaned against the wall near the door, took a drag on his cigarette and said with a sandpaper rasp, "So you're the new guys."

We introduced ourselves. He said his name was Frank. Then we all looked at each other for a while without saying anything.

"What can we do for you, Frank?" Russ asked.

"Nothin'," he answered. "It's what I can do for you."

"What's that?"

"Warn you," he said.

"Warn us? About what?"

"The Indian. Two doors down. He's crazy."

"Crazy how?"

Frank took another drag on his cigarette and exhaled a plume of smoke into our room. "He's got demons in him," Frank said. "Bad ones."

Russ and I didn't quite know how to respond to that, so Russ said, "Well, thanks for the warning, Frank. But if you don't mind, we need to get some sleep."

"There's a Mexican on the first floor you don't want to mess with, either," Frank said. "Says he killed a guy once. Probably just talk, but you never know."

"Thanks," I said rather weakly.

"You ever kill anyone?" Frank asked. By the expression on our faces, he could probably guess that the answer was no.

"Well don't," he counseled.

I nodded, as if to acknowledge that this was, indeed, good advice.

"I've killed people," he said, taking another drag on his cigarette. "Not a lot. But a few. In 'Nam."

Silence.

"I know guys who did a lot worse," he said, exhaling a plume of smoke into our room.

"What's worse than killing?" he asked, rhetorically. "Plenty. It's how you kill. *Why* you kill. *Who* you kill. Not everyone deserves to die. Even in war, there are limits. Or at least there should be."

Then he launched into a story: "Me and four other grunts were out on patrol. In the jungle. Hot as hell. Air thick as spit. Mosquitoes the size of Volkswagens. But that wasn't the worst of it. The worst part of being on patrol is not knowing if you're gonna make it back. Any second you could get a bullet in the head and bam, it's over. Know how you get around that? You have to pretend you're *already* dead," he said, turning his index finger into an imaginary bullet and tapping his forehead. "You have to accept the inevitability before it happens. If you don't, you'll go crazy," he added, as if he'd thwarted the demons of craziness and was now offering us sage advice from his perch atop Mount Sanity. "We were making our way through the jungle, single file, me in the lead, when we came to a clearing. The ground was covered in blood. Flies were buzzing like bees. The stench was sickening. The smell of death, hot and thick in that jungle heat? Nothing like it. Once it gets in your nose, it never leaves. Wanna know why? Because it ain't human, not anymore. It's steaming hot jungle rot, the body breaking down, returning to the Earth, Mother Nature reclaiming her own. And what was that smell? Hanging from a tree branch above the clearing was an entire Vietcong family—mom, dad, and three kids, one of them no more than two—who had been strung up by their feet and gutted. At first, I only saw their backs. But when I walked around to the other side of the clearing I could see their intestines hanging out, dangling there like a bunch of wadded-up rope. Their eyes had been poked out too, and somebody had cut off the dad's dick."

Frank paused to let us fully imagine the horror he was describing.

"You wanna know who did it?" he asked. We did not dare guess.

"We did, that's who," he said. "The good, ol' U, S, of A."

Frank took a drag on his cigarette to let the gravity of this assertion sink in.

"Why?" he mused, stabbing the air with his cigarette. "Why would we do such a thing?"

Then he answered himself. "Because *that's who we are.*"

Over the ensuing weeks we would come to understand that this scene in the hellscape of Vietnam was the defining moment in Frank's life, the moment when his spirit shattered and the splinters of the person he once was were strewn in all directions, never to be assembled in quite the same way again. He visited us frequently, late at night, sometimes drunk, sometimes high, always angry, and told us his war stories, the incidents that had riddled his life with holes he could not fill. He was not like this before the war, he claimed. The war had *done* this too him. The things he'd seen he could not un-see, no matter how hard he tried to erase them from his memory. Haunted by images of death and depravity, tortured by the moral vacuum at the center of the conflict, he roamed the halls of our little tenement talking to anyone who would pretend to listen.

To me, his stories were tales of the bullet Russ and I had both dodged. The draft was suspended in 1973, this was 1979, so we were the first generation of American men who did not have to fear being conscripted into military service. I was always aware of this generational cut-off because I had a friend in high school who was passionately involved in protests to drop the requirement that young men register for the draft—a fail-safe the government still requires, in case there is another war in some godforsaken part of the world that may require filling body bags with the carcasses of kids who aren't lucky or rich enough to avoid such a fate. At the time, I was of course relieved that I would never have to go to war involuntarily; I also felt somewhat guilty about it. In a way, selling books was a substitute, an alternative way of testing my own mettle in foreign territory, albeit without the fear of annihilation. It was a way of finding out how much I could endure, how self-sufficient I could be, how deep my inner resources really were. It was also a sort of punishment for being privileged, a kind of self-flagellation for having the kind of childhood and upbringing that others can only dream about. And as forms of self-flagellation go, selling books door-to-door was quite effective. It teaches humility, patience, courage, and resolve, and it forces the salesperson to confront the limitations of their willpower, that part of the psyche that allows people to overcome their fears and inhibitions to do something they really, truly, do not want to do.

CHAPTER 21

Sunday was our only day of respite, though not exactly rest. Every other Sunday, all the student booksellers in Iowa, Illinois, and Missouri met in a central location for our regional sales meeting. At the first meeting, held in Springfield, Illinois, there were about one-hundred students like us, all of whom had just endured their grueling first week in "the field." The Field is in fact a perfect metaphor for bookselling, because it captures the whole idea of being abandoned alone in the middle of nowhere with no help. Add the word "battle" to that field and the metaphor is even more apt.

Everyone had their stories. There was the guy who slept in his car for four days; the girl who tracked down an old boyfriend and crashed at his place; the guys who slept in a barn for two nights until a farmer kicked them out. There were people who hadn't sold a single book all week, and whose despair was written on their faces in a sheepish sheet of shame. Russ and I could identify with these people. We too had struggled to get a foothold on survival, and though we hadn't been completely skunked in our first couple of weeks, the enormity of the challenge to sell "a mere two books a day" had become disheartingly obvious.

The people we couldn't identify with were the ones who had actually found a benevolent host family to stay with, or who had sold twenty or more books their first week and seemed to be cruising on easy street. Gifted with some blessed combination of good luck and great salesmanship, these people seemed to have an almost super-human ability to bend the universe to their will. For every story of someone else's defeat, they had a tale of victory. For every admission of doubt or failure, they had an inspirational story about overcoming adversity and/or encountering truckloads of generosity from unexpected places. We had one of those stories too—a pimp named Love Train who bought us a couple of hamburgers—but most of our tales were of the hard luck and woe variety. Not many good things had happened to us since we landed in Davenport, and the list of bad things that had happened made us look like we were somehow cursed, as if our struggles were some sort of karmic retribution for wrongs committed somewhere along the way, in this life or a past one. And if that was the case, we somehow deserved it. Or brought it on ourselves. Or were simply incompetent.

The managing class of the Southwestern Company had a different explanation. To them, it was clear that we did not have enough faith in God and were not right with The Lord. The gist was that we could expect bad things to keep happening to us as long as we refused to accept Jesus Christ as our Lord and Savior. The Devil would continue to bedevil us until we learned to walk the path of righteousness with Almighty Him by our side, helping us open people's doors and wallets in service of the Lord's grand mission—which was, of course, higher sales figures.

"Jesus wants you succeed," they told us. "All you have to do is let him into your heart."

"Jesus too suffered rejection, yet he persevered."

"With Jesus in your heart, you are never alone."

Indeed, a solid portion of our Sunday get-togethers sounded like a southern Baptist revival meeting. Older, more experienced salespeople evangelized about the strength Jesus gave them and how their faith got them through the hardest parts of the bookman's day, when the only word you've heard all day is "no" and you just want to quit and go home. When hopelessness and despair invade your heart, they'd say, the only thing that can drive it out is a good long talk with your buddy, Jesus, who will counsel you to stop feeling sorry for yourself because, you know, things could be worse. You could be wearing a crown of thorns and be nailed to a cross while angry villagers hurl goat dung at you and stab you in the side with long, sharp lances. Compared to that, what's a few hours of door-knocking? It's nothing, they'd insist. You're just throwing yourself a pity party. Feeling sorry for yourself. Losing sight of the big picture. Jesus loves you and wants to show you The Way, they'd say. And for right-thinking book-people everywhere, the Lord's ultimate message was crystal clear: Stop whining and get back to work.

Left virtually unmentioned during our first meeting was the fact that about half the kids from the original group in Nashville had, like our man Greg, already up and quit. If it was mentioned at all, this embarrassing reality was spun as a testament to our superior character and moral fiber, not as an indictment of the Southwestern Company itself. These were all students who had been hand-picked and trained by the company, dispersed into America by the company, and asked to sell books on behalf of the company, yet a conspicuously high percentage of these students still elected to walk rather than put up with the company's nonsense. What did that say about the Southwestern Company itself? What did it say about the company's recruiting methods? The effectiveness of its sales training? The appeal of its value proposition to aspiring college students? The wisdom of its sink-or-swim selling philosophy?

No one dared ask.

The company treated these defections as an unfortunate but necessary culling of the herd, and emphasized that those who had quit hadn't really quit on the company, they had done something much worse—*they had quit on themselves.*

Quitting on yourself was of course the most damnable crime in book-dom. Quitting didn't just mean you were a weak, pathetic loser who couldn't make the grade; it meant you had made the worst mistake of your life by choosing the path of least resistance, by retreating, by taking the coward's way out. It meant that you had given up on the idea of success, and had embraced a morally reprehensible attitude of failure, setting you up for a life of misery, disappointment, poverty, and sin. People who quit were weak in character and corrupt in spirit. They had no grit, no fire in the belly. They were the kind of people who always chose the easy way, the path of sloth and self-indulgence, and people like that were soft tubs of mediocrity who would never amount to anything in life. People like us—people who stayed and fought and persevered—were the leaders and succeeders of the future.

Or at least that's what they wanted us to believe. It's also what we wanted to believe about ourselves. We who stayed did not want to believe we were chumps, that we had allowed ourselves to be manipulated and misled by a bunch of evangelical con men who preyed on our fear of failure. We did not want to think we were the stupid ones, or that those who had the guts to quit were the ones with the strongest character and the most internal resolve. No, we wanted to believe that the hardships we were enduring were the fire necessary to forge the steely spirit of success we all not-so-secretly desired. That's why we were there—to learn the shamanic rituals of success, the habits and attitudes that would ferry us forward into prosperity.

It would be interesting to study the career trajectories of those who quit selling books that summer and those of us who stayed. I'm willing to bet that many of the quitters went on to have illustrious careers precisely because they had the guts to say, "Hell no, I'm not putting up with that shit anymore." Knowing when to say no is a useful skill in life, arguably more useful than learning how to ignore your screaming inner rebel in the name of "self-discipline." Learning how to endure the unendurable has its downsides, too. I, for one, have stayed in far too many job situations that in retrospect I should have abandoned; remained stuck in too many relationships that I should have ended sooner; put up with far too many lousy friends and lazy co-workers; accepted way too many people at face value; overlooked countless insults and indignities simply to keep the peace; swallowed heaping gobs of pride; choked on the loss of my own moral compass; and generally failed to stick up for myself, to do what in my heart of hearts I really wanted to do. All because I could. All because I learned how to do it—in school, during Hell Week, on the streets of Davenport. All because I had convinced myself that in order to succeed I somehow had to suffer. A logical trap that turned into a bizarre tautology: The more I suffered, the more successful I'd be.

Equating suffering with success is of course ridiculous. But in the 1970s, it was practically an article of faith. When I was in high school, the phrase "No Pain, No Gain" was plastered on the wall of the weight room, where pumping iron to the point of agony was viewed as the path to manhood, the surest way to gain strength, endurance, and the attention of girls, who tended to gravitate toward guys with well-toned musculature (not, as women's magazines would have us believe, the boys who made them laugh). Ben Franklin is said to have originated the phrase with his admonition, in *Poor Richard's Almanac*, that "there are no gains without pains." But the idea itself goes back centuries. Almost every spiritual practice in existence embraces the idea of struggle and sacrifice as a path toward enlightenment. The Bible itself is full of characters—Job, Abraham, Elijah, Jonah, Job, Moses— who must endure almost unimaginable levels of pain and heartbreak before God lifts an eyebrow and decides they've had enough. Jesus himself is the living embodiment of Nietzsche's dictum that "to live is to suffer," and that the point of survival is to try to find some meaning amidst all that inevitable pain.

But is all that pain really inevitable? Is it really necessary to suffer in order to grow? To learn? To identify one's talents and develop them to the best of one's ability? Maybe, in a sense. But there's a huge difference between self-discipline and self-flagellation, between doing what you want to do with conscious and deliberate dedication, and punishing yourself for the heck of it. Not that punishing oneself doesn't come with its own perverse sort of pleasure—it does—just that the underlying psychological motivations behind that kind of thinking tend to be counter-productive and, taken to the extreme, self-destructive. Unfortunately for those who try it, self-punishment does not lead directly to spiritual purification, it leads much more directly to feeling shitty about yourself. And when you feel shitty about yourself, you are more likely to succumb to despair, to drink and smoke and seek out a drug that can make you feel better.

In America, however, there is a grand paradox at work. On the one hand, the ethos of capitalism grants people the freedom (if not the obligation) to make the most of their talents and abilities to pursue "happiness," primarily through personal success and prosperity. On the other hand, there are so many social, cultural, and institutional barriers to achieving that sort of comfortably prosperous "happiness" that most people inevitably fail. And they feel bad about failing. They get angry. And they get angry because they realize they were sold a pack of idealistic lies. They grew up believing that the so-called American Dream is available to anyone who works hard. Then they find out—a bit too late in most instances—that it isn't. In reality, turning that dream into reality involves a great deal of luck, even if you have the desire and perseverance to meet all the myriad challenges of life head on. Conversely, if you are content with your lot, happy in your mediocrity, and have scaled back your expectations to a reasonable level, you are said to be doing something wrong, settling for less, not living up to your potential. In America, one is not supposed to sit back and enjoy life too much; one is expected to be perpetually dissatisfied, and to address that dissatisfaction with an ever greater commitment to work, even if that work consists mainly of soul-destroying tedium.

Those who question the universal applicability of the "no pain, no gain" philosophy are often treated to the story of the butterfly—how, to escape from its cocoon, the butterfly must first struggle and squirm to build its strength, so that when it emerges from its chrysalis, it is strong enough to fly.

It's a lovely metaphor. And for those whose job it is to inflict pain—P.E. teachers, for instance—invoking the struggle of the butterfly is an excellent way to justify the systemic torture of pubescent bookworms who have no interest in lifting anything heavier than a dictionary. But as words to live by go, they are somewhat problematic. If every gain must be preceded by pain, what are we to make of gains that do not involve pain, or gains that involve a pleasurable version of "pain," such as the artist's drive to paint, the musician's desire to play, the athlete's desire to excel? Why couldn't a catch-phrase like "No Pleasure, No Treasure" be equally true?

I'm sure there's an alternative universe out there where I win arguments like this. Unfortunately, I don't live in that universe; I live in this one, where, for reasons that aren't entirely clear to me even to this day, my eighteen-year-old self *chose* to endure the agony and humiliation of my fraternity's Hell Week, and *chose* to subject himself to the absurd indignities of door-to-door book-selling. And he chose it not because it was the easiest thing he could do with his summer, but because it was the *hardest*. My eighteen-year-old self needed a test—of his manhood, if you will: of his endurance, his inner strength, his capacity for suffering. And he found it on the streets of Davenport, Iowa.

CHAPTER 22

One of the things we discovered at our first Sunday regional get-together was that there was another team of booksellers who were working in Bettendorf, Davenport's tonier neighborhood to the north. They were right next door, in other words, and they were . . . female.

Dana was from Kansas University, and Jackie was from the University of Missouri. Dana was attractive and cheerful and smart. She had an infectious laugh, and her teeth were disconcertingly straight and white and large, as if her orthodontist had implanted in her gums a row of perfectly chiseled dinner mints. Jackie was on the homelier side. She had an unruly nest of curly brown hair and lived in an awkward body with a low center of gravity. But she was kind, and she had a sardonic, goofy sense of humor.

The truth is, I don't remember ever meeting Dana and Jackie. All I remember is that one day Russ and I were alone in Davenport, with no friends and no one but ourselves to rely upon for moral support. And then we weren't.

When our Sunday meeting was over, we bummed a ride from Dana and Jackie back to the Quad Cities. Dana had a green Chevy Impala, a big ugly road beast with squishy shocks that made it feel as if you were riding on a bag of marshmallows. But having a car—or knowing someone who had a car—was a huge advantage in bookselling. It meant you could precisely target different neighborhoods, and didn't have to waste time taking the bus or walking to get there. And when the car always arrives with two women in the front seat, it means you have companionship, people to talk to, people to flirt with—indeed, people who might one day agree to have sex with you.

But I'm getting ahead of myself.

On the way back from our first Sunday meeting, the topic of discussion among our newly formed foursome was why the folks running the Southwestern operation did not inform us of each other's existence in the first place? From a management perspective, keeping us apart perhaps made sense because four college-age men and women in the hormonal prime of their lives might find ways to distract each other. But they had to know we'd eventually find each other, so they also had to know that any attempts to keep us apart would be futile. Mike, our district manager, had been in regular contact with all of us, yet he had chosen not to disclose each other's proximity. Why?

"Because Mike is a dick," was Russ's analysis.

"Because Mike is dedicated to making our lives as difficult as possible," was my assessment.

"Because Mike is a double-dick-faced douche-monster who wants to get in my pants," was Jackie's contribution, adding, "*Wants* being the operative word there."

"Because Mike knew we'd hook up eventually, and knew we all had a lot to work through in the first week, and didn't want to spoil the surprise," Dana said. "But now that we've all got places to stay, we can focus and get down to business. You know, when we're not busy distracting each other."

It was early evening when we got back to Davenport. Constant conversation and laughter had made the trip go by in a flash. On the road, we had quickly discovered that we all got along, and that we all shared a similar skepticism about some of the Southwestern Company's persuasion tactics, especially the whole "Jesus is your buddy" trope, which struck us all as vaguely creepy. Perhaps it's a cultural thing, but Southern evangelicals in expensive suits with coiffed hair and cufflinks are a curious breed. How anyone can be fooled by their faux sincerity is a mystery. The Reverend Billy Graham is the model, of course. By 1979, Graham had already established himself as a "spiritual adviser" to several U.S. presidents, including Dwight D. Eisenhower, Lyndon Johnson, and Richard Nixon. His relationship with Ronald and Nancy Reagan would eventually become national news, of course, but that particular turn of the screw hadn't happened yet. The only exposure a kid from California like me had to Graham were his sermons on Sunday morning television, which struck me—a kid raised by scientific rationalists—as an absurd form of spiritual theater. Southwestern execs struck me the same way, except that their evangelism was more corporate, and therefore more sinister, because it was aimed at leveraging the Lord's eternal love for humanity to make more money—for them.

Though Dana and Jackie technically lived in Davenport, their accommodations were close the city border and they worked in Bettendorf, so they had never laid eyes on the seamier side of the city. As we approached our tenement house that day, their assessment of our neighborhood was not very charitable. Dana called it a "slum," and Jackie said it was "too close to home." They weren't wrong. Lower-class neighborhoods in America all share the same dispiriting sense of squalor, due in no small part to a losing battle with entropy. The houses were small and in various states of disrepair. Peeling paint. Rotting wood. Crumbling sidewalks. Tall weeds. Cars on cinder blocks. Half-dismantled engines in the garage. A conspicuous lack of mufflers on the cars that did run. Blaring stereos. Radios tuned to the game (there's always a game). Overflowing trash cans. Roaming dogs of no particular breed in search of discarded pizza and day-old French fries. Old people sitting on their porch, watching the goings-on with quiet resignation. The occasional glimpse of a child, barefoot and unsupervised, playing too close to the street.

Our neighborhood had it all—and, we soon learned, even more.

Russ and I did not want Dana and Jackie to see where we were living, partly because we were ashamed, and partly because getting out of the car felt, well, dangerous. To wit: Parking on our block turned out to be impossible because all the available space was taken up by motorcycles. Harley Davidsons. Big, shiny noise machines, more than fifty of them, parked in neat rows along the street, each one a trusty gleaming steed of leather and chrome. Their riders were gathered on the front lawn of the house next to ours, drinking beer from kegs and grilling burgers and dogs on a barbecue made out of an old oil drum cut in half with an acetylene torch. Men with beards and tattoos milled around, telling jokes and laughing. An old sofa had been pulled out onto the front yard, on which several women of various ages sat, silently observing the anarchy and trading a knowing glance every now and then.

A closer look at the gang affiliation on their jackets provided no comfort whatsoever. The gang was called "The Grim Reapers," its insignia a portrait of the infamous Reaper himself in a red hooded robe holding a scythe with a blade twice as big as his head.

So yes, we were apparently living next door to a motorcycle gang that worshipped death by throwing a barbecue and listening to Willie Nelson on a thirty-dollar radio held together with duct tape and tin foil. My ability to survive in the world until that point depended partly on avoiding these types of people, so I—as well as Russ and Dana—tried hard not to make eye contact with any of the Reapers as we approached our own dwelling.

Jackie, however, had a different reaction. Instead of averting her gaze, she spontaneously blurted, "Whoa, party!," then strode up to the nearest Grim Reaper and introduced herself.

We were aghast—and frightened.

It wasn't hard to imagine what we looked like in their eyes. We were clean-cut kids with neat haircuts who were, at that moment, wearing khaki shorts and Polo shirts and carrying bright-red sales cases. If there is a cultural opposite to the Grim Reaper, were were it. Consequently, it also wasn't hard to imagine that we were the kind of people they hated. Given the opportunity, they might drag us out into the woods and skin us alive, I thought, then use our blood in some sort of sacrificial rite that granted membership to the person who held the knife and slit our throats, while a throng of bikers chanted pagan poetry and held torches under a full moon at midnight.

While Jackie made small talk, we hung back in the hope that she would soon come to her senses. Instead, she waved us over and introduced us to a guy named Lurch, who stood about six-foot-seven and was one of the scariest motherfuckers I've ever seen. Arm tattoos. Nose ring. Head bandana. A beard you could strain soup through. The whole terrifying package.

Lurch shook our hands and invited us to join them. He pointed to the beer keg, and told us to help ourselves to some food. "Any friend of Jackie's is a friend of mine," he said, even though he had only known Jackie for a grand total of two-and-a-half minutes.

Lurch, it turned out, was one of the nicest guys you'd ever want to meet. Polite. Well-spoken. And, bizarrely, more curious about us than we were about him.

"So Jackie tells me you guys are trying to sell educational books door-to-door to put yourselves through college," he said as he took a sip of beer. "If you don't mind my saying so, that's fucking crazy."

"Couldn't agree with you more," Russ said.

"It's also pretty ballsy," he said. "No way I could do that."

"Neither can we," I replied, "which is why we are currently living in the fine establishment next door."

"So you're neighbors?"

We nodded. Reluctantly.

"Welcome to the neighborhood, then!" Lurch exclaimed. Then he called a few people over—guys with names like Chubbs, Knuckles, Dogpatch, and Flea—and introduced us. The strange thing was, he introduced us as though we were one of them, as if we belonged there (though we manifestly didn't), and were actually welcome. He explained to his biker buddies what we were doing in Davenport, and they all laughed, as if the absurdity of it was instantaneously obvious to all. But it wasn't a dismissive or contemptuous laugh; it was a laugh that communicated a strange form of respect. They seemed to understand intuitively that what we were trying to do was hard, that it was unusual, and that knocking on doors all day took a certain amount of renegade courage. They did not seem to judge us at all by how were were dressed or how we looked, only by the fact that we were trying in our own way to get ahead in the world, and that our odyssey of ambition had landed us on their doorstep—an ironic turn of events that they seemed to find amusing.

The more we talked to them, however, the more I realized they felt kind of sorry for us. Sorry for feeling like we had to punish ourselves in an obviously shitty job just to get an education and join the rat race like everyone else, rather than roam the countryside on a rumble-bike like them, free to do whatever they wanted, whenever they wanted, with whomever they wanted, under the influence of whatever mind-altering substances they wanted, regardless of what the law, society, or anyone else had to say about it. They also felt weirdly protective of us, almost paternal, as if we were wayward children who needed just enough supervision to prevent us from running into the street and getting hit by a car. After a couple of beers and a burger and quite a few laughs (at our expense, mostly), they offered precisely the same sort of protection that our old pal Love Train had offered: To wit, if anyone in Davenport ever fucked with us, they instructed us to inform the offender that we were friends with the Grim Reapers, and if said idiots continued fucking with us, the Reapers themselves would find them and fuck *them* up, but good. By which I took them to mean that they would murder the offenders in cold blood and bury their bodies in the woods.

It's disconcerting to have one's stereotypes turned on their head. We had been in Davenport for less than two weeks, and by far the nicest people we had met were a flamboyant pimp and members of a notorious motorcycle gang.

Go figure.

After we said our thanks and goodbyes to the Grim Reapers, Russ and I escorted Dana and Jackie upstairs to our room.

They were horrified.

"How can you live like this?" Dana asked.

"The sheer luxury of it can be a bit overwhelming at first, I'll admit, but you get used to it after a while," I offered.

"This is awful," Jackie hissed under her breath.

"We have to get you out of here," Dana said with an air of urgency that I took to be a product of her shock.

"It's not like we have much choice in the matter," I explained.

"The good news, I guess, is that it can't get much worse than this," said Dana.

"Oh, but it can," Russ corrected. "And believe me, this is several steps up from 'worst,' which is where we were before this."

They were shocked. The reason they were shocked, we soon learned, is that they apparently had very little trouble finding an excellent place to live. Without even trying very hard, they had gotten a lead about a guy who was going to be out of town for the summer and needed someone to house sit while he was gone. They contacted him, the deal was struck, and they were now living on the second floor of his place. What they didn't tell us was that his "place" was a modest-sized mansion, and that the "second floor" consisted of four bedrooms, a bathroom, a kitchenette, and a formal library. They had hit the jackpot, in other words, and were living precisely the way the company had described. Better even. And they had fallen into this sweet arrangement through pure luck and happenstance. It didn't hurt that they were responsible-looking young women, I'm sure, but still, their success at finding suitable accommodations made us look like chumps. And when we described in greater detail the indignities we had already suffered, as well as the treatment we had received from the police, from our district manager Mike, and from pretty much everyone who wasn't a biker or a pimp, they found it hard to believe. Hard to believe that we hadn't bailed on the whole project, that is, and gone back to our respective sun-baked sanctuaries in the Southwest.

But there we were.

The project to remove us from our circumstantial hellhole was complicated by the fact that the one rule Dana and Jackie had agreed to in their housing arrangement was "no guys." Were it not for this clear and unambiguous stipulation, they would have invited us to live with them in a heartbeat, they said. Furthermore, the "guy" who owned the house had yet to leave for the summer and was still living on the first floor. So bunking with them was not an option.

Finding a new place to live wasn't much of an option either, though, because money was still extremely tight. We were barely covering our expenses as it was. Saving up enough money for a down-payment on another place would take some time. At least a few weeks. In the meantime, we assured the ladies that the place wasn't as bad as it looked (a lie), and that we had every intention of leaving as soon as possible.

Mollified for the moment, Dana and Jackie left. They would be back in the morning at 8 a.m. sharp, they said, and we would all go out for breakfast. Then we'd sing the Book(Person) song and go sell some Volume Libraries. That's what we were there for, after all, and now that we were all a team, helping each other succeed was our highest priority.

After Dana and Jackie left, Russ and I could not believe that fortune had finally smiled on us so generously. Not only had we met two not-unattractive women with whom we could share our misery, they also had a car and a decent fund of cash (from Dana's parents), all of which meant that we might survive for another couple of weeks after all.

But there had to be some ground rules, we agreed. "Whatever we do, we cannot sleep with them," Russ declared, and I concurred. No matter how tempting it might be to try, and even if the opportunity presented itself, the best way to mess up the whole arrangement up was to introduce the specter of sex and romance into the mix. We shook hands on it, then went to bed with a strange feeling in our guts—a feeling of optimism about the coming week and all it might entail.

CHAPTER 23

Dana and Jackie arrived rather too promptly the following morning, chipper to a fault and ready to meet the day in a way we were not. Frank had paid us another visit the previous night and had eaten up two precious hours of sleep with more of his "you would not believe the horrors I have seen" Vietnam stories. At some point during his retelling of a firefight that involved snipers, napalm, mud, snakes, and a stray cow, I found I could half-listen to Frank and half-sleep at the same time. But half-sleeping is not the same as sleeping, so both Russ and I were a bit on the groggy side when the girls picked us up. In the car, on the way to breakfast, Dana turned on the radio and a voice came blaring out of the speakers.

"Spike at the Mike here, coming to you from Twinkie Boulevard on the shores of the Mississippi River. Not all of us have recovered from the rigors and libations of the weekend, I know, so we're going to start the day out with a song assassination. That's when we take a song that needs to die, and we kill it. Here goes . . ."

Then the all too familiar strains of my most-hated song in the world began to play: "Muskrat, muskrat, candlelight. Doin' the town and doin' it right. In the evening. It's pretty pleasin'."

"Noooooo," I cried—and just as I did, the rat-a-tat of artillery fire ripped through the speakers and stopped the song in its tracks. Then Spike made some squeaky noises that I think were supposed to be muskrats getting riddled with bullets. I laughed and applauded. Spike at the Mike had "assassinated" that damn song, the one that had haunted me during my fraternity's Hell Week, the song that had kept me awake in a cold shower, the song that bounced off the bathroom tiles and reverberated in my head for hours that night. How many times had I wanted to kill that song? Too many to count. Now Spike had done it for me, killed it dead before it had a chance to get to the swirling and twirling and tangoing part, or any other part of the song for that matter.

"There it is, folks. 'Muskrat Love' dead and gone!" Spike laugh-yelled into his microphone. "Some songs should not be allowed to exist, and that's definitely one of them!" Spike opined. "Every morning we kill a song that needs to die. The list is long, especially now that Foreigner has a new album out. So be patient. Death will eventually come to a song you hate. Or at least a song I hate. Now for some real music," he added, then started playing something by the Stones.

"Spike" was a humorous morning shock-jock of the sort that ruled the airwaves in the 1970s, the heyday of classic rock. He was more entertaining than most, and listening to his show became a morning ritual for us. Hearing him dispatch such treacly Top 40 hits as "We Are Family," (Sisters Sledge) "Dreamweaver," (Steve Wright), "Two Tickets to Paradise," (Eddie Money), "Dust in the Wind" (Kansas), "How Deep is Your Love," (Bee Gees), etc., was cathartic. He had what I thought of as a well-aimed disdain for the sort of saccharine, empty wailing about obsessive love that I also hated, and he seemed suspicious of any song that the management of his radio station made him play more than ten times a day. I was sick of these songs after hearing them only a few dozen times on the radio; I could only imagine the sort of loathing one might develop if broadcasting those songs was your job. Spike seemed to maintain his sanity (and the devotion of his listeners) by attacking the hand that fed him, an act of defiance that also served as a sort of meta-commentary on the state of popular music, the tyranny of corporate broadcasting, and the ridiculous frequency with which some songs were played in order to attract listeners and boost ad revenue. The business model was: play the songs on the Billboard Top 20 as many times a day as you can. That's it. And they did, which is why the mental soundtrack of people over fifty sounds so much like a Fleetwood Mac album.

Ironically, listening to any "classic rock" station on FM radio now isn't much different from rock stations in the 1970s. Eighty percent of the songs are the same—big hits by so-called "supergroups"—and the rest are forgettable imitations by various rock bands who emulated their heroes and manufactured appealing but highly derivative variations on the same theme. The band Boston was iconic for its highly analytical approach to rock-and-roll thievery. Rather than simply write songs, the leaders of that band created a database of popular songs and their musical structures—keys, chord changes, lyrics—and came up with a template for the most popular chord progressions and song structures, then built its music around that information. It's a tribute to Boston's creativity that its songs do not sound obviously derivative, but they are, in the most scientifically accurate way possible at the time. Their music represented an artistic breakthrough of sorts, an innovative blending of new-fangled technology and age-old musical knowledge for the specific purpose of creating popular music that just about everyone would like. And it worked. Everyone liked Boston. For a while. Until their songs—along with bands like REO Speedwagon, Journey, Styx, and yes, Fleetwood Mac—were aired so relentlessly that a kind of popularity fatigue set in, an aesthetic backlash against the prevailing notion of "popular" music. At least that's what happened to me. And to Spike. And to a lot of other people. This led to a kind of anti-pop-culture creed. To wit: If it's popular, it must suck. Or, like a Dorito, its inherent mediocrity must be so well-manufactured that you don't really notice—in fact, you might even like it—until the bag is empty and you start feeling sick to your stomach. Over-consumption of anything will have pretty much the same effect, I suppose. In most cases, however, the object of one's indigestion can be purged. Over-consumption of certain types of music sticks with you for life.

CHAPTER 24

Over the next couple of weeks, our foursome settled into a comfortable routine. The girls picked us up in the morning, we all went out to breakfast, then the girls dropped Russ and me off in our respective territories. At the end of the day, around 6 p.m., they picked us up and took us home. Sometimes we went out for dinner too, but more often than not we simply went home and made ourselves a peanut butter and jelly sandwich. We lived on PB&J, partly because we were broke, partly because we were lazy, and partly because we were scared to use the kitchen facilities in our building for fear that we might meet someone else like Frank. At the end of the day we were usually too exhausted to do anything but read a bit and go to bed. On most nights we were in bed by 10 p.m., even though it wasn't entirely dark yet. The next morning we woke up and did it all again—day after day after day.

At the end of each day, we naturally shared stories about the people we'd met and reported the number of books we had sold. Dana and Russ settled into a groove where they were selling one or two books a day. I was still struggling to sell even one book or set of children's books per day, and often returned to the group only to report that I hadn't sold anything. We all got skunked every now and then, but I seemed to get skunked more often than anyone else. And there is no worse feeling than spending an entire day knocking on people's doors and persuading absolutely no one to listen to you. The heavy emotions usually hit somewhere in the early afternoon, after four or five hours of failure. Loneliness, anxiety, depression, despair—they came in waves, coupled with a less-than-helpful internal dialogue about the futility of the whole enterprise and the folly of even trying. After all, one could just as easily sell no books by going to the movies, or playing a round of golf, or taking a long bike ride. The difference was that not selling books in those ways did not come with so many heaping piles of misery and heartache. (Although there are times on the golf course when those emotions do come bubbling to the surface on occasion.)

The surprise performer in the group was Jackie. As it turned out, Jackie had a substantial advantage over us all in the selling department, because she looked, acted, and talked like an average Midwestern girl. There was nothing remarkable about her, and that was her ace in the hole. She understood Midwesterners in a way that Russ and I could not, and she spoke to them in a language we did not understand and could not fake. I once complained to her that when I spoke to the people in Davenport they looked at me like I was an alien, and that they all seemed to have the words "I do not trust you" tattooed on their foreheads. She knew I was struggling, and made a suggestion.

"Can you do a Southern accent?" she asked. (As it happened I could, because I was born in Texas and lived there until I was nine.) "Try putting a little drawl in your voice, and talk quieter and slower," she advised. "You're too loud and you talk too fast. It makes people think you're trying to pull a fast one over them. You'll do better if you talk slow and don't project too much confidence."

I had nothing to lose, so the next day I tried it, and had my best sales day ever! I also had more fun than ever. For the first time I actually enjoyed selling. Whenever I pretended to have a Southern accent, and approached people with a kind of aw-shucks innocence, it seemed to disarm them, to give them permission to let their defenses down. I didn't understand why this happened, but I certainly took advantage of it. Indeed, many of my days in the book-field were spent talking as if I were a character in a Tennessee Williams play.

Over time, I developed a kind of "character" for book-selling: he was a well-meaning young man from Amarillo, Texas, who was putting himself through college because his father died in a car accident (a head-on collision, the other driver was drunk), and whose mother worked double shifts as a checkout clerk at the local grocery store to make ends meet. He loved his mother, and was so grateful to her that he couldn't in good conscience burden her with the cost of his education. Selling books was a way to honor the sacrifices his mother had already made on his behalf, and help him realize his mother's deepest wish for him: that he get a good education and "make something of himself" in this world. Buying a book from him wasn't just a financial transaction, it was a kind of charitable donation, a way of helping a young man realize his mother's dream. Sometimes his mother had diabetes or lupus or some other disease that made her life that much harder. Sometimes his father died in a farming accident, or swerved into a tree to avoid hitting a deer, or fell off an oil rig in the Gulf of Mexico and drowned. If more details were necessary, he also had a sister with Down syndrome or muscular dystrophy, whose care and feeding consumed most of his mother's energy and resources. He did what he could to help, he told them, but had come to the conclusion that the best way to help his mother was not only to remove the yoke of his existence from her, but to get a good education and a well-paying job so that he could take care of his mother and sister in the future.

The ruse worked, for several reasons. For me, playing a character, rather than being myself, helped depersonalize the daily barrage of rejection and failure. It was like wearing an impenetrable shell, one that made it easier to swat away the slings and arrows of outrageous daily door-knocking. It was also more fun. Knowing that I was fooling people into believing I was someone else, and knowing that I could use that tragic persona to manipulate them into feeling sorry for me—well, it made me feel powerful. It was like a magic trick, except that if I did it right, they never found out it was a trick.

My carefully constructed ruse eventually backfired, of course. One afternoon, my well-practiced, three-rap door knock was answered by girl about my age. Blonde, gorgeous, sweet, and kind, she immediately invited me into her home and, because I was a sweaty mess, she offered me a glass of lemonade. We sat in the living room and began to talk. Without thinking much about it, I turned on the drawl and started spewing my usual stream of tragic bullshit. On her, it worked better than I could have ever hoped. She was fascinated, and kept asking me questions about my childhood and upbringing.

"What kind of place is Amarillo?
"Did your father and mother love each other?
"Where is your sister now?
"How does your mother care for her?
"Do you have other family in the area?"

Each question forced me to make up more details, to fill in the blanks of a story I hadn't thought through entirely and often changed depending on my mood, the person I was talking to, and whatever heart-wrenching story I could dream up on the spot.

She responded the way a good, honest person does:
"Oh my, how sad."

"Your poor mother."

"Such a shame."

"I can't even imagine."

"You poor thing."

We talked for hours that day—me spinning an ever-thicker tangle of lies, and her responding with sincere, heartfelt compassion. Me pretending to be a heroic hick trapped by unfortunate circumstances, and her listening to my every word with an open, honest heart—a heart I was mocking at every turn.

I also got her story: She had graduated from high school but never thought about going to college, because she didn't think she was smart enough. Besides, she was needed at home, she said, where she was the eldest of six children and the de facto head of the household. Her mother was alive, but she was an unemployed (and unemployable) alcoholic who had pretty much abandoned all responsibility for her children. Her parents were divorced, and they lived on a combination of alimony and disability payments. She was the rock in this hurricane of dysfunction, I came to understand, and it was obvious that she was lonely, because she had just spent three hours talking to me.

I too was lonely. By the time I left her house that day, I was also in love. Not only was this girl gorgeous, she also seemed to me at the time to be the kindest person I'd ever met. After encountering so much hostility and indifference from Davenport's population in general, to be treated with such genuine decency was practically a revelation. Talking to her was an addictively pleasant diversion from selling books, and I wanted more of it.

So did she, evidently. Before I left she asked me to stop by the following afternoon. If I was in the neighborhood, that is. I promised her I would definitely stop by, because yes I was going to be in the neighborhood, and in any case was in town for the rest of the summer. In fact, nothing could prevent me from visiting her, because after weeks of drudgery and disappointment I had finally found someone with whom I could simply talk, without all the complications of trying to sell her something.

I was still trying to sell her, of course—on a completely fictional version of me.

Fooling her was cruel, I knew, but once I'd started I could not stop. If I did, the game would be over. Besides, I was normally a bit shy around girls, and adopting the Southern persona helped me quell that anxiety and fake confidence as well. Normally, girls did not hear stories of my childhood and remark about how "brave" and "strong" I was for enduring such hardships and still having the wherewithal to persevere and, of all things, go to college—something no one in her family had ever done. It felt good to have someone feel sorry for me, to have her respect me for my "ambition," and admire me for having the "courage" to talk to strangers all day long (another thing she said she could never do).

Culturally speaking, we were complete opposites. She was ultra-Christian; I was an atheist. She came from a family with legitimate problems; I came from a family with "first-world problems"—that is, problems that arise out of too much privilege, not a complete lack of it. Her family was lower middle-class, mine was upper middle—maybe even upper—class. And, of course, she was honest. I, on the other hand, was a lying sack of scum.

The following day, I arrived mid-afternoon at her house, a small but tidy rambler that housed seven people by my count—herself, five siblings, and her mother. The house had been relatively empty the day before, save for one or two intrusions by some kids I judged to be around seven or eight years old. This time, the whole family was there—mom, sisters, brothers—and the atmosphere in the house was chaotic, with the bustle and hum of too many people crushed into too small a space. The girl (let's call her Grace, because that should have been her name) tried to shoo her siblings out of the living room in order to give us some privacy. It didn't work very well, though, because they all seemed to be keenly interested in me. They hovered and lurked and tittered as if we were in an episode of *The Waltons* and I was the handsome stranger who'd come to court the oldest daughter. Which, to be fair, was a fairly accurate description of what was going on from their point of view, and maybe even from hers.

I had planned that day to tell her of my deception, to come clean and admit that I had misrepresented myself. But it was clear from the beginning that she had told them "all about me," and that my story had metastasized into a thing that had a life and will of its own. I couldn't take anything back, because it was clear that my visit the day before had been the subject of much speculation and discussion around the family dinner table, and my presence again suggested to them—and to the mother, apparently—that something close to a marriage proposal was in the air.

All of this took me by surprise. Our discussion the day before had been easy and free, but our conversation that day was stilted and forced. Both of us had become paralyzed by self-consciousness, and neither of us knew how to get past it. Finally, to break the tension, I decided to come clean and admit the truth. In the nicest way I could think of, I explained to her—in my normal voice—who I really was, why I'd let the Southern charade go as far as it did, and why now I felt she should know the truth.

When you're young and unskilled in the nuances of love, you think you're going to get credit for telling the "truth," because isn't it better to tell the truth than perpetuate a lie? Yes, it is. But in matters of the heart, it only works if you tell the truth from the beginning. Correcting the record after the fact isn't quite as effective.

She didn't yell at me or scold me. She did something much worse: She began to cry. Softly at first, then with little gasps that felt like knife stabs in my chest.

"You should go," she whispered between sobs. I didn't want to leave, but the time had come, I knew, to accept the consequences of my deception.

From time to time, as the weeks went by, I entertained the idea of stopping by her house and trying, yet again, to apologize. But I didn't. There was no point. She and I were never going to date. The only reason we even talked to each other in the first place was that we were both caught in circumstances largely beyond our control (her moreso than me), and because both of us were lonely to talk to someone our own age, and to entertain the idea, however fleetingly, that we might find a way to escape the lives we were currently leading but not really enjoying.

I never told anyone about her. Not Russ. Not Dana. Not Jackie. She was my secret. A shameful secret, but a secret nonetheless.

CHAPTER 25

One of the most useful skills I developed in the book field was a rather all-encompassing obsession with frugality. Borne of necessity, since I was barely making enough to pay for rent, this preoccupation with penny-pinching became a game of sorts, one at which I was particularly adept, due in part perhaps to my Scottish roots and to my predisposition (unhealthy at times) to accept any sort of challenge as an opportunity to prove that I can beat anyone, at anything. Within the Southwestern universe, there were awards and various types of recognition for people who saved a high percentage of the money they earned. So, since I wasn't beating anyone in the overall money-making department, I set my sights on winning the frugality awards. This meant taking a solemn personal pledge that I would only spend money if it was absolutely necessary. It also meant accepting the various monikers for the sort of person I aspired to be— "cheap-skate," "tightwad," "mooch," "skinflint," "bum," "leech," etc.—as the cost of not doing business with anyone, for any reason. The only way I could make this kind of inverted thinking work was to turn the money-for-food conundrum into a game. And in order to turn not spending money on food into a game, I had to trick my brain's reward system into believing that it was more fun to avoid spending money on food (or anything else) than it was to part with my hard-earned cash. Thus, I had to teach my brain to experience extreme frugality as a form of pleasure, or success, and to experience spending money as painful, or a form of failure.

Thinking this way—that saving money = success, and spending money = failure—is an interesting exercise in cognitive dissonance. On one hand, the economic engine of capitalism both requires and encourages constant consumption, regardless of income (otherwise, credit cards would not exist). On the other hand, if the American public ever started thinking that every dollar they spend counts against them in the scorecard of life, the economy would soon grind to a halt. Capitalism is based on the idea that people have never-ending needs and desires, and that eliminating those needs and fulfilling those desires is the key to happiness. But the truth is, people don't "need" much to survive, and everything beyond survival is just icing on the proverbial cake. If you don't care about icing, and are just trying to ingest enough cake to get through the day, you don't need to burden yourself with the pressures of status and conformity and pleasure-seeking.

If you break down the spending of an eighteen-year-old living week to week in a run-down tenement house, there is only one way to curtail spending, and that is to avoid buying food. For most people, the best way to stretch a food dollar is to buy groceries at the store and prepare meals at home. We didn't have a kitchen or a refrigerator, though, so the only food we could keep in our room was peanut butter, jelly, bananas, apples, and trail mix. As we have already explored, fast food is a relatively inexpensive way to lard one's arteries with calories—but during an average day of selling books in the neighborhoods of Davenport, the nearest McDonald's might be several miles away. Dumpster diving is always an option for finding free food, of course, and the logical place to do it is in the back of a grocery store or restaurant. But if you've ever tried back-alley dumpster-diving before, you know that a wide variety of unsavory characters long ago staked out the best territories as their own. And if you decide one day to encroach on their turf—to steal food from their kitchen, as it were—you can expect to encounter some resistance. If that resistance does not involve the point of a knife, you can consider yourself lucky.

Fortunately, I stumbled upon a way to obtain virtually unlimited amounts of free food through a discussion with my district manager, Mike. One day, I complained to Mike that I tended to get very hungry in the middle of the day, and that more often than not there was nowhere I could go to even get a quick snack, much less a decent lunch. By the time dinner rolled around I was famished, I told him, and during that hungry time my desire to sell books was sorely compromised.

"Here's what you do," he advised. "Next time you're hungry and giving a demo to Mrs. Jones (the book business's all-purpose nickname for every housewife in America), ask her if you can buy a peanut-butter-and-jelly sandwich from her for a quarter. Explain that there are no stores or gas stations nearby, and that you have a strict schedule to keep. Ninety-nine times out of a hundred they will take pity on you.

They'll make you a sandwich, give you a glass of lemonade or a Coke to go with it, and they will not take your quarter. I've eaten free that way for years. Trust me, it works."

There was a kind of genius to this approach, I thought. By offering to pay for the sandwich, you could deflect the idea that you were mooching while simultaneously communicating that you needed to be fed. By offering such a pittance—a quarter!—you basically ensured that they would refuse the money. And by going for peanut butter and jelly, you could not be blamed for needing something to "wash it down," so some accompanying liquid refreshment was all but guaranteed.

The first time I tried this ruse, I could not believe how well it worked! Not only did I get more than I asked for—a ham sandwich with chips and a Coke—the woman I asked sent me on my way with an apple and a granola bar for the road.

Once I realized that I could coax free food out of unsuspecting housewives, doing so became part of my daily routine. Conning people out of food was much easier than selling books, and the gratification was instantaneous. Even if I didn't sell a book to someone, I would exact my revenge by trying to get something—anything—out of them, even if it was only a glass of water.

One day, Russ and I decided to take a few hours off and go see the Delta Queen, a restored paddlewheel steamboat that ferried passengers up and down the Mississippi River in the time-honored tradition of American folklore. Russ and I had never seen an actual paddle-wheeler, so we figured that the educational opportunity offered by the docking of the Delta Queen in Davenport was significant enough to abandon bookselling for a few hours. Russ was an avid photographer, so he was eager to point his lens at something interesting. I was interested in Mark Twain and jazz and not knocking on doors if I didn't have to. Hannibal, Missouri—Twain's home town—wasn't far down the river, and the Delta Queen was the sort of boat he is said to have captained. Indeed, the young Samuel Clemens supposedly chose the name "Mark Twain" because that was the term boatmen yelled out to indicate that the water was only two fathoms (or twelve feet) deep. As for jazz, one of the other ways in which the Delta Queen and other riverboats like it served the cities along the Mississippi was by carrying bands of musicians from New Orleans to St. Paul and back. Louis

Armstrong cut his teeth playing in dance bands on elegant riverboats like the Delta Queen, and Davenport's own Bix Beiderbecke is said to have been so enchanted by the music that came to town along the river that he roamed the docks in search of inspiration for his own musical adventures. Davenport's annual Bix Beiderbecke Festival, held in the first week of August, pays homage to their hometown hero, and I wanted to understand better how awareness of (and interest in) America's only homegrown music—blues and jazz—was spread in the days before radio. I also wanted a bag of powdered donuts, and the Hostess Thrift Bake Shop was on the way.

Having procured the donuts, Russ and I ventured down to where the Delta Queen was docked and had a look around. No one was on board. In fact, the only person minding the ship was a grizzled old fellow who looked like he'd been doing the same job for eighty years and was still wondering why he'd never won an Employee of the Month award. He was asleep, in other words. When Russ approached him, he barely lifted an eyelid as Russ explained that we were journalists from *Time* magazine doing a story on historic riverboats, so could we possibly have a look around? He nodded his assent, and we boarded.

After half-an-hour of poking around, we'd seen pretty much everything there was to see. Paddlewheel steamboats look a lot more interesting from the shore, it turns out, and even though the Delta Queen was relatively large—it had sleeping cabins and a restaurant—it wasn't exactly a Princess cruise ship. It did not have a pool, and you could not hit golf balls off the back into the Mississippi River. It did have history and charm, though, and I resolved that one day I would cruise down the Mississippi River on such a ship, to New Orleans, where I'd drink gin fizzes and dance to Dixieland jazz, eat muffuletta sandwiches and steep myself in the music and culture of America's most European city.

(Note: I have yet to take such a cruise, even though for thirty of the years between now and then I've lived within a mile of the Mississippi River, in St. Paul. I've seen plays on riverboats, eaten fine meals on them, attended parties, even gambled (and lost), but I've never taken a paddleboat river cruise of any kind in my life. Why? I have no idea.)

On the way back, I had to use the bathroom. Unfortunately, we were in the industrial part of Davenport, near the Wonder Bread factory on River Drive—aka "Twinkie Boulevard"—so there were no public buildings nearby. I couldn't just step into an alley and take a leak (it wasn't that kind of emergency), and the situation was getting desperate. Russ spied a small, square, cinder-block building not far away. It didn't look promising, but I had no other options. So I walk-ran toward it, trying desperately to keep everything in that wanted to come out.

The door was open, and there, in the lobby, was a restroom. Whew.

When I'd finished, Russ was sitting in a chair the lobby. "Do you know where we are?" he asked.

"No."

"Look around," he said.

On the wall there were a bunch of rock posters and some signed photos of B-level celebrities, like the blonde guy from *Starsky & Hutch*, and Erik Estrada, who, in the 1970s, seemed to be everywhere. More to the point, there was a broadcast booth, and through a wall of Plexiglas we could see a radio announcer jumping in and out of his chair, gesticulating wildly and ranting about something. The show was being broadcast through a tiny speaker in to the lobby, and, strangely enough, the voice sounded familiar.

"You know who that is?" Russ asked.

I did not.

"Listen carefully."

It only took a few seconds for me to realize that the announcer in question was none other than Spike at the Mike, our radio hero!

As it turned out, there were only two people in the building, Spike and his producer. During a commercial break, Spike himself came out to the lobby to greet us. He didn't have any guests scheduled, and it wasn't a building that got many visitors, so he was curious as to who the hell we were. We introduced ourselves, and I told him how much I appreciated his machine-gunning of my most hated song, "Muskrat Love," adding that if he needed suggestions about other songs to kill, I could certainly help. Then I offered him a donut.

"Are you kidding? Every song I play deserves a quick and merciless death," he said, donut powder clinging to his lips. Then he asked, "So what brings you boys to this part of town?"

We explained that we were there for the summer selling educational books to the good people of Davenport, and that we were doing it to earn money to pay for college.

He thought that was hilarious. "You've got to be kidding me," he said. "This is the best summer job you could find? You guys are genuinely pathetic."

We were indeed pathetic, we assured him, and recounted a few of our adventures in Davenport thus far, from Love Train to the Salvation Army drunk tank to our keg party with the Grim Reapers to living next door to a Vietnam vet who never quite came back from the war. Every once in a while he'd stop us and go back into the booth to do a segment, then return when a song was playing. He seemed to enjoy our stories, so I told him how we went about conning housewives out of lunch by offering them a quarter for a peanut-butter-and-jelly sandwich. He laughed so hard I thought he was going to puke.

Once he'd regained his composure, he said, "You guys gotta come on the air with me. This is too good."

And so, Spike ushered us into his broadcast booth. When the song that was playing finished, he introduced us: "Folks, I've got a special treat for you this afternoon. I'm sitting here in the studio with—what are your names? (We told him.) They're in town for the summer, selling some kind of educational encyclopedia thingy door-to-door to raise money for college, I'm guessing so they never have to sell anything door-to-door again. Am I right, boys?"

"You are absolutely right, Spike," I said.

"Because as jobs go, this sucks pretty much as hard as a job can suck, right? The only thing worse would be working in the Twinkie factory across the street."

"The good thing about Twinkies, though, is that they can't slam a door in your face," Russ quipped.

"But if someone slams a Twinkie in your face it's a different story, because they have the side benefit of being delicious and semi-nutritious," Spike retorted.

"I'm told the cream filling is also excellent for your skin," I said.

Because we were frequent listeners, we knew that Spike operated in the realm of hyper-kinetic nonsense. Still, it was surprising, when one of us got off a good line, to see him jump out of his chair and yell, "Touchdown, Green Bay!," then jut his arms in the air as if he were a referee at the Super Bowl.

"Now folks, we've got a lot of Bible thumpers and Moonies running around this summer, but I want to assure you that these guys are not them," Spike said. "These guys are tall and good-looking, in a generically preppy college-boy way, and they'll be carrying around a red case that could double as a baby coffin in a pinch. You'll know it's them when one of them asks you if they can buy a PB&J off you for a quarter. How sad is that?!!!," Spike spat into his mic. "Please, mothers of Davenport, these guys are from the West coast. They are unfamiliar with our ways. If they ask, don't make them grovel—just give 'em the damn sandwich!"

After the interview, I offered Spike another powdered donut. He took three and thanked us for coming in. It was the highlight of his day so far, he said, and would probably be the highlight of his week, considering that he was basically trapped in a cinder-block building working for a Top-40 radio station in a secondary market that did not always appreciate his brand of humor. That's what we liked about him, we said, and he sighed. "Maybe I'll get a job in L.A. someday," he said. "In the meantime, I've got songs to kill and a soul to destroy, so I better get back to it."

CHAPTER 26

Outside the studio, the hulking gray Hostess factory loomed over River Drive, the street Spike always referred to as Twinkie Boulevard. The sun was high in the sky and the heat of the day was starting to build, thick and moist, like a sauna without any therapeutic benefits whatsoever. The last thing I wanted to do was get back to my territory and start knocking on doors, but there was quite literally nothing else for us to do in Davenport. We weren't scheduled to meet up with Dana and Jackie for another seven hours. I suggested that we stop by the diner for an early lunch and visit Madge.

"A capital idea," Russ agreed. "Anything to avoid going back into the field."

"Touchdown, Green Bay!" I exclaimed, and we began walking toward the diner where we'd met Love Train on our first day in the city. A lot had happened since then, and he'd appreciate the stories, we thought. No matter how many times we went back to that diner, however, we never saw Love Train again. Madge didn't know where he'd gone; he just stopped showing up. Maybe he'd found another hangout. Maybe he'd moved. Maybe he was in jail. Maybe he was dead. Anything seemed possible with Love Train.

Madge was not at the diner that day, either. Her shift did not start until 3:00 p.m., it turned out, so Russ and I ordered a couple of burgers and planned the rest of our day. There wasn't much to plan, of course. What lay ahead after lunch was five or six hours of trying to sell a book hardly anyone seemed to want. That wasn't the hardest part, though. For me, the hardest part was fooling myself into believing that something good was going to happen—that dipping the leaky bucket of my psyche into that eternal wellspring of hope was going to yield anything other than thirst and misery and despair.

At such times, the Bookman Song can only take you so far. Door-to-door selling is a soul-crushing experience, so those who do it need to be fortified with some sort of spiritual protection. Whether it's Jesus, God, Bhudda, Vishna, Allah, Krishna, Scientology, psychology, science, mysticism, or magic, one needs something stronger than the thin eggshell of ego we all use to protect ourselves from the world's indignities. As I've mentioned before, the Southwestern higher-ups descended from door-to-door Bible salesmen, so when the going got tough, they recommended getting better acquainted with Jesus. So did my manager, Mike. So did a lot of other people.

Somehow, reading the Bible was supposed to make me feel better. In theory, I was supposed to compare my current circumstances with those of Jesus and think: Hey, things could be worse. I could be wearing a crown of thorns and hanging on a cross with nails pounded through my hands and feet while an angry mob throws rotten fruit and feces at me. Thinking that way may help some people, in the same way that it helps a man with a raging sinus infection to think he's lucky because, hey, it's not brain cancer. I wanted the Bible to help me. I wanted to believe. I tried to believe, in fact, but I couldn't make my brain do the sort of logical loop-to-loops necessary to believe in something as patently ridiculous as the "story" of Christianity. Nor was I moved by the idea that God had "sacrificed" his only begotten son so that humanity can be saved—since, from God's point of view, it's pretty obvious that dying is no big deal. Plus, if God already planned to resurrect Jesus after the crucifixion, the whole drama is nothing more than an arresting bit of street theater, a show put on for the plebeians to give them something to argue about for the next two-thousand years. It was obviously a con, and humanity's record of not being fooled by con men isn't encouraging, especially if the people you are trying to fool are poor and illiterate and in desperate need of reassurance that their lives are not just a pointless slog to the grave.

All I saw in Jesus was a guy who walked all over the place trying to sell a message no one wanted to hear, only to be rewarded with an excruciatingly painful death. Yes, the man got resurrected. But did he then go out and resume the activities that led to his demise? Did he spend his post-resurrection time trying to perfect his message and convince more people to buy what he was selling? No, he did not. Jesus may have come back to life after being pilloried by the hoi polloi, but he did not make the same mistake again. After the Resurrection, Jesus allegedly appeared to Matthew, Mark, and John in disguise, said a few words of encouragement to them, then skedaddled off this Earthly plane in favor of a less humiliating existence somewhere in the celestial great beyond. His message, as far as I can tell: Life on

Earth sucks. Thirty-three years is all I can take. I'm outta here! After the resurrection, the man stuck around for forty days—less than a month and a half!—then called it quits. To me, that's not an affirmation of life, it's an invitation to suicide. (Though to be fair, Jesus did end up selling quite a few books with this stunt.)

But that's just me. Luckily, because I don't believe Jesus was anything more than a rabble-rousing rabbi who pissed off the elites of his day, I don't feel a tempting pull into the great unknown. I'm stuck in the here and now. But it's also true that since I was not raised in a Christian household, and did not find inspiration or comfort in the idea that Jesus had it worse than me, I was in a pickle. Russ was a semi-devout Christian, and did seem to find strength in the words of God. I did not (and still don't) believe the Bible was written by anyone other than a bunch of semi-literate teenagers a couple centuries after the fact—by which time, my journalistic instincts tell me, the "story" of Jesus's resurrection had likely accumulated a few poetic flourishes to make the tale sound more magical and fantastical than it really was—you know, so people would pay attention. Or maybe the real story was just too sad. ("Tell us the story of Jesus again, Isiah, but this time with a happy ending. It's been a tough day, and we could all use a lift.") Hyperbole, wishful thinking, and a propensity for grandiose bullshit are qualities too engrained in human nature to ignore. To believe that those who wrote the words in the Bible were reliable narrators is to believe that people who sit around telling stories every night haven't always engaged in some entertaining exaggeration every now and then. I mean, look what happened when a bunch of lumberjacks in the Northern territories started one-upping each other around the campfire. Paul Bunyan, that's what—a man so big and strong and fearsome that he could kick Jesus's ass in a heartbeat.

Sans the comfort of Jesus, however, I was left to my own devices—my own limited inner resources, that is—to overcome the darkness that came with every Davenport dawn.

In 1979, the market had not yet been saturated by "self-help" books. There were the classics—Norman Vincent Peale's *The Power of Positive Thinking*, Napoleon Hill's *Think and Grow Rich*, and Zig Ziglar's *See You at the Top*—but these were more accurately described as "motivational" books, and they were written for despondent salesmen who need a kick in the ass to get out there and keep selling. I read all of them, but only ended up feeling worse, because the Holy Grail of success was, for me, so goddamn elusive.

For many weeks, I carried one of these books with me into the field. Often, instead of selling, I'd park my ass under a tree and try to milk some inspiration from their pages, usually to no avail. My personal experience was that yes, a story about a blind beggar who becomes a billionaire could be inspiring while I was reading it, but the emotional lift didn't last much longer than that "clean" feeling after you've brushed your teeth.

For instance, the first few sentences of Peale's *The Power of Positive Thinking* are, "Believe in yourself! Have faith in your abilities! Without a humble but reasonable confidence in your own powers, you cannot be successful or happy."

As empty platitudes go, it's not the worst advice. But did it help? No. Because the more time I spent selling books, the *less* confidence I had in my ability to sell *anything*. Ironically, before I started selling books—back in those heady days before the summer began—I was brimming with so much confidence that I felt invincible. Several weeks in the book field had destroyed that particular self-delusion. My former, seemingly reasonable confidence had been replaced by the humblest realization of all—that I totally and absolutely sucked at *everything*. The only things I seemed to be improving at were procrastination and self-pity. I had become very good at those, and no book of wise and encouraging words could prevent me from getting better at them.

Sometimes, I'd read an allegedly inspirational book and it would lead me in the opposite direction. One book that fell into my hands during this time was *Illusions: The Adventure of a Reluctant Messiah*, by Richard Bach. Bach is better known as the author of *Jonathan Livingston Seagull*, a parable about a seagull who gets bored of being a mere seagull and seeks a more fulfilling life through the perfection of flight, a passion that gets him kicked out of his flock and eventually kills him. But hey, he died free, doing what he loved.

An insipid book, yes (film critic Roger Ebert is said to have remarked that JLS is so shallow it had to be marketed to adults, because children would see right through it.) But millions of people loved it, launching it to the top of the *New York Times* best-seller list. Lots of people, that is, who don't want to be an average, garden-variety seagull. Personally, I think it would be fun to be an anonymous seagull, flying and squawking through life in some quiet harbor where tourists and their food scraps are plentiful. But that's just me.

Illusions is about a guy who is sick of being the Messiah and gives his "savior handbook" to a friend of his, the narrator of the story. Now, *Illusions* may very well be a profound book, since it basically paraphrases a lot of other profound books, especially the ones that tell you that reality is just an illusion, so stop getting so worked up about it all. In the book field, in my state of mind at the time, that message was actually quite welcome. If I could tell myself that none of this was real, that I was just walking through some sort of elaborate dream that I myself had cooked up, then maybe it didn't matter if I failed to get my ass in gear. But then I'd be reading along and run into a passage like this from the Messiah's Handbook: *"You're always free to change your mind and choose a different future, and a different past,"* and it would drive me absolutely crazy. Why? Because I was desperately trying to choose a future in which I sold several books every day, made a ton of money, and laid the groundwork for a lifetime of success—so that I could look back on my past and congratulate myself for being so goddamn awesome. But it wasn't working out that way, which suggested that perhaps I should be choosing a different future, one that did not involve being told time and again that success did not lie behind the door on which I was currently knocking. I could have quit anytime, of course, but at the same time I couldn't—and didn't—because I had been taught (very well, as it turns out) that people who abandon their commitments and responsibilities just because their life isn't as fulfilling as they'd like it to be—just because they are "bored" of being a seagull, for instance—are basically selfish, narcissistic assholes who care more about themselves than others, and can't be relied upon for anything. Other passages from the Messiah's Handbook carried the same basic message. *"Your conscience is the measure of the honesty of your selfishness. Listen to it carefully,"* was another one. So, you know, as long as you're *honest* about your selfishness, it's all good.

Another book that fell into my hands during this period was called *The Greatest Salesman in the World*, by Og Mandino, perhaps the most iconic inspirational book for salespeople ever written. (Why the guys who write these books—or purport to write them, because most are actually ghost-written by someone else—have names like "Zig" and

"Og," I do not know. Zig Ziglar's real first name was "Hilary," though, so maybe he got tired of being mistaken for a girl. And Og Mandino's real first name is "Augustine," a pretentious, three-syllable mouthful to be sure. For the purposes of name recognition and regular-guy bona fides, though, nothing works better than a monosyllabic grunt. Zig and Og are legends in the sales world; Hilary and Augustine are not.)

Set in ancient Babylon, *The Greatest Salesman in the World* is a book of life lessons (which also happen to be sales lessons) wrapped in a laughably "ancient" parable. The parable is about a poor camel herder who receives from his dying mentor a series of ancient scrolls that purport to reveal the secret not only to great salesmanship, but also happiness, personal fulfillment, success, and peace of mind. There are ten scrolls, and, according to the instructions in the book, the true student of sales (and life) mastery is supposed to read and digest one scroll per month for ten months. At that rate, it'd take the better part of a year to read. I did not have that kind of time, so I read the whole thing in an afternoon.

(Humorous side note: An oft-quoted zinger from Mandino's motivational mentor Zig Ziglar is: "Rich people have large libraries and small TVs. Poor people have small libraries and big TVs." The implication is that rich people "enrich" themselves by reading, while poor people waste their time watching too much TV. Fast forward to 2018: The president of the United States is a billionaire and proud non-reader who watches cable news shows all day on multiple screens in the White House. Did Zig get it wrong? Not entirely. Spiritually speaking, Donald Trump may very well be the poorest person in the world.)

Mandino's manifesto has had many imitators. Indeed, since the 1970s an entire genre of inspirational business books has been created using the same formula—based on the Bible, of course—in which a simple, charming parable communicates a treasure trove of essential truths. The "truths" themselves are typically contained in a secret document whose ancient origins are murky, but whose timeless wisdom cannot be denied. In *The Greatest Salesman in the World*, the scrolls run through the typical bromides to love yourself and persist in the face of adversity. Once again, however, when it came to inspiring me to get out there and sell more books, Og's advice failed to do the trick.

Scroll #2, for instance, begins, "I will greet this day with love in my heart."

Where to begin with that one? Sounds simple, but what does greeting the day with "love in your heart" actually mean? In my experience, people who are a little to loose with their love are not the sort of people one wants to be around. That's what the Moonies do, and it creeps people out. Besides, the Bible's admonition to "love thine enemy" has to be the most ignored passage in history. No one does it, least of all people who call themselves Christians. That's because nobody knows what it means to love their enemy. And even if they did, they wouldn't do it, because it's so much more satisfying to hate one's enemies. Christians, it seems, love nothing more than to hate non-Christians. They may wake up with love in their heart (for themselves and their dog), but by the end of the day they seethe with the hatred of a thousand suns, then tune in to Fox News to swallow a few more gallons of gasoline. It's bullshit, pure and simple—and no one delivers it purer and more simply than Og Mandino.

Moving on, Scroll #3 begins, "I will persist until I succeed."

Again, this is solid advice insofar as it goes, which is not very far. How long must I persist? What will success look like when it happens? And when I succeed, doesn't it follow that I must have persisted, making the whole statement a closed, self-fulfilling circle of carousel logic? It does take persistence to succeed, of course, and it's just this sort of master-of-the-obvious "wisdom" that makes books like this so infuriating. The writer slaps some vacuous pronouncement on the page—"Be true to yourself," "Don't be ordinary, be extraordinary," "Succeed you must, there is no fail"—then sits back and lets the reader flail and wallow in their own inadequacy, in the sudden and discomfiting realization that they cannot possibly live up to the sentence on the page. It's maddening because such pronouncements have the feel of truth, but are in fact complete nonsense. Fill a book with such pronouncements and the collective "inspiration" it allegedly provides is little more than the distance between the reader's reality and the writer's gift for bullshit. The jolt of motivation is supposed to come from the sudden and inescapable awareness that you, poor human, have not lived up to your own expectations for yourself—or worse, that you have failed to live up to other people's expectations. But who among us has achieved all our goals and reached complete personal fulfillment? Who among us isn't wracked by insecurities about the limit of our own talent, intelligence, and abilities? No one, that's who.

Those who claim otherwise are lying, usually to coax you into buying their book.

But at least Scroll #3 makes a shallow sort of sense, as long as you don't examine it too closely. Scroll #5, not so much. Scroll #5 commands the aspiring sales giant to recite the pledge: "I will live this day as if it were my last."

Again, this is the kind of nonsense that passes for wisdom in the business world. It's profoundly stupid advice to begin with, but it's especially ridiculous for salespeople, because if it really were your last day on Earth, selling anything to anyone would be pointless. Sales books make it sound like selling is the end-all and be-all of life, but it's not. A truer aphorism would be, "I will pretend to live this day as if it were my last, but I'm pretty sure it's not, so I'm going to hedge my bet by going out and making a little money so that I don't starve tomorrow when the sun rises and it turns out that, nope, it's just another day."

Honestly, for me, the only scroll in Og's beloved manual of eternal sales wisdom that made a lick of sense was Scroll #7: "I will laugh at the world." To this day, that's the only advice from Og's book that I've ever found helpful. I applied this concept immediately when I read *The Greatest Salesman in the World*. Sitting under a giant oak tree on the outskirts of Davenport, near a tract of suburban sprawl filled with potential customers I was ignoring, I laughed at Mandino's book a lot. I also cursed it, because—like the Bible and the Bee Gees and Shakespeare and *Star Wars*—it was one of those things that millions of people supposedly love, but I did not. Why didn't other people's collective love for these things transfer to me? I didn't know; I only knew that it didn't, which left me feeling more alone than ever.

Later in life, I learned that Mandino's method sounds suspiciously like Ben Franklin's "Thirteen Virtues," a system Franklin devised over the course of his life to improve his own character. Supposedly, Franklin wrote up a list of thirteen virtues—Temperance, Silence, Frugality, Sincerity, Moderation, etc.—and meditated on one of them each week. After thirteen weeks, he started over. In a year, then, he could cycle through his virtues four times, and, by "virtue" of repetition, engrain them indelibly into his character. The funniest one from Franklin is: "Chastity: Rarely use venery but for health or offspring; never to dullness, weakness, or the injury of your own or another's peace or reputation." The funny/ironic/hypocritical part: Franklin was a legendary womanizer who sired at least one illegitimate child, and who apparently felt that regular sexual dalliances with women not married to him were always healthy, never dull, and were best enjoyed with women whose reputations could not be sullied, and whose peace of mind was not a major concern. Prostitutes, in other words.

That's the problem with a lot of these books. They are filled with seemingly sage advice that sounds good on the surface, but if you dig a little you find that: a) the wisdom itself is just a series of empty platitudes, b) the author of the book isn't exactly an exemplar of their own advice, or c) it's mostly derivative, poorly plagiarized, warmed-over nonsense that the author is trying to pass off as wisdom.

Exhibit A in my admittedly sweeping indictment of inspirational business books is the one credited with starting it all, Napoleon Hill's *Think and Grow Rich*, which has allegedly sold more than one-hundred million copies worldwide since its publication in 1937. (Though, as we will soon see, any "fact" associated with this book is likely to be only partially true or entirely fabricated. The book's true sales could be anywhere from twenty to 120 million copies, depending on the dubiousness of the source. No one really knows.)

Nevertheless, if you ask a successful businessman in the U.S. to name the most influential book they ever read, many will cite Hill's dubious "masterpiece." Indeed, the basic precepts laid out in its pages amount to a manifesto of American capitalism. Which explains a lot, because the truth is that Hill was a con man, and the book that made him famous was just one of dozens of get-rich-quick schemes he concocted during his lifetime, many of which involved money-laundering and fraud. Not that the "ideas" in the book can't be applied to achieve financial success (one does need to think and persevere to succeed, after all)—it's just that the book's content is almost entirely a product of Napoleon Hill's imagination. In other words, it's fiction passed off as fact—fake news for the Industrial Age that, eighty years later, almost everyone believes is real, because that's what Hill told them.

In the book, Hill claims to have been tasked by business magnate and serial philanthropist Andrew Carnegie to interview five-hundred of the most successful men in business (Henry Ford, Alexander Graham Bell, and John D. Rockefeller among them), who collectively revealed to him "the secret" to living well and getting rich. The task is supposed to have taken him twenty years, and Hill claims to have received no compensation for his efforts other than the knowledge these men shared with him. (Payment would have required tax records, after all, and, as we all know, con men do not like people looking too closely at their tax returns.) Instead, Hill's "payment" was the treasure trove of wisdom he received from these men, which he claims to reveal in the pages of *Think and Grow Rich*. Elsewhere in the book, Hill claims to have "analyzed" more than 25,000 people over the course of twenty-five years. Which isn't impossible—it averages out to about three people a day for a quarter of a century—but it is improbable to the point of absurdity. Funnily enough, only a few pages after he makes this ridiculous claim, Hill goes on to tell a story about Henry Ford and the importance of ignoring people who say things are "impossible." Maybe, in this instance, Hill was simply practicing one of the principles of business success he gleaned from so many conversations with men of extraordinary achievement. One problem: According to the Andrew Carnegie Foundation, there is no record whatsoever indicating that Napoleon Hill ever met Carnegie, or that he ever interviewed any of the five-hundred titans of industry he claims to have "researched" on Carnegie's behalf. Hill also claims to have been a trusted adviser to presidents Theodore Roosevelt and Woodrow Wilson. There is of course no record of Hill ever meeting either man, or ever visiting the White house. But Hill doesn't stop there. Following the con-man's mantra—the bigger the lie, the better—Hill claims to have been in the Oval Office when Woodrow Wilson was negotiating the armistice ending World War I—and that Wilson *asked his advice* on the matter!

Clearly, Hill thought he could get away with this whopper because, in the days before the Internet, it was more difficult to fact-check a bullshitter. In fact, many of Hill's claims are positively Trumpian in their grandiosity. Coincidentally (or not) Hill, like Trump, was also sued for operating a fraudulent "college"—The National Automobile College—that was supposed to provide the training necessary to get a job in the auto industry. It did nothing of the sort. The National Automobile College was nothing more than a multi-level marketing scheme made to look like a legitimate educational enterprise.*(Hat tip to Matt Novak, for his 2016 Gizmodo article, "All-American Huckster: The Untold Story of Napoleon Hill, the Greatest Self-Help Scammer of All Time.")

In *Think and Grow Rich*, Hill distills the wisdom he supposedly gleaned from his non-existent interviews into a "Philosophy of Achievement." There are thirteen principles to Hill's "Philosophy of Achievement," (sound familiar?) but they—and all the other success advice peddled by the business-motivation industrial complex in the past eighty years—can be summed up in the age-old axiom, "If at first you don't succeed, try try again." Ancient wisdom it is not—the phrase is credited to educator Thomas Palmer, who used it to describe the attitude schoolchildren should have toward their homework—but it gets to the nub of the matter: success does usually require some effort on the part of the person who wishes to succeed.

Ironically, one of most appealing aspects of *Think and Grow Rich*—as well as other such paeans to magical thinking as *The Lazy Man's Guide to Riches*, and the 2006 best-seller *The Secret*—is the idea, suggested in the title, that success can be achieved through little or no effort—that is, by merely thinking. (The idea that thinking isn't work is a popular and enduring delusion, entertained primarily by people who don't think, and therefore don't know how much work it really is.) How? By programming the subconscious mind, through pure thought alone, to guide one's conscious mind and physical body to "transform" wishes and desires from the dream world into the physical world. This power goes by many names: Hill calls it the secret of the "Master Mind," *The Secret* calls it "The Law of Attraction," and Norman Vincent Peale calls it "positive thinking." In each case, the basic assertion is that people have more control over their fate than they think; that the laws of the universe are somehow organized to reward those who follow their passions; and that all one needs to enjoy the delicious fruits of success and happiness is to wish for them really, really, really super hard.

Shakespeare, as always, said it pretty well: "Which dreams are indeed ambition, for the very substance of the ambitious is merely the shadow of a dream." That may sound like a mystically relevant endorsement of the same basic idea, but the character who says it is Guildenstern, in *Hamlet*, who is an incompetent, dishonest buffoon.

At the time I was reading these books and trying to apply the wisdom therein to my day-to-day struggles in the book field, I did not know any of this. All I knew was that I wasn't exactly setting the world on fire, and, despite my best efforts, saw no way to improve other than to follow the example of people who supposedly knew what they were talking about. Deep down in my bones it felt wrong, but I was in no position to question their advice. In fact, I desperately needed the words of these supposed sages of success to be true—or at least helpful. But no matter how much I read, or how diligently I tried to apply the principles of success in those pages, my sales skills did not improve. And because they didn't improve, I felt more like a failure than ever.

Now, the thing about motivational self-help books is that even if you strip away all the hypocrisy and bullshit, there is still a grain of truth in them. There's nothing profound about this particular truth. Set goals, work hard, stay focused, don't give up, believe in yourself—these are the principles of achievement no matter what the objective, whether it's learning to play the piano or starting a multimillion-dollar corporation from scratch. What these books usually fail to mention is that while failure along the way is an absolute certainty, there is no guarantee whatsoever that one's efforts—no matter how sincere, well-meaning, or diligent—will end in success. More than 90 percent of all new businesses fail, after all, and for the people involved, that failure often represents the evaporation of their hopes and dreams, not to mention the disappearance of their life savings and an overwhelming sense of humiliation and defeat. What most sane people do in those situations is to re-define "success" on their own terms rather than chase it on someone else's. That is, they lower their expectations to the point where their dreams align more closely with their unfortunate reality.

In lectures, Napoleon Hill liked to talk about how Thomas Edison "failed" 10,000 times before he found a way to make his electric light bulb work. The story is supposed to be inspirational—like the fact that Babe Ruth struck out more than anyone else in baseball history—but all it really tells us is that Edison was mono-maniacally obsessed with his light-bulb invention, and that he was a persistent SOB who never gave up, even when he probably should have. But who really wants to live like that? Is that kind of devotion truly necessary to succeed? And if it is, is it worth it? Furthermore, should we as a society really be encouraging citizens to focus their energies on attaining a single goal? Rather than, say, becoming well-rounded, educated citizens with many different interests and an abundant curiosity about art, music, literature, and drama, as well as the emotional skills necessary to have good friends, sustain a lasting relationship and be a responsible parent?

I'll wager that most people would rather not focus their efforts on achieving a single goal which, if they fail to achieve it, will destroy their lives. No, they'd prefer not to risk it. They'd rather go to work, get a paycheck, come home to the wife and kids, eat some dinner and watch some TV. For most people, the price of "success" is too high, the journey too hard, the sacrifice too painful. Or worse, they convince themselves otherwise and spend years chasing an elusive phantom.

But no matter: What all of these books have in common is that they encourage people to risk everything in pursuit of a dream or an idea, no matter its quality or practicality, based solely on the faith that it will somehow work out, because—according to the magically self-serving laws of The Universe, which of course wants you to experience the joy of unfettered free enterprise—you have the power to will your dreams into existence. If you, the reader, take their advice and it doesn't work out—if you risk everything and go broke, get divorced, lose custody of your kids, and lose yourself at the bottom of a martini glass—the writers of these books have a convenient out: If you happen to fail, it's because you didn't try hard enough, you lost your faith in yourself and your project, or you just need to keep trying. In other words, it's *your* fault. If you haven't succeeded yet, it just means you haven't failed enough. Keep trying, they'll say. Don't give up. Success is just around the bend. There's never any mention of the millions of hopeful entrepreneurs who crash and burn flying too close to the sun of their own ambition, only the glorification of perpetual struggle. In the parlance of business, dreams that go up in smoke aren't failures, they're learning experiences. At the end of the day, the only advice these authors ever give people who are wrestling with their inner doubts and demons is: ignore them. After you've licked your wounds, dust yourself off and get back in the saddle. The funny thing is, these same people are the sort of knuckleheads who say that the "definition" of insanity is "doing the same thing over and over again, expecting a different result." Using that logic, someone who tries ten-thousand times get a light bulb to work would be considered clinically batshit:

"I'm worried about Tom. He's been working on that light-bulb thing for years. He just won't give up."

"Yes, but is he happy?"

"No, he's miserable. Throws things. Swears all the time. Why, last week he tried a filament made out of cesium, and ended up smashing the whole thing with a hammer. He almost electrocuted himself."

"Has he lost interest in other aspects of his life?"

"He has no other interests. Just that stupid experiment."

"Ah, well, obsessive-compulsive behavior can be difficult to live with."

"The man is a selfish jerk. Who cares about light bulbs? I mean, what's wrong with candles? You light them, they do their job, end of story. It's not like they need to be improved."

"At least he's passionate about something."

"One person's passion is another person's delusion."

"Do you think Tom is deluding himself?"

"I think he needs to spend some time in a hospital somewhere to work his shit out, not some dusty lab."

"Have you signed the commitment papers?"

"I have them right here. In triplicate."

The actual definition of insanity is: "Mental illness of such a severe nature that a person cannot distinguish fantasy from reality, cannot conduct his/her affairs due to psychosis, or is subject to uncontrollable personal behavior." Ever met an entrepreneur who has burned through his cash reserves and is looking for a way to save himself? "Insane" is sometimes the kindest thing one can say about such people.

Napoleon Hill claims that success begins with a "white-hot desire," and is fueled by faith.

Indeed, the iconic American entrepreneur is someone who is so fixated on their own idea—their fantasy—that they will do almost anything to make it a reality. In the throes of their *idée fixe*, dedicated entrepreneurs aren't afraid to max out credit cards, take out second mortgages, borrow thousands from their family, or even go bankrupt a few times—because they *know* in their heart and gut that eventually *they will succeed*. The word "no" is not in their vocabulary, and they are proud of it—because only hyper-rational losers give in to their fears and doubts. Only average, mediocre people succumb to the oppressive weight of reality. There is no room for such equivocation in the psyche of the heroic entrepreneur, only a dogged willingness to endure whatever misery their project requires of them, whether or not it makes sense to anyone else, and regardless of the odds they will succeed. No matter. Their behavior may seem oddly intense, and the decisions they make may seem insane to some, but as long as they're motivated by the goal of business success, it's all good.

To put it another way, if these people were playing blackjack, they would believe with a white-hot certainty that if they just keep playing—if they never give up—the cards will eventually smile on them and they will go home rich. Lots of people have gone broke thinking like that. As the saying goes, "Las Vegas was built one quarter at a time"—by people who believe, or at least hope, that they'll hit a jackpot on the next spin of the slots. There are a lucky few who happen to be sitting in front of a slot machine when it pays out, but the vast majority cash out and go home losers. In fact, the only sure winner in a casino is the casino itself. The house never loses because all the odds in a casino are rigged in the house's favor, with each game returning anywhere from three to twenty percent, depending on the skill of the player or lack thereof. By contrast, the odds of succeeding in business are less than ten percent. Out of a hundred people who chase their dream of entrepreneurial success, then, ninety of them will come up short, no matter how white-hot their desire, and no matter how dedicated and persistent they are. Because those are the odds of the game. Everyone thinks they are going to win. Everyone wants to win. But everyone can't win, because the game won't allow it.

Of course, everyone thinks they are going to win until they don't. That's one of the most valuable lessons competitive sports teaches children. When I was young, I was considered a pretty good tennis player, and played the junior tournament circuit in southern California. I was the captain of my high-school tennis team, and, because we had a lot of good players, our team was one of the top ten high-school tennis teams in the nation. I wasn't even the best player on that team, but I convinced myself that if I trained hard and dedicated myself, I could excel in college and become a professional tennis player. Rather than go to a smaller, more modest school where my tennis talents might be appreciated, I chose instead to attend the University of Arizona, a Pac-10 tennis powerhouse. I tried out for the team and barely made it as a reserve doubles player, the lowest of the low. Only the top six players got full-ride scholarships, so I made it my personal mission to play my way into a scholarship. Somehow, I convinced myself that winning a scholarship was possible. But after a few weeks of getting my ass handed to me in match after match against better, stronger, faster players, it soon became clear to me that I was deluding myself. At some point I had to face the fact that there were hundreds of tennis players my age who—by virtue of talent, coaching, physical abilities, mental strength, or whatever—were simply better than me. Yes, I could keep trying. I could ignore all the accumulated data illuminating rather starkly that, in the big picture, I was at best a mediocre tennis player. But I could not lie to myself anymore; I could not claim that I was winning when, time after time, the scorecard said otherwise.

"A man's reach should exceed his grasp," goes an old motivational maxim—meaning, I suppose, that one should always leave room for improvement. *How far* one's reach should exceed their grasp is the question. Accepting that my tennis dream was a receding fantasy well out of reach by the tender age of eighteen was a bitter pill to swallow. But swallow it I did, because the alternative was chasing a dream that was never, ever going to materialize. In fact, of all the hundreds of amazing players I knew in junior tennis and in college—guys I was certain were going to be the next John McEnroe or Jimmy Connors—only two of them turned pro. One of them, Michael Chang, won the French Open—but everyone else didn't. We all had the same dream back then, but the rest of us had to replace the professional-tennis dream with another, more realistic dream, one that didn't require a 130 mile-per-hour serve, freakishly responsive fast-twitch muscles, and almost super-human vision. (A recent study of professional baseball players found, for instance, that the average baseball player has close to 20:10 vision. In other words, pro ballplayers can see at twenty feet what the rest of us see at ten feet. Professional baseball players are, in fact, a self-selected population of people whose extraordinary eyesight gives them an overwhelming advantage over the rest of the population when it comes to hitting a baseball. Extraordinary eyesight allows them to track a ninety-mile-per hour fastball and "see the seams" on a looping, dipping curveball. A kid can wish all they want to be a professional baseball player, but if they don't have better-than-perfect vision, it isn't going to happen.)

To proponents of positive thinking, this kind of reality check constitutes "negative" thinking, because it allows the demon word "can't" to displace the cheery optimism of "can." No matter how you look at it, though, the truth is that everyone has wishes and dreams that are never going to come true. And it doesn't matter how earnestly they wish for their heart's desire, or how hard they work to achieve their seemingly impossible goals—life simply isn't going to give them the rewards they seek.

It isn't necessarily wise, however, to chuck all of one's idealism into the existential trash bin at the tender age of eighteen. Nor is it useful when one is trying to find ways to combat an overwhelming sense of futility and a creeping case of nihilistic despair. Also, the question has to be asked: What does it say about me personally that I went straight from disillusionment on the tennis court to disillusionment in the book field? The answer is that I wasn't looking for disillusionment in either case; I just happened to find it.

Perhaps it was inevitable. After all, life is in many ways a progressive series of disillusionments, of curtains pulled away and scales peeled from the eyes of the innocent. From the moment a kid learns the truth about Santa Claus and the Tooth Fairy, the compact of trust between children and adults is broken. As a parent, it is fun to envelop your child in a magical world of make-believe, a world where a fat man in a puffy suit can slide down a chimney ten inches wide and deliver presents to every kid in the world by, say—as I said to my own kids—traveling through a cosmic wormhole where space and time are compressed, which, according to Einstein's theory of relativity, allows Santa and his reindeer to travel at or near the speed of light.

Eventually, the kids catch on, of course, because even a kid knows that Einstein had very little to say about Santa Claus. When a kid learns the truth about Santa Claus, however, the next logical question is: What else are my parents lying about? And the answer is: quite a lot. But we lie to protect children from the cruel realities of the world. And as adults, it is our responsibility to dole out "reality" in small doses, to gradually introduce the idea that champagne wishes and caviar dreams are just that—wishes and dreams—and that most people have to settle for diet Coke and a tuna-fish sandwich.

With each successive grade in school, we up the ante and insist that children need to work harder, study more. All through school, the great sorting happens. Those who are good at school and "do their homework" are gradually separated from the rest of their peers and put in advanced-placement courses, where the intellectual distance between them and those left behind grows exponentially. Those students then go on to the "better" colleges and universities, where they distance themselves even further from the hoi polloi, who inhabit the vast universe of averageness and mediocrity that good students are taught to disdain. Then, in college, even the best students learn that not all avenues of ambition are realistically open to them. Gradually and grudgingly, they come to understand that part of growing up is giving up on your dreams and "getting real." Suddenly, what was important isn't anymore; what's important now is what sort of job you plan to get after college—how you plan to pay for your own rent and food, and, eventually, the house and car and kids and toys you are eventually going to want, even if you don't know it yet.

Unfortunately, one good way to create a generation of disenfranchised young people is to pump them full of idealism and set them loose into a world that doesn't care a whit about their passions or their talent. That's what happens in America today: Kids are told they can be anything they want to be, that there are no limits to what they can achieve, that the world is their proverbial oyster and all they have to do is sit around and wait for that gorgeous pearl of a life to form. When it doesn't happen, the kids get angry. They say, "You tricked us," "The system is rigged," "It's all bullshit," "Everything is a lie"—and they are right. Nobody grows up dreaming about being a mid-level marketing executive at a large corporation. Nobody, when they are young, has a deep passion for accounting or an overwhelming desire to study tax law. These are professions people choose after their primary passion, whatever it is—sports, music, art, theater, dance, writing, science, literature, etc.—has flamed out and they are forced to choose some other, lesser life. Granted, one of the great things about capitalism is that it provides plenty of jobs for people who don't have much passion for their work. But what that leads to is a nation of people who aren't very happy—a nation of people who pop anti-depressants like tic-tacs, swallow or inject any substance that dulls the pain of "reality," and spend an inordinate amount of time and money on ways to calm their frazzled nerves.

To be fair, the deception used to be worse. When I went to college, tuition was cheap and one could realistically conceive of becoming a professor of English literature, say. The idea was not completely absurd. Now, the economic realities of virtually any artistic endeavor are well-known, and it is equally well known that the best path to a life of prosperity is through a STEM job (Science, Technology, Engineering, or Math). So, in a sense, kids today are growing up in a world that is infinitely more candid about the economic realities that await them in adulthood. But they are also growing up in an extraordinarily sophisticated dream factory, one that preys on their hunger for transcendence and their wish for the world to be other than it is. When they learn, as they inevitably do, that the world isn't perfect—that there's still a lot of work to be done and that the adults running the show don't necessarily know what they are doing—they feel betrayed. Is it any wonder they don't trust us?

These days, many colleges are dropping majors in languages and the humanities in order to avoid leading students down the primrose path to Ph.D. purgatory, where hyper-educated scholars in post-structural gender dialectics spend their days making lattes and wondering where their lives went wrong. Corporations and businesses claim they value people with so-called "critical-thinking skills"—the one thing of value that humanities majors supposedly acquire through all that book-learnin'—but in practice, the last thing companies want is people who think for themselves and approach their jobs (and their superiors) with a critical mindset. People who can think critically are the key to creativity and innovation, they say—the sort of "problem-solvers" who can think "out of the box" and offer "dynamic" entrepreneurial solutions that enhance a company's global competitiveness. In reality, however, most companies hate people who are independent, creative thinkers. People who think critically tend to challenge authority, demand respect, have a low tolerance for stupidity, and do not always follow orders, especially if they have a better idea, which they almost always do. Middle-management drones feel threatened by such people, and if one of them happens to squeeze through a company's personality-filtration process and get hired, they are immediately subjected to the sort of petty, vindictive, back-stabbing office politics that they—having read *Animal Farm, 1984, All the King's Men, Babbitt, Don Quixote, Fahrenheit 45, Germinal,* and *The Metamorphosis*—instinctively abhor. Trapped by the dual imperatives to pay back their student loans and acquire decent healthcare benefits, creatively inclined independent thinkers usually find themselves working in jobs that barely keep them awake, much less engaged and motivated. It doesn't take long for their supervisors to identify them as "unhappy" or "not a good fit" for the company culture. That's why most companies prefer to hire people who are content to sit in their cube and shut up. Creative thinking leads to job dissatisfaction; too much of it will get you fired.

Still, the business world tends to fetishize words like "imagination" and "creativity," and handsomely rewards people like Steve Jobs, Bill Gates, and the Dyson vacuum-cleaner guy—but only if their ideas end up turning a profit. Outside the world of business, people who actually use the full magnitude of their imagination and creativity— painters, novelists, playwrights, composers, dancers, musicians, and other artists of all kinds—are treated with contempt. The only members of this creative cohort that business-people respect are those who succeed in the marketplace, who turn their creativity into profit. All the rest—which is to say the overwhelming majority of artists—are seen as sad, impractical people who are wasting their time on self-indulgent nonsense that nobody wants to read, hear, or watch.

In this and many other ways, the idealism and trust of our nation's youth is being systematically destroyed. As they grow older, young people discover that, despite everything they have been told, society is not arranged for them to pursue their passions; it is organized primarily for companies to make money. Sure, there are companies that do useful and necessary things on their way to a healthy bottom line, but many do not. Companies like Coke, Pepsi, Nabisco, Kellogg, Keebler, Kraft, Nestle, and hundreds of others do little more than sell sugar in various forms, contributing to society mostly in the form of an epidemic of diabetes and obesity. That may sound bad, but in the business world, adversity is just opportunity in disguise. That's why, in 1978, the H. J. Heinz Company started Weight Watchers, which has itself become a $1.5 billion company. Heinz ketchup is far and away the most popular ketchup in the U.S., and twenty-five percent of every bottle is—no surprise here—high-fructose corn syrup.

Entrepreneurial capitalism runs by the motto: "Identify a problem or need, then provide a solution." Companies like Heinz take that creed a step farther by creating the problem, then offering the solution, then pretending they are doing something socially responsible by addressing the "problem" they created, in this case by starting a company that purports to help people shed the pounds they gained eating hamburgers and hot dogs and other foods laced with its parent company's signature product. It's a beautiful circle of complete and utter bullshit—like killing someone's cat, then showing up at their door with a basket full of kittens and a brochure on the plight of feral felines. But if you are at a baseball game and have a hot dog in your hand, the one condiment that most Americans must have on their dog is a ribbon or two of Heinz ketchup, myself included. Nothing is better on a hot dog. Or a burger. Or fries. It's the perfect complement to a meal of fat and salt, the sweet counterpoint that completes the circle of deliciousness we have all been trained to love.

CHAPTER 27

The day was disgustingly hot. Which is to say, if Russ and I spent much time walking around outside, we'd end up disgusting people. This we knew, because both of us had shown up on people's doorsteps dripping with sweat, shirts soaked through, asking them to let us into their homes. And both of us had seen the grimace on those people's faces when they opened their door, the expression that said, "You've got to be kidding." Not only am I not interested in what you're selling, that look said, I am even less interested in allowing you to enter my home and drip sweat all over my kitchen floor. Plus, you probably stink, and the mere fact that you're standing there asking me to let you into my home calls your mental health into question. So no, you can't come in.

Trying to sell books under such circumstances was futile, and we knew it. So did Dana and Jackie, apparently. They showed up at the diner as we were finishing our lunch, having declared the day a total loss. It was early afternoon, the heat of the day was upon us, and they wanted to do something "fun." We'd ditched a few sweltering afternoons already. Sometimes we sought refuge in an air-conditioned movie theater, or just drove around to keep a steady breeze flowing over our skin. This time, Dana and Jackie wanted to go swimming, and had identified a small beach where we could all go, for free, and dunk ourselves to our heart's content.

The beach itself was located off a small tributary of the Mississippi River. It was not a beach in the sense that I understood the word. It was more of an inlet with a ribbon of dark, muddy sand, and the water itself was on the brackish side, with little tufts of algae floating on the surface and clouds of silt suspended in a murky, uninviting soup of industrial toxins, the kind that scientists in the 1990s would link to an epidemic of mutant frogs and three-legged salamanders.

Normally I would not even have considered swimming in water that foul, but these were not normal circumstances. Relief from demon heat was our top priority that day, and submerging ourselves in the Mississippi River was one way to achieve it. They don't call it the

Muddy Miss for nothing, however, so one way of understanding our mindset that day is that the oppressive heat of the day outweighed any misgivings we might have had about swimming in the fetid waters of America's scummiest river. Besides, the girls (ahem, women) wanted to do it, and if they were willing to swim in the Mississippi, macho pride demanded that we do it too. Besides, Jackie, who was from Missouri, claimed that she swam in the Mississippi "all the time," ha ha ha. And, since she hadn't sprouted any extra limbs out of her neck and her body wasn't scarred with lesions from flesh-eating bacteria, we could safely assume that a brief dip in this toxic stew wouldn't do us much harm.

Foolishly, I believed her. (Although in retrospect it's probably more accurate to say that I, at that age, was in the habit of ignoring all warning signs of potential danger, and actually enjoyed taking foolish risks for the pure, idiotic hell of it.)

And so we swam.

The following evening, after Russ and I got home, a violent thunderstorm was raging outside. Iowa thunderstorms are not like regular thunderstorms, which rumble in the distance and light up the sky with brief flashes of lightning and drop a few chunks of hail here and there. No, Iowa thunderstorms are epic, and they come at you like the fury of the gods. They arrive as a wall of wind pushed by a collision of low and high pressure. They accelerate from 0 to 80 mph in a matter of seconds, toppling trees, ripping off roof tiles, hurling trash and debris everywhere.

They fume and spit and howl. Jagged bolts of lightning rip the sky apart. Rain bounces off the window panes like little nails. Thunder explodes like a series of concussion bombs, rattling the windows and reverberating across the plains, warning all the creatures below that chaos and mayhem are coming, so take cover now, or risk being lifted off the ground and tossed half a mile by a tornado; risk having your corpse discovered the next morning by a farmer assessing the damage to his property, tsk-tsking you for not respecting the strength and power of nature or the indiscriminate essence of its destruction; risk losing everything, because you were too stupid or arrogant or dismissive to believe that, given half a chance, Mother Nature would not hesitate to end you.

Those are the stakes in an Iowa thunderstorm; the things are fucking dangerous.

On this particular evening, my right ear had been bothering me all afternoon. Pressure had been building inside my ear canal, and little darts of pain seemed to be burrowing their way toward my brain stem. As the night progressed and the storm intensified, so did the pain in my ear. I tried everything I could think of to alleviate the pain—Q-tips, Tylenol, ice—but nothing worked. The pain in my ear grew sharper and stronger. I tugged on my ear lobe and banged the side of my head. I lay on the bed and hung my head upside down. Every time a thunder bomb went off, it felt as if someone were kicking an ice pick into the middle of my skull. After a while, the pain became so intense that all I could do was lay on the floor in a fetal position and cover my ears with my hands. It didn't help, though, because the pain was inside me, in my head, and I couldn't get it out. I thought my head was going to explode.

Interestingly, when you are in so much pain that you think your head is going to explode, several thoughts immediately occur to you: 1) You begin to wonder if it is indeed possible for your head to explode; 2) If so, you begin wishing it would happen soon, if only to relieve the pain; 3) If your brain does explode, you wonder if it will be messy—that is, will it be a tiny controlled explosion inside your head, like a stroke, or will your head detonate like a grenade, splattering your brains to kingdom come? After that, it's not your problem, you figure. There are people whose job it is to collect corpses and clean up spontaneous brain combustions. The longer the pain persists, however, you begin to wonder why your head hasn't exploded yet, because it doesn't seem possible that the pain and pressure can get any worse. And yet it does, causing you unimaginable agony. The sweet relief of annihilation never comes. You have no choice but to suffer and moan, because the entirety of your existence is focused on the blinding white torture machine between your ears. Nothing else matters. Nothing else exists. Only pain—hot, sharp, relentless pain, the kind of pain that makes childbirth sound like a warm bubble bath; the kind of pain that makes a root canal feel like the tickle of an ostrich feather; the kind of pain that can only be survived if you do not have a shotgun in the house. Because if you did, and you could choose between continuing to suffer and never suffering again, you'd immediately blow your brains out.

Unfortunately, I did not have access to a shotgun or any other kind of firearm. Frank, our freaked-out veteran friend, might have had one under his bed. He might even have shot me if I asked him to. We'll never know. What I do know is that the only person in the world who could help me at that moment was Russ, and he was terrified on my behalf.

"Dude, you're starting to worry me."

"Aaaaaaannnnnnhhhh."

"Is there anything I can do?"

"Agggggggghnhhhnnn."

"Are you going to be okay?

"Unnnnnggggggghhhhh."

"Maybe if you eat something."

"Ohhhhhhhnnnnnnn."

"Or suck on a LifeSaver."

"Grrrrrrrrrnnnnnnnnnnn."

"I could try to find some aspirin."

"Phhhhhhmmmmmmttt."

"Maybe we could sing the Bookman song."

"Ahhhnnnnnnnnnngggggg!!!!!"

To be fair, Russ was in an awful position. Back in 1979, cellphones didn't exist, and Russ and I did not have a phone in our room. The only people he could call for help were Dana and Jackie, who lived three miles away—but they did not have a phone either. There was no internet, so Russ couldn't Google my symptoms or watch a YouTube video on how to alleviate traumatic head pain. He had no way of knowing what was wrong with me, only that I was curled up in a ball on the floor like one of those bugs that recoils and wraps around itself when you touch it. Furthermore, a punishing thunderstorm was raging outside, so he'd be risking his own life if he ventured outside to, what, ask the Grim Reapers for their help? (Come to think of it, they would have been the logical people to ask for a gun, or for some drugs that might have done the trick, but, being a Christian do-gooder, that option apparently didn't occur to him.)

At some point, Russ apparently concluded that I might actually die, and that he needed to take some action. What that action was, I didn't know. All he said to me was, "Wait here. I'm going to go get some help."

For the next hour or two (I don't know how long it was, because it seemed like a week) I lay on the floor, writhing as the icepick in my ear stabbed and jolted and tortured me. Time only flies when you're having fun. When you are in primordial pain, time slows to a crawl so that you can savor the agony. Evolutionarily speaking, I suppose this is the body's way of getting your attention, of communicating to you that there is an emergency somewhere in your flesh sack, and if you want to return to the realm of timeless pleasure, you had better deal with it.

Only later did I learn what Russ had done. In the middle of that raging storm, he had run the three miles through the streets of Davenport to Dana and Jackie's house. They all piled into Dana's car and returned to pick me up. Then they all three took me to the nearest emergency room.

At the ER, a doctor informed me that the cause of my pain was an ear infection. He asked me if I'd gone swimming lately, or spent a lot of time around little kids. I told him it was a bit of both, but that I suspected taking a dubious dip in the Mississippi River may have had something to do with it.

"You swam in the Mississippi?" he asked, incredulously.

"Yeah."

"The Mississippi River is basically a sewer—you know that, right?"

"I know it now," I said.

"Nobody in their right mind would swim in it," he said. "What were you thinking?'

"I have no idea."

The good doctor then reached deep into my ear canal with a pair of tong-like pincers and pulled out a plug of ear wax the size of a pencil eraser. A roaring rush of sound sent a fresh jolt of pain through my head as he held the nub of gunky wax buildup to the light for me to see. "You might want to clean your ears every once in a while too," he said, "because if you don't, a wad like this can build up and cause, well, an ear infection."

The doctor sent me home with some Tylenol and a bottle of antibiotic goop, with instructions to put three drops of the goop into my ear three times a day for a week. The infection should be gone by then, he said, and I should be back to my normal self, provided I did not immerse my head in a septic tank anytime soon.

The strange thing about this tale is that the week after my emergency-room visit—the week I spent popping painkillers and dripping antibiotic goo juice into my ear—I had my best sales week ever. Even though I felt miserable and basically walked around like a zombie that week, people opened their doors for me and bought books right and left. I had no idea why. I don't know what I did differently that week; I still don't.

When, at our weekend meeting, I told my manager Mike what had happened (sans the little detail about all of us bailing on the book biz that sizzling afternoon and going swimming)—that I had gotten an ear infection and had spent the week only being able to hear out of one ear because of the medication—he immediately deduced the reason for my sudden spike in sales: "It's because you couldn't hear the word 'no,'!" he exclaimed with the absolute certainty of a preacher. "Next week, you should plug your other ear up and see how you do. Your sales volume will probably triple!"

For Mike, every cloud had a shiny silver lining. To find it, all you had to do was grin like an idiot, say something stupid, and believe every word.

My own theory was that because I felt so awful that week, the act of selling books door to door did not feel as loathsome as usual. In fact, because I felt so bad, selling during that week was a welcome distraction. The alternative was to wallow in self pity and think too much about how crummy I felt. My previous misery (the daily door-to-door) had been temporarily displaced by an even greater misery (the earache), which rendered my former misery less miserable by comparison. In this contextually warped frame of mind, I had somehow struck the right balance of persistence and nonchalance, that golden demeanor of placid doggedness that melted Midwesterners' hearts and made them want to save me from myself. How else to explain the woman who, seconds after seeing me on her front stoop, exclaimed, "You poor thing!" and, ten minutes later, wrote me a $79 check for a *Volume Library*?

That kind of thing never happened to me, except for one golden week when it did.

CHAPTER 28

After the ear infection cleared up and I got my hearing back, things returned to normal on the sales front. Which is to say, I returned to my normal shitty sales self. In order to stop the slide, Mike arranged for me to go out on a few sales calls with one of the company's most accomplished veterans, a woman who had been selling books every summer for four years, and who had broken every sales record in the books. Her numbers were consistently astounding, and she agreed one day to take me around with her, to show me how it was done.

This woman, let's call her Anne, was unremarkable in every possible way, except for the fact that she could, by reputation, sell mud to a pig. Like Steve, her specialty was farmers, an alien species from Midwestern mythology that I had never encountered, and one that, on the surface, seemed unpromising in the extreme.

Our selling philosophies couldn't have been more different. I approached selling more-or-less like trick-or-treating, which is to say that a promising neighborhood to me was block after block of tidy homes crammed in tight so one didn't waste time in transit from door to door. More houses meant more opportunities to make a pitch, increasing the statistical likelihood of making a sale. Anne didn't seem to care that, in her territory, the houses were a mile or two apart with nothing but corn and soybeans in between. It also didn't seem to faze her that she was selling to farmers, people who most likely didn't go to college and for whom education was an afterthought—for whom, in fact, education was likely a threat. I mean, if I were a farmer who wanted to pass my land and all its responsibilities on to my son or daughter, the last thing I'd want them to do is go to college. Yes, they could study agricultural management, but they could also study a lot of other subjects—subjects that might open their eyes to the fact that farming is a very nineteenth-century way of making a buck.

To Anne, however, farmers were just as likely to buy a book as anyone else. The difficulties of her territory did not seem to concern her, and she refused to use them as an excuse not to sell. Her attitude was supposed to inspire me, I think, but it just made me feel small for not being able to sell in the relative abundance of Davenport proper.

The day I accompanied her, we drove for about half an hour into Iowa's interior, where farms are the only sign of civilization. She wore denim overalls, which I thought was an obvious ploy to make herself look like she belonged behind the wheel of a tractor—a ploy any actual farmer would immediately see through. She said she wore them because they were "comfortable," but I didn't believe her. As we approached our first farmhouse, she instructed me not to talk, and to pay attention to her delivery—the pace and cadence of her voice, the elements of her pitch, her transition to the close, etc.—so that I could learn the secret to her success. She had long ago abandoned the idea that she had to knock on a hundred doors to sell two books. There was no way she could visit that many farms in a day, so she had to make each visit count. Closing percentage was the only statistic she cared about—and, according to company lore, she had a closing rate of close to fifty percent. Which is to say, she sold a book to every other person she talked to, and only needed to talk to four people in a day to sell two books. Her target was five books a day, however, not two, and, according to her own estimate, she was able to bank anywhere from $12,000 to $15,000 a summer, a number I found entirely inconceivable.

The first thing I noticed about Anne's sales approach was that she talked to farmers like they were her aging grandparents. She did it in a super nice way, but to me she sounded condescending, as if these were just simple folk who needed help making any decision whatsoever.

Our first prospect was a farm wife whose husband was out in the field, but who welcomed us with a friendly smile and invited us inside. Anne complimented her on keeping a lovely home, and asked if there was a comfortable place in the house where they could sit. She did it exactly the way we were taught in training back in that Nashville motel, and the woman replied by guiding us to the kitchen table, where, without prompting, she served us cookies and lemonade. I found this suspicious, because no one had ever offered me anything unsolicited. Then, wasting no time, Anne segued into her demonstration of the *Volume Library*. The most peculiar thing I noticed was that she followed the Southwestern Company's goofy, ridiculous script almost to the letter. And, when the farmer's wife asked questions or offered an objection—like, "Oh, I don't think our granddaughter would use this"—Anne countered the objection using the language provided by the company—"But you can see how this would help if she did use it, can't you?"—and nodded her head yes, precisely the way we had been taught. None of this was language that came comfortably out of my mouth, because I thought the company "script" was cheesy and stupid and awkward. Not Anne. She rarely strayed from the company-approved script, and she did not deviate when it came time to close the sale—that is, to get an order and some percentage of cash as a down payment. Anne did not ask for half-payment, though, she asked for the whole $79, claiming that full payment just "made everything easier."

Then a funny thing happened. At precisely the moment my inner dialogue was going, "Oh my god, I can't believe this chick has ever sold a book in her life," and "How she thinks she's going to get a dime out of these people, I don't know," the farmer's wife reached into a ceramic jar on top of the refrigerator, retrieved four crisp twenty-dollar bills, and handed them to Anne. Anne gave her a dollar in return, had her sign the order, then thanked her and we were gone. The whole thing took fifteen, maybe twenty minutes at the most, with cash payment in full. It was astonishing.

So astonishing that I didn't believe it.

As we drove away, I said to Anne, "So this was a setup, right? I mean, that was way too easy to be real."

Anne assured me that it wasn't a setup. She just knew these people, she said—knew how they think, what they want, what their pain points are, etc.—and knew how to talk to them about it.

I still didn't believe her. "What about the cash?" I said. "Who has a wad of cash sitting around waiting for some book person to come to their door?"

"All farmers keep a few hundred dollars in cash around for emergencies," she said. "I always get cash."

I never got paid in cash. I was lucky to get a check that didn't bounce. "But it's not like you used your awesome knowledge to improvise the most persuasive possible argument in there. You followed the company script almost exactly."

"The script is everything," she insisted. "When you get off script, you get into trouble. I learned that a long time ago."

"Well I still haven't learned it, because the script is so goddamn stupid!" I cried.

"And how's your 'smart' approach working for you?" she zinged.

She had me there. The only reason I was riding around with her was because I was having trouble selling "up to my potential." And the reason, she surmised, was that I was trying to sell books without the benefit of decades of sales experience to help me—decades that were distilled into that idiotic, grammar-challenged, soporific presentation that I could not bring myself to memorize or mouth.

We visited two more farms that morning, and she sold a *Volume Library* to each one as easily as she had the first. It was crazy. In the span of a couple of hours she had sold more books than I had in the entire previous week. And her day had just gotten started. She sold all the way to sundown, she said, because evening is actually the best time to talk to farmers. Not the morning. That's how good I am, she seemed to be saying: I can sell books to anyone, anytime, anywhere. What's your excuse?

After lunch, Anne drove me back to Davenport and let me loose in a stretch of suburban sprawl that I would have thought was prime sales territory twenty-four hours earlier. After a morning with Anne, though, I began to think that maybe the only people in the state of Iowa who read books were farmers who have nothing else to do at night but sit by the fire for hours poring over Proust. Maybe I had been duped into thinking that the suburbs were havens of middle-class aspiration hungry for the advantages of a good education, eager to grab any possible foothold on a better life. Maybe I had it all wrong. Maybe it was America's farmers who were eager to better themselves through education so that they could avoid turning into some sad, industrial-age labor statistic. Maybe it was the farmers who understood that their way of life was doomed, and that the only way they were going to survive was by learning how to do something else—something that wasn't threatened by technical progress, giant corporate conglomerates, or the cruel vicissitudes of Mother Nature; something that didn't require so much sweat and toil and heartache; something that allowed them to make a living from the relative safety and cleanliness of a modern office building, where air-conditioning and business suits and vending machines make life better for everyone.

Clearly, I was confused. Accepting the idea that I was a lousy salesperson was difficult. Watching someone like Anne make it look so easy just made my incompetence that much more humiliating. Until I rode around with Anne, I didn't realize how bad a salesperson I really was. Her success was supposed to inspire me, but it only made me feel worse.

CHAPTER 29

Still, I felt better than a lot of other people. One of the more disorienting aspects of our regular Sunday meetings, which were meant to inspire us and foster community, was the dwindling number of students who attended. Each week, dozens of students who seemed on top of their game the week before simply didn't show up. By the fifth or sixth week, there were only thirty or forty of us left. The majority of kids who had started with us had quit, and most of them disappeared without any sort of explanation, never to be seen again. It felt as if, every Sunday, we were soldiers coming back from the front, and we were not supposed to talk about those we left behind. Instead, we compared stats, told stories, sang the Bookman Song, and tried not to notice that everyone around us was dropping out, electing to return to their former lives rather than suffer the frustrations and indignities of another week in book-selling hell. Every week, the message we got was that those of us who had chosen to stay were the proud, the brave, the strong, and that every week we remained committed to our goals we were strengthening our character and proving to the world—and to ourselves!—that we were winners. The fate that awaited anyone who quit was a flaming pit of shame and humiliation, of dreams deferred and fortunes lost, a lifetime of losing, an eternity of infinite regret. The only way to avoid such a fate was to stick it out, to ignore the ominous and ill-considered decisions made by other, lesser people, and honor the promise we'd made—to ourselves!—so that at the end of the summer we could enjoy the deep and lasting satisfaction of a job well done. Armed with a character forged in the fires of book-dom, and with habits of success handed down from the masters, we would naturally establish ourselves as superior competitors in the Darwinian jungle that awaited us after college. In fact, when we got back to school and people asked us, "What did you do over the summer?," and we told them, their regard for us would soar, our self-esteem would skyrocket, and we would instantly take our rightful place as leaders in a world of followers, wolves in a world full of sheep, successful über-students whose future success was a foregone conclusion. Whatever path we chose, whatever profession we embarked upon, the confidence we gained from our book-selling experience would give us the edge we needed to excel, from the mail room to the boardroom and everything in between. Whatever we did in life, we were going to be kicking ass, not kissing it.

The drumbeat of positivity was relentless. Not that we all believed it. We wanted to, of course. We wanted to believe we were better. But it was hard to escape the nagging notion that we were the ones being duped—that the only thing we were proving was that we had the capacity to endure grandiloquent amounts of bullshit and ignore the most obvious distress signals in the endless and often fruitless pursuit of what amounted to a little bit of pocket money.

There were other measures of success, however.

Each Sunday, Russ and I met up with a guy named Bob, who shared our skepticism but also refused to quit. Bob was a decent-looking guy from who knows where. The only facial feature I remember about him was that he had a bushy black mustache, and his hair was on the longish side, which made him look like a cross between Tom Selleck and Jesus.

The other thing about Bob that differentiated him from everyone else is that every Sunday he came armed with a story or two about the young housewives he had slept with that week. To him, banging lonely housewives had become a perk of the job, and he kept track of his conquests in the same way everyone else kept track of their book sales.

These revelations were astonishing to me. According to Bob, he could barely go a day without encountering some hot, young mom who practically ripped his clothes off the moment he walked through the door. It happened all the time, he claimed, and he could not understand why we weren't taking advantage of this hormonal bounty ourselves. They were there for the picking, he insisted, low-hanging fruit on the tree of desire, waiting to be plucked by any reasonably well-endowed bookman who knocked on their front door.

This had not been my experience. Yes, I had given book demos to some attractive moms barely out of high school, but they were usually surrounded by several needy children and a farting dog or two. Most had at least one kid who had just learned how to walk and was therefore in need of constant surveillance. They all looked tired; night after night of sleep deprivation left their eyes flat and their skin pallid. Their houses were usually a mess, littered with toys and dirty dishes and discarded clothes. And the smell of various body secretions—shit, urine, vomit, breast milk, and spittle—did little to encourage adding another to the mix. Besides, even if they did let me into their den of shame, the majority of these haggard suburban housewives sat on the couch and listened to me with that "how long is this going to take?" look on their face, the one that lets you know rather unmistakably that they are annoyed by your presence, do not intend to buy anything, and can't wait for you to leave. Because, you know, they've got shit to do.

It's hard enough to sell a book. How one transformed an exhausted prisoner of parenthood guarded by an army of toddlers into a quivering siren of sexual abandon was beyond me. Granted, my own sexual experiences up to that point had been a discomfiting mix of embarrassment and terror. Still, I couldn't help wonder how a guy like Bob could fall so easily into the arms of a woman, any woman, when I, living in the same world, doing the same thing, could not fathom how the opportunity would even arise. Was there some secret bat-signal that people who wanted to fuck knew about but I didn't? Was there some bizarre pheromonal phenomenon at work? On some primal level, did people who wanted to have sex with each other just "know" it? And if so, how did they learn to recognize these signals and communicate them to each other?

The whole dance was a mystery to me. Then again, the same thing had happened back in college. During my freshman year, it seemed as if everyone was having sex with everyone else, while I sat on the sidelines listening to their erotic escapades, wondering how I could get in on the action. Whenever I came close, the door always shut, because the girl with whom I wanted to have some wild sexy time wasn't ready, willing, or drunk enough to comply. My only consolation was that Russ, too, found the idea of spontaneous door-to-door sex with customers a bit far-fetched.

"He's full of shit," was Russ's assessment. "Even if he did get laid, it was probably with a goat or a sheep, something with four legs that can't talk back."

Sex with farm animals. There was another predilection I didn't understand.

One morning, Dana and Jackie dropped me off in my territory, and soon it began to rain. Not hard, but steady enough to soak me if I stood out in it too long. From a selling standpoint, rain was not necessarily bad. If I showed up at someone's door while it was raining, it boosted the chances they would invite me inside. It also gave me an excuse to linger and maybe weasel a snack for the road. Sitting around doing nothing while it rains is also boring, so the rain itself usually motivated me to get out there and bang on some doors, especially doors with porches or some kind of overhang that served as shelter, if only for a short time.

That morning, the first door I knocked on was answered by a woman who, when she saw me standing in the rain, immediately invited me inside.

"You poor thing," she said, ushering me into her living room. "I just made coffee. Would you like some?"

Free coffee at 9:00 a.m.? Of course.

She brought out the coffee in a small pot, along with two generous pieces of coffee cake. Even if I didn't sell anything to this woman, the stop was already a success, I thought.

The woman's house was small and not exactly tidy. My habitual survey of her living room revealed someone who did a lot of crossword puzzles (judging from the newspapers on the floor), and collected little glass-blown animals—unicorns, seahorses, and little medieval-looking dragons—the kind of thing you see at state fairs, where some guy sits in a Plexiglas booth and heats little tubes of glass with an acetylene torch, then proceeds to shape globs of molten glass into the most amazing shapes, and you can't help wondering: Why is someone capable of producing such delicate artistic masterpieces cooped up in a booth at a fair, hawking his goods the same way other people hawk corn dogs and mini-donuts? She had a nice little collection of these critters in a beautiful cherry-wood cabinet. Unfortunately for me, that meant that either she didn't have small children, or her children were older—or, worst of all, she had no children at all and had invited me inside simply out of the goodness of her heart, because it was raining outside.

"So, what brings a handsome young man like you to my doorstep at this hour of the morning?" she asked.

I told her what I was selling, and asked if she had any children.

"No," she said, "but I do have nieces and nephews."

"Great," I said. "May I ask how old they are?"

The age question determined what I would try to sell her. Young children got the kid's books demo, while older children got the *Volume Library* demo. Her nieces and nephews were all under five, which meant trying to sell her some kids' books for a birthday present or something. Such demos were usually a longshot, but it was raining fairly hard outside, so I figured what the hell, at the very least I could practice my sales pitch while I waited for the deluge to let up.

Halfway through my demo she stopped me and said she would happily order three sets. Just like that. No persuasion or haggling necessary. I could not believe my luck. Three sales first thing out of the chute, in the rain, to someone who doesn't even have kids. What were the odds? You never know, I thought—sometimes a sale lurks in the unlikeliest of places.

As I packed up my case and retrieved my receipt book, the rain was pouring down steadily outside, with no sign of stopping.

"I can't let you go outside in this," the woman said. "You're welcome to stay as long as you like."

I thanked her and mumbled something about how I might stick around for a few minutes to see if the rain let up. Then she asked me a question that caught me off guard: "Is it true what they say about traveling salesmen?" she asked.

"I don't know," replied. "What do they say?"

"That, you know, you meet lots of lonely women, and there are lots of opportunities to . . . make them feel less lonely?" At which point she spread her legs and leaned over so that I could see her breasts swaying beneath her shift—breasts for which the adjective "pendulous" was invented.

Then it finally sunk in: This woman is hitting on me.

Now, in Bob's world, this may have been one of those situations that he seemed to run into so often: lonely woman looking for sex from the door-to-door book stud. But in my world, this was an awkward situation that was rapidly turning into a terrifying dilemma—the dilemma being that I absolutely, one-hundred percent did not want to have sex with this woman. My admittedly shallow reason: She was fat and ugly.

In general, I have nothing against people who are grossly overweight, or people whose physical appearance won't land them on a magazine cover anytime soon. The chemistry of desire is a different animal altogether, though, and the body usually has its own ideas about what it finds attractive and what it does not. Mine did not find this woman attractive in the least. In fact, I found her rather grotesque, and the thought that she wanted to have sex with me right then there was as repulsive as it was frightening.

"Uh, may I use your bathroom?" I deflected.

I needed to buy some time to figure out an elegant way to escape, yes, but also to get her money. She hadn't signed her order receipt yet, and she hadn't written me a check or given me any cash for a down payment. So I was in a bind.

As I sat on the toilet, trying to develop an exit strategy, I noticed a stack of magazines. The magazine on top was a Penthouse, and several of the ones underneath it were among the raunchiest X-rated publications available at the time: *Screw*, *Hustler*, *Swank*, and plenty more *Penthouse*s. At the time, Larry Flynt, the publisher of *Hustler*, was involved in the first of many First-amendment lawsuits—evidence to my fraternity brothers, at least, that his magazine was the best (and worst) on the market. I had only seen one or two copies of *Hustler* in my entire life, so I picked one up and rediscovered what I already knew—that it was too raunchy for my tastes. *Penthouse* was more in line with my adolescent sexual preferences, which is to say naughtier than *Playboy*, but not as sick as *Hustler*.

In addition to the air-brushed photos of women in various stages of rapture and undress, *Penthouse* had something the others didn't: its Letters section. When I was growing up, the *Penthouse* Letters section was where we found out what really went on in small Midwestern colleges, where we learned about the range of orifices available for sexual experimentation, and how many ways there were to turn an ordinary social situation into an orgiastic free-for-all. Many of the letters were written by people who evidently read the Letters section itself, and didn't believe what they read—*until it happened to them*. Deep down everyone knew these letters weren't real, that they were absurd fantasies cooked up by writers who specialized in a peculiar form of erotic prose based on a thesaurus of sexual euphemisms unavailable to ordinary people like me. At one point, in my search of practical applications for my budding literary aspirations, I briefly entertained the idea that I too might get paid to make up sex stories for *Penthouse*. I even tried writing one once, but discovered that my sexual imagination was not up to the task. The problem: more research—in the form of first-hand experience—was needed, in order to make my adolescent imaginings sound more realistic. I have since discovered that allowing too much reality to creep into a sexual fantasy is inadvisable. But that's a story for another book.

Sitting on that toilet, magazine in hand, I realized that the woman out there in the living room was an avid reader of the *Penthouse* Letters section as well, and—like everyone who read those letters—she probably hoped that something worth writing about might happen to her someday. Today, maybe. Right now, if possible. With this young man who knocked on her door in the middle of a rainstorm and hadn't left the house yet. Who was now sitting in her bathroom, amid stacks and stacks of pornographic magazines, hopefully getting the hint that if he had half-an-hour or so to spare, she would let him do *Penthouse* letter-like things to her, and vice-versa.

The thought terrified me.

"You okay in there?" she asked in a sing-song voice dripping with what I guessed was anticipation.

I pretended not to hear her. Outside, the rain was coming down hard and straight, with no sign of letting up. The logical thing to do was stay inside and wait it out. But that was no longer an option. I had been in the bathroom for such a long time that it was starting to seem strange, even to me. I had to make my move.

So I flushed the toilet, washed my hands, and went back out into the living room.

"I thought you'd gotten lost in there," she said, coyly.

"Indigestion," I replied. "Must've been the sausages I ate for breakfast. Probably weren't cooked enough."

"I like sausages too," she said, creepily.

"Normally I go for bacon, but they were out," I said.

"I like the way bacon sizzles in the pan, don't you?"

"I like the way it doesn't upset my stomach," I said, patting my belly.

"I hope you feel better soon," she said. "Maybe I can help with that."

I could take it no longer. I had to get out of there. But it was still raining outside, and I didn't have a poncho with me, so I knew I was going to get soaked the minute I stepped out the door. Of the two options, however—getting raped by a sausage-loving porn addict or getting soaked by a somewhat-less-than-gentle summer rain—the latter seemed preferable. So I grabbed my sales case and made for the door.

"You can't leave yet," she said.

"Bookmen are like mailmen," I informed her. "Neither rain nor sleet nor snow nor pelting rain shall keep us from our appointed rounds. Besides, I have a schedule to keep. Thank you for your hospitality," I said, "but I must be on my way."

"Don't I have to pay you?" she asked. I had forgotten completely about the books and the sale, but at that point I didn't care, and I didn't dare stop moving toward the door, for fear that if I did, something irrevocable and traumatizing might happen.

"Not to worry," I said. "Your books will be delivered in about a month, and you can pay for them then." This was a lie—I was never coming back to her house—but I had to cut things short and make my escape.

"Again, thanks and have yourself a lovely day," I said as I opened the door to let myself out.

"Do you really have to go?" she asked, this time in a plaintive, almost forlorn tone of voice that indicated how sad and lonely she really was, and that she understood all too well why I was leaving. She knew I found her repugnant. She knew I was scared of her. She knew that the fragile fantasy she had nursed until that moment was not going to come true, and that for her, like so many people, the closest she was going to come to having surprise morning sex with a door-to-door salesman was in the letters section of her favorite magazine, where people who are not her enjoy the kind of life she can only imagine.

"I really do," I said, and stepped out into the rain.

CHAPTER 30

Over the years I have fantasized about what might have happened that rainy morning if the circumstances had been different—if the woman in that house had been as attractive and lonely and willing as a magazine letter-writer. For the rest of that summer, in fact, the hope of experiencing a revised version of that tale haunted me throughout the day. Sometimes, I'd knock on a door and, when an attractive young mother answered, I would think, this could be the moment! But it never was. Not once in the remaining days of that summer did the opportunity to engage in anything other than polite chit-chat present itself. This was disconcerting, because many of the mothers I met that summer were in their twenties, were attractive, and—if they had had the slightest inclination to do so—would have succeeded immediately in seducing me. Then, at the age of eighteen and for all intents and purposes a virgin (save for one spectacularly inept episode in high school), I was about as primed for sex as anyone could be. Had I been truly motivated, of course, I could have tracked our friend Love Train down and requested professional assistance. But I was more mystified than desperate. Whatever frustration I felt from not being able to have sexual intercourse with my customers was a hell of my own making. After all, I had almost no experience. I knew what to do in the clinical sense, because I had paid very close attention to the mechanics of the matter in my tenth-grade life-education class. But how one managed to get through all the anxiety and self-consciousness and potential shame of any given sexual encounter was beyond me. At that point in my life, I could not imagine how to have a relaxed, mutually fulfilling, flesh-based encounter with a woman. It seemed impossible. But that didn't stop me from fantasizing about it.

By that time in the summer, I knew my sales pitch so well that it only took a small fraction of my mental capacity to deliver it. That left the rest of my brain free to wander whatever terrain it felt like. In practice, this meant that I could sit in front of someone and move my mouth and turn pages and ask questions and nod my head without having much conscious interaction with my body at all. Often, it felt as if I were standing outside my body, watching myself with a sort of curious detachment, unable to fathom what I was doing or why. During those moments, it was entirely possible for my body to be giving a sales pitch while my mind occupied itself with other thoughts. And one of the ways I entertained myself was by trying to imagine what the person I was talking to looked like when they were having sex.

Imagining what people look like during sex is surprisingly difficult. Next time you're in a grocery store, give it a try. That grandma squeezing the Big Boy tomatoes? She's no stranger to fleshly pleasures, of that you can be certain. But it's hard to picture her in the throes of ecstasy because she's old and wrinkled and fussy about her produce. Likewise, the dude behind the meat counter might be hung like an ox and amaze his partners with his freakish stamina in the sack, but somehow the sexual side of his nature is hard to see when he's asking you how thin you want your sandwich meat sliced. The same goes for everyone else in the store. They're all people—sexual beings hardwired to fornicate—but they all manage to hide that side of themselves beneath layers of indifference, fatigue and, quite often, fat. It shouldn't be that difficult to mentally peel a person's clothes off and flop them on their back. But it is. And it shouldn't be that difficult to imagine them in the middle of the act itself, because everyone looks pretty much the same when they're having sex, like they just put their hand on a hot stove or stubbed their toe on a rock.

Once, I sat on a city bus full of people and tried to imagine what each person might look like in *passione flagrante*. Couldn't do it. No matter who it was, there was something about them—their body shape, demeanor, clothes, hairstyle, hygiene—that prevented me from seeing their sexy side. Now, it's quite possible that this deficiency of erotic imagination resides in my head, and my head alone, and that other people are perfectly capable of envisioning their fellow citizens moan and quiver and throb. But for reasons I don't understand, I can't look at a cashier at Target, say, or a man wearing cargo shorts, and see the sexy inside them. My mind resists the image, the way most people cringe at the idea of their parents in bed, even though they themselves are incontrovertible evidence that their parents do engage in ejaculatory activities every now and then.

Unfortunately, this imaginative liability also proved true with young mothers in Davenport, even if evidence of their sexuality was right in front of me, running around the room in diapers. I'd be delivering my sales pitch, trying to imagine what might happen if I could sell her on the idea of a little harmless afternoon adultery, but the image refused to come into focus. I could not imagine how it might happen, or what it would look like if it did happen. So of course it never happened.

Nor did it happen anywhere else. Through the first six weeks of our ordeal, by some miracle of self-control and circumstance, Dana, Jackie, Russ and I had kept our collective promise not to have sex with each other. This may sound like an impressive act of self-control, but it had more to do with the fact that we were always together, all the time, so if a twosome decided to break off and do their own thing, it would have been a conspicuous breach of protocol. There simply was no opportunity to pair off. And even if there was, doing so would have been an unconscionable betrayal of trust.

That all changed, however, when Russ and I decided to move in with Dana and Jackie.

As I mentioned earlier, Dana and Jackie (unlike us) had landed in the sweetest possible living situation. In the first week of the summer, they had been invited to house-sit a mansion in one of Davenport's "transitional" neighborhoods on the north side, closer to their territory in Bettendorf, but not exactly in it, or of it. Though the house itself was once quite grand, the neighborhood around it was, at the time, transitioning decidedly downward.

Like many river cities in the Midwest, Davenport was a bustling port town at the turn of the century, a hub of economic activity that led to a building boom in the 1920s. (Interestingly—and entirely beside the point—in 1922, Davenport's first radio station, and only the second licensed radio station in the country, WOC, began broadcasting with a new format: talk radio. In 1933, the station hired as a staff announcer a young man with a smooth voice and gentle sense of humor. The man's name: Ronald Reagan, future president of the United States. Even more interestingly, and not entirely beside the point for Americans living in the 21st century, WOC still broadcasts today, and is one of the most popular talk-radio stations in the Midwest. Its highest-rated show: Rush Limbaugh.)

During the late 1800s and early 1900s, shipping magnates, agriculture executives, and local business scions were fond of building Victorian-style mansions on the gently sloping hills along the Mississippi River. Most had been torn down by the 1970s, but the one Dana and Jackie lived in was still standing, even though the neighborhood around it had become a somewhat less desirable location to live. The guy who owned the house was in the process of rehabbing it, and was concerned that if he left for any length of time, word in the neighborhood would get out and the place would be ransacked. He wanted to leave town for the months of July and August to vacation in Europe, and needed someone to watch the place. When Dana and Jackie contacted him, he made them a deal: they could have the second floor of the mansion all to themselves, if they agreed to watch the place and contact him if anything bad happened. A housekeeper came once a week to keep the dust on the first floor at bay, but otherwise they could have the place to themselves.

It was a huge house. As I recall, the upstairs had four or five bedrooms, a couple of bathrooms, and a study. Plenty of room, in other words, for four people to live comfortably without stepping all over each other.

Moving in with them was Dana's idea. Until then, we lived across town. Every morning, Dana and Jackie drove to our place, picked us up, dropped us off in our selling territory in the morning, and picked us up in the evening. It was a tiresome routine, and it manifestly sucked for us every time they dropped us off at our hovel and drove away. We had come to depend on each other for companionship and moral support, so separating each evening was difficult.

As time went by, we found ourselves spending more time in the evening with Dana and Jackie, talking and laughing and playing cards until it was time for us to go home. One night, we didn't go home—we crashed at their place. The next morning, everything was much easier on them and us, because we were already together. Then, because our place was so sketchy, and driving across town was a hassle, Russ and I gradually started sleeping over at Dana and Jackie's more and more often.

One evening, after dinner, Dana just came out with it. "You should move in with us."

By then, for all intents and purposes we were already living with them, so it wasn't so much a suggestion as an admission of our current reality. One of those realities was that the owner's housekeeper only came during the day, when we were all out, so the place was always empty at night and in the morning. So what did it matter if we moved in? No one would know. Yes, our living there would technically violate a secondary part of their housesitting agreement, which was not to have any parties, and not to make a habit of bringing boys home with them. We danced around those semantics by reasoning that we weren't "boys" in the pejorative sense; rather, we were business associates, and residing with our colleagues was a sensible business decision. Besides, we spent so much time selling books—from 9 a.m. to 7 p.m. most days—that we'd be asleep most of the time we were there.

So it was decided. And the great thing was, we didn't have to do anything to move in except stop paying rent on our old place. All our stuff was already there, in our backpacks and selling cases.

What changed, of course, was the sexual dynamic of our relationship with Dana and Jackie. It was entirely possible for us to sleep with each other, if we chose. Opportunity was not the problem anymore. The problem now was that there was too much opportunity. We each had separate bedrooms, but there was nothing preventing any of us from sneaking into another's room in the middle of the night—nothing other than our mutual pledge not to. Russ and I discussed the issue again, and agreed that sleeping with Dana and/or Jackie was a bad idea, and that we should do everything in our power to avoid it. But, under the circumstances, it was also understood that we were only human. A situation might arise in which we did not have the power to resist. If, for instance, Dana snuck naked into my bed one night and begged me to hold her, to comfort her, to temporarily banish the agonies of our daily struggle with a little harmless connubial bliss—well, what kind of monster would I be to deny her? Likewise, Russ could not be blamed if a similar situation arose and he were put in the position of having to deny an eager young woman the pleasure of some carnal stress relief. So we modified our pledge somewhat, to: try not to have sex, but if it happens, oh well.

The problem, really, was Dana.

She was beautiful, smart, funny, sensible, and flirtatious—just the kind of girl one would choose to date if one were in college looking for a girlfriend. Russ and I were both half in love with her already, so the match was already lit. All it needed was a little fuel. Dana herself was problematic though, because she simultaneously stoked the fire and doused the flames. On our first night as official roommates, she established the ground rules.

"Just so we understand each other, there is not going to be any sex," she declared. "So don't even think about it."

"But what if you try to seduce us and we are powerless to resist?" I asked.

"Funny," she replied.

"What if I sleepwalk into your room and accidentally slip my penis into your vagina?" Russ asked. "Would you classify that as sex, or the unfortunate result of an unavoidable sleep disorder?"

"I would classify it as rape," Dana retorted. "How about you, Jackie?"

"Rape, definitely," Jackie concurred. "Good for five to ten years in prison, I'm guessing."

"What if . . . ?"

"This is not some Lysistrata situation, where we are withholding sex as some sort of punishment," Dana interjected. "We are taking sex off the table because, if it were on the table, everything would get weird and uncomfortable. You know it. We know it. I'm just putting it out there."

"That you're not going to put out."

"Exactly."

And so it was agreed: We shalt not have sex with each other under any circumstances whatsoever.

Having laid the ground rules, however, Dana was also fond of testing them. She liked back rubs, for instance, and, after a long day in the book field, would beg me to rub the kinks out of her back and shoulders. She'd lay on her bed face down and indicate with her hands where the trouble spots were. My job was to gently knead her shoulders, then her back, while she made little moaning noises to indicate when I'd hit the right spot. After that, she'd ask me to dig my elbow into the two large muscles in her lower back. At the end of a massage, she always wanted me to give her "the tingles." That is, starting with her lower back, she wanted me to ever so lightly run my fingers up her spine and into her neck to the base of her beautiful skull. After I did that two or three times, she'd turn over and say it was "my turn." She didn't do massages, but she did like to give me "the tingles" by running her fingernails lightly along my skin and up my back to my neck. And yes, it felt good, really good—too good. The tingles did not relax me. On the contrary, by the time she was done, I was usually so revved up that I was terrified I might try to break our covenant. But I enjoyed the contact so much that I rubbed her wherever and whenever she asked. I looked forward to it, in fact, because touching her skin and tingling her back was often the highlight of my day.

For her, the arrangement was safe because we had an "understanding"—we were roommates now, so any touching of the flesh was purely platonic. I don't think she experienced the same thrill of sexual possibility, either, though I like to think there was at least a little bit of a spark there. For me, of course, every evening was fraught with exquisite tension. Secretly, I was relieved that I had an excuse not to take things any further. But I could not deny that there was a part of me—a part located six inches below my belt—that wanted desperately to find out what would happen if things did go further, if things got really weird and uncomfortable. But somewhere deep inside we both understood that it wasn't going to happen—or, at the very least, that it shouldn't happen, because introducing actual sex into the equation would complicate things immeasurably.

Jackie was another story. The trouble was, neither Russ nor I was attracted to Jackie, and that fact alone was uncomfortable. It wasn't Jackie's fault, but with all the attention focused on Dana—and to be fair, Dana did require a great deal of attention—Jackie kind of receded into the background. Also, Jackie did not seem interested in pursuing anything more than a cordial friendship with either of us, and did not seek the sort of affections that Russ and I showered on Dana. Had one of us been attracted to Dana and one to Jackie, things might have turned out otherwise. But that's not how it was, and this obvious imbalance of affections led us all to more or less honor the pact we had made. Sex might have been in the air, but that's as far as it went, a tantalizing wisp of possibility that swirled around us but never materialized into anything more substantial.

Or at least that what I thought at the time. Later events called all of these assumptions into question. At the time, however, I was under the impression that all of us were playing by the same rules.

CHAPTER 31

Week after week after week of door-to-door bookselling takes its toll in many ways, not the least of which is an intense feeling of loneliness and isolation. Talking to people in order to sell them something is not the same as actually talking to someone. Selling is not communication, it is manipulation and persuasion. The interaction between salesperson and customer is transactional; there is nothing about it that feeds the human need for true connection and communication. Unless you're the kind of person who enjoys chatting with people for the heck of it—or better yet, are the kind of person who enjoys manipulating people with the raw power of words (You can see how a book like this could help your child succeed, can't you?)—door-to-door sales is not for you. If one does not enjoy door-to-door sales, and isn't the kind of person who likes talking to people they don't know, the obvious question is: Why do it?

Money is one reason. Desperation is another. For some people, door-to-door selling is the only job they can get. But one of the most common reasons people choose to sell things door-to-door—one of the reasons I chose to do it, in fact—is to overcome their fear of rejection. Of all the skills door-to-door selling teaches a person, this psychological fortification against the pain of being told "no" is the most appealing one, especially for people who have never done it.

I say "appealing" because many people think of the ability not to be hurt by rejection as a kind of superpower. If you are a college student, for instance, it means you could walk up to any young man or women at a local mixer and strike up a conversation—or at least attempt to—without the fear of being ignored or dismissed or embarrassed. If you are interviewing for a job, it means that the sting of being told no, they hired someone else, won't hurt. If you are an actor or performer, it means having a thick enough skin to withstand audience indifference or hostility, bad reviews, and the withering psychological toll of unsuccessful auditions. If you are a writer, it means not having to suffer whenever your work is deemed insufficiently brilliant to appear in a publication that, by all appearances, is in the business of publishing less-than-brilliant writers. And if you are a regular human being, as most of us are, it means not having to feel inferior whenever your averageness is exposed, as it often is, at the worst possible time.

Fear of rejection is primal. Human beings are hard-wired for community; they want to belong; they want to be loved; they want to be admired, praised, and accepted. They do not want to be criticized, demeaned, humiliated, isolated, alienated, or lonely. In primitive civilizations, rejection from the tribe meant shame, starvation, and—eventually—death. In modern society, however, the main result of rejection—the reason people want to avoid it so much—is that it hurts. Rejection is painful. It burns to the very core of who we are, in the deepest, most vulnerable part of our psyche. People naturally want to avoid that pain, so they look for ways to go around or through it without getting burned.

Much of modern psychology is built on the premise that one can overcome fears by facing them. And if one were to devise an experiment that forced people to face their fear of rejection, time and time again, it would look a lot like door-to-door sales. Being told no, no, no, no, no, no, no, no, no, no, over and over again has the cumulative effect of making rejection seem like an ordinary, everyday occurrence. And when it happens several times an hour, desensitizing oneself to the hurt becomes a matter of survival. No one can endure that much rejection without developing some coping mechanisms, and many people feel they need this sort of psychological armor in order to succeed in life.

Former president Ronald Reagan (who, in 1979, was one year away from being future president Reagan) had a favorite story that is widely interpreted as a parable that addresses the theme of rejection. And it does, sort of. But how you interpret the story says a lot about how you interpret the world—and, in turn, how much credence you lend to the power of cheerful optimism.

The story, which Reagan thought of as a "joke," goes like this:

Once, there were two six-year-old boys who happened to be twins. Worried that the boys had developed extreme personalities—one was a total pessimist, the other a total optimist—their parents took them to a psychiatrist. First, the psychiatrist treated the pessimist. Trying to brighten the boy's outlook, the psychiatrist took him to a room piled to the ceiling with brand-new toys. But instead of yelping with delight, the little boy burst into tears.

"What's the matter?" the psychiatrist asked, baffled. "Don't you want to play with any of the toys?"

"Yes," the little boy bawled, "but if I did, I'd only break them.

Next, the psychiatrist treated the optimist. Trying to dampen his outlook, the psychiatrist took him to a room piled to the ceiling with horse manure. But instead of wrinkling his nose in disgust, the optimist emitted just the yelp of delight the psychiatrist had been hoping to hear from his brother, the pessimist. Then he clambered to the top of the pile, dropped to his knees, and began gleefully digging out scoop after scoop with his bare hands.

"What do you think you're doing?" the psychiatrist asked, just as baffled by the optimist as he had been by the pessimist.

"With all this manure," the little boy replied, beaming, "there must be a pony in here somewhere!'"

Setting aside for the moment the neuroticism of parents who would take their six-year-olds to a psychiatrist, the moral of this story, to Reagan and millions of other people, is that having an optimistic attitude can make even a giant pile of shit seem like a promise of better things to come. Also, that optimism is a preferable outlook on life than pessimism.

Reagan himself was a legendary optimist, yet it seems to have occurred to pretty much no one that the steaming pile of shit in this story could easily represent the Reagan administration itself—or rather, the empty promise of Republican governance. Nor does it strike many people as odd that the hero of the story—the optimist—is deluding himself. Because there is no pony in that room. There will never be a pony in that room. Yet the story asks us to entertain the idea that it is better to believe a lie—or worse, a fantasy of our own making—than to accept, or even acknowledge, the truth. The story also does not tell us what happens to the little boy's cheerful attitude after hours of shit-scooping and still, no pony. What becomes of his beaming optimism after days of searching? Weeks? Years? Decades?

Of course, this kind of magical thinking is what gave us President Ronald Reagan, trickle-down economics, George W. Bush's "mission accomplished," and, eventually, Donald Trump. And it all starts with the willingness to believe in something that doesn't really exist.

For the past thirty years, the American middle class has been digging through pile after pile of shit in pursuit of an illusory "happiness" pony that they're never going to find. Why? Because while they were digging, their government long ago killed that pony and fed it to the military-industrial-corporate-entertainment complex, who outsourced it to China and Thailand. Granted, the Declaration of Independence doesn't promise actual happiness, only the right to pursue it—but a society can take only so much shit-shoveling before people start to wake up and think, hey, maybe they lied to us about that pony. Or worse, maybe we convinced ourselves that all that shit came from a horse, when they could have just trucked it in for the purposes of a dubious social experiment. One has to ask: How long will people dig through pile after pile of shit before they give up? Or before they decide to stop digging and go confront the people who set the experiment up? Or before they decide the people running the experiment are the problem?

Those are questions for another time.

The point I'm trying to make has to do with the psychology of rejection, people's desire to avoid the pain of rejection, and the tools of emotional resilience—some healthy, some not—that are required to insulate oneself from this most primal and unwelcome of feelings. In the Reagan/pony story, the boy who won't play with the toys for fear of breaking them is presented as the "pessimist," but is his outlook really pessimistic? Perhaps his parents have yelled at him for breaking toys in the past, so he is understandably leery of adults asking him to play with toys. Or perhaps his parents are lawyers, and he is simply hyper-aware of the potential insurance implications if he did happen to break a toy. In any case, what he's really trying to do is avoid getting into a situation where his decision to "play" results in some sort of reprimand. Likewise, the supposed "optimist" in the story tells himself there is a pony beneath all that shit in order to avoid the sadness he will feel if there isn't a pony—if, that is, the truth is something other than what he believes. Optimism, in this case, is the antidote to cynicism and disappointment. It's also a complete fantasy.

The depressing thing about unbridled optimism is that it actually works to combat negative feelings, even if—and sometimes especially if—by embracing an optimistic outlook one is simply fighting facts and reason with hopes and wishes. Salespeople of all kinds need optimism because the facts of their working life—that 98 out of 100 people don't want what they're selling—are so depressing. In order to avoid the sting and burn of almost universal rejection, salespeople the world over adopt a "fake it 'til you make it" style of surface cheer, which is why so many sales folk feel creepily friendly. The reason it feels creepy is that the friendliness of a salesperson is entirely false. That too-big smile and overly firm handshake? Pure theater. Inside, as they are shaking your hand asking what they can help you with today, most salespeople are seething with a toxic mix of contempt and disdain for their customers, not to mention a Freudian boatload of shame for not being able to make money in a more culturally respected way. As they are talking to you, they are also steeling themselves against the statistical likelihood that you are going to walk away without buying anything from them, robbing them of their commission and wasting their time. The only way to survive this kind of repeated, daily rejection is to pretend that it isn't happening—to convince yourself that the rejection isn't personal, that the next person you talk to offers another sales "opportunity," and that your inability to sell is not an indication that you are a lousy salesperson, just part of the daily diet of humiliation and heartbreak that must be endured in order to eventually succeed.

Selling is like fishing, after all. People can fish for long hours without catching anything if they believe in their heart that there are fish in the water and that some magic combination of bait and technique (movement, depth, glitter, stink, etc.) will result in a bite. Belief that it is possible to catch a fish is all a fisherman needs to keep fishing. If the fish aren't biting, imaginary "nibbles" are enough to keep hope alive for hours. But if the fisherman has no hope whatsoever of catching a fish—if, say, they are fishing in a toxic-waste dump—the lack of hope will sap their resolve and it won't take long for them to pack up and go home. The same psychology applies to selling. The difference is that when fish aren't hungry, they don't tell you to your face that your approach to catching them sucks. Fishing would be a very different experience if every perch that circled a hook suddenly rose to the surface and spat, "Get off our lake, fisherman. We don't like the bait you're dangling."

When they fail to catch anything, however, fishermen do not feel rejected. Disappointed and frustrated maybe, but not rejected. The sting of failure isn't personal. When a human being says no directly to your face, though, it does feel personal, and it hurts in a way that most people hate. The question is: Why? In the forests and savannahs occupied by early humans, fear of rejection probably served some important evolutionary purpose, because being rejected from the tribe meant going it alone, which meant a slow and agonizing death. Unfortunately, fear of rejection is entirely counterproductive in a competitive meritocracy. It serves no useful purpose. In fact, it gets in the way of everything—everything from getting a job and finding a spouse to identifying and pursuing one's passion in the face of overwhelming obstacles.

If your mental wiring does not demand that you fear rejection, you have a distinct advantage over other people. That's one reason sociopaths are so successful in business and other professions. Sociopaths aren't derailed by other people's opinions. They don't get flustered when people disagree with them. It doesn't bother them when other people get upset by something they've said or done. In fact, studies have shown that sociopathic tendencies themselves may be an evolutionary response to the circumstances of life in contemporary Western society—Nature's way of insulating us from hurt feelings, so that we are free to control and manipulate people without the nagging inconvenience of an old-fashioned moral conscience.

In any case, many people feel that if they could just numb themselves to the pain of rejection, they'd be much better equipped to deal with life. I thought so too, and, as I mentioned earlier, it's one of the reasons I decided to sell books door-to-door in the first place. Did it work?

Yes and no.

One of the things I did learn from selling books was that it is possible to take a lousy situation and reframe it in your head to make it seem less lousy. This is a handy skill. Suppose, for instance, that you are in the grocery store and they are out of the peanut butter you like. A lousy situation, to be sure, one that would upset anyone whose brand loyalty has been built up over time. I mean, if you've spent your life eating Skippy Super Chunk, and suddenly its place on the shelf is empty, leaving you to choose between various formulations of Jif and some organic brand of "all natural" peanut butter that contains no emulsifying agents to prevent the messy separation of oil and peanuts, and by the way contains *only* peanuts and nothing else—well, you have to agree, that would be infuriating. But if you think about it differently—if you can reframe it in your head—you can view the lack of your desired peanut butter as an opportunity to try some other brand of peanut butter, or maybe another peanut-butter product altogether, one that mixes the jelly in with it, say, or provides you with layers of yummy marshmallow cream. Or you could take a step further and abandon the whole peanut-butter-and-jelly paradigm altogether, viewing the lack of Skippy as a "message from the universe" telling you to try some other kind of sandwich: turkey or pastrami, maybe. And if you end up liking one of those other alternatives, you could look back on your whole "what, no Skippy Super Chunk!" experience as a net positive, since it introduced you to other sandwich possibilities, thereby enriching your life and making you appreciate Skippy Super Chunk all the more.

Unfortunately, what I also learned is that no matter how much rejection you expose yourself to, it is pretty much impossible to remove all the sting, all the time. Which is fortunate. Because while it may sound wonderful to be impervious to emotional pain, such a mindset is not a very stable foundation for one's mental health. Many people spend their lives trying to numb themselves to the pain and hurts of their childhood, or to forget the formative indignities and outrages seared into their souls. But the mechanisms people use to anesthetize themselves from that insistent ache within—alcohol, drugs, sex, work, exercise, television, etc.—tend to lose their effectiveness over time, and the hurts themselves tend to re-assert themselves in ways that make everyday life even more unpleasant and difficult. For many, the ability to withstand or ignore a great deal of personal pain is viewed as a sign of strength, especially in men. But true strength is achieved by having the courage to remain open and accepting of one's feelings, and to remain vulnerable enough throughout life to experience pain, and to work through it in real time, in the moment, while it is happening. It takes a tremendous amount of courage to remain emotionally open enough to allow people to hurt you, but the reward is a much stronger connection to one's own humanity. When people cut themselves off from their own pain, they tend to lose the capacity for empathy, for appreciating other people's pain—and that, in a nutshell, is a large part of what is wrong with our country. So many people are in so much pain themselves, and so engrossed in the project of reducing or eliminating their own personal pain, that they have exhausted the ability to empathize with others. The only thing worse is to somehow achieve that rarified state of mind in which other people's pain and anger is of no consequence, because it is not "rational," or because it does not happen to affect them personally. That's why all superheroes have a flaw to ground them. Kryptonite is Superman's connection to human nature, a cosmic reminder that he is not entirely impervious to pain, injury, or death. None of us are. The irony is that by embracing vulnerability and openness in our relationships with others and the world around us, we have the power within us to vanquish the emotional bogeymen that haunt us, and to neutralize the pain and fear that so often controls—or derails—our lives. Unfortunately, it is extremely difficult to be both an emotionally bulletproof success machine *and* someone with an open, honest heart who is willing to risk being hurt in the interest of better personal relationships and more resilient mental health. The two rarely go together, because one usually obliterates the other.

CHAPTER 32

No two days of door-to-door selling are alike. If doors are opening and books are selling, the day can whiz by in a blink. If not, the day can be tortuously long, each minute an agony unto itself. More often than not, however, days in the book field were marked by jarring ups and downs. After a sale, it could feel as if I was walking on a cloud, both my feet and mood as light as a marshmallow on Mars. At other times, the feelings of loneliness and futility would feel so oppressive and heavy that I could barely move.

The pain of a bad day usually peaked around three o'clock in the afternoon, after several hours of unsuccessful knocking. It wasn't just the constant rejection; the stifling heat and other-worldly humidity also took their toll. Iowa in mid-summer is renown for this one-two combo of meteorological misery, which makes everything heavy and wet and slow, as if you are walking on Venus, a planet named after the goddess of love but protected by a veil of gas so toxic it could melt the skin off a rhinoceros.

On days when people who have central air-conditioning allowed me into their house, there was respite from the heat. But on days when no one wanted to open their door, there was no refuge. On such days, the heat seeps through your skin and into your muscles and bones, finally taking up residence in your heart, where it accumulates weight like water dripping into a sponge. The trouble is, everyone else in Iowa feels the same way during summer, and the last thing people want to do under such circumstances is discuss the value of curiosity and knowledge. It is difficult to have a lively mind when everything around you is telling you to slow down and take a nap. And it is almost impossible to get excited by new ideas when your brain is telling you that the most important thing you can do at the moment is stand in front of a fan.

In the middle of the afternoon, the relentless depletion of heat and failure also magnified the loneliness—the feeling, deep down, that no one in the world quite understood what I was going through. And how could they know? How could they know what it felt like to be paralyzed by despair in some generic Midwestern neighborhood where the most exciting thing to do on any given afternoon is run through the sprinkler until someone yells at you to stop. How could they appreciate the sense of isolation that envelops you are in a place where no one knows you, no one wants to talk to you, and pretty much everyone you do talk to wishes you would go away?

These days, of course, it is almost impossible to imagine an eighteen-year-old in that particular situation. After all, with a cellphone in your pocket the antidote to loneliness is just a couple finger taps away. But cellphones did not exist in 1979. If you wanted to "text" someone, you had to send them a letter though the U.S. mail. If you wanted to call someone, you either had to have a phone (which we didn't), or you had to use a payphone—which, by definition, required money. A local call might only cost a quarter, but calling someone long distance was an entirely different story. To call someone long distance from a payphone in 1979, you either had to call "collect," which meant the person receiving the phone call had to agree to pay for it—or you had to make your way to a bank in order to obtain a roll of quarters, which you had to feed into the phone every few minutes in order to keep the conversation going. Talk was not cheap, either. In the continental United States, talking to anyone long distance cost $10-$20 per hour, or about $35 to $70 in 2018 dollars. That's a lot of quarters.

For the entirety of my book-selling ordeal, I had kept one promise: I had not called my parents. Not once. Not even to check in and let them know I was alive. I had written a couple of letters, but that was all. And I had stuck to communicating via letter because it is much easier to shade the truth when you are in complete control of the words and no one can interrupt you to ask an uncomfortable question. Every once in a while, however, a boy needs to talk to his mother. And though I knew I shouldn't, and had promised not to, I found myself on one particularly despondent afternoon wanting desperately to talk to mine.

To the suits in the company, of course, my desire to talk to my mother was nothing short of treason.

In the Southwestern training program, the admonishment "whatever you do, do not call your parents" was drilled into us hard. The company encouraged us to think of us as adults who did not need our parents. Indeed, they sought to undermine any hint of parental influence or authority by warning us that our parents would not—indeed, *could not*—understand the strength of our commitment to book-selling. Parents were portrayed as soft sacks of emotional mush who would of course respond to any sign of distress from us with entreaties to return home, back to the safe bosom of our childhood. Parents, we were told, were inherently incapable of seeing the "big picture," the broad canvas of possibilities that would naturally accrue from our fierce independence and dedication to a cause greater than ourselves, the call to spread knowledge and freedom throughout the land, thereby releasing the poor and uneducated from the invisible shackles of ignorance and paving the way for a generation of ambitious young scholars to grow up and make the world a better place. Parents were small-minded and selfish; all they wanted was to keep their "babies" close to them, to protect them, so that they wouldn't get hurt. What parents didn't "get" is that ambitious young people like us needed to encounter pain and adversity in order to strengthen our character. What parents didn't "understand" was that our commitment to selling books was stronger than our need to make our parents feel less anxious. Indeed, parental anxiety itself was presented as an obvious sign of weakness; irrefutable evidence that our own strength and fortitude was much stronger than the fragile nervous systems of those who bore and raised us.

"We are giving you what your parents can't—the freedom to be yourselves, to be the best *you* you can be." That was the company line. It was a lie, of course. The truth was that the very existence of parents was a thorn in the company's side. The company's existence depended entirely on its ability to recruit and manipulate young people into selling its product, and the parents of those young people were an obvious impediment. Unlike their inexperienced and idealistic offspring, parents were more likely to smell the bullshit and alert their children to it; parents who knew what their children were going through would of course cry foul; parents who were especially enraged might even file a lawsuit. Parents were the enemy, and in order to fight them the company had to be very good at dividing and conquering, building a bizarre "us or them" alliance that transformed our parents into adversaries. Attempting to talk to them was considered a betrayal of first principles, of the promises we had made to ourselves, a sure indication that we were cracking under the pressure and seeking "permission" from our parents to give up and go home.

There would be times in the book field when we would of course want to talk to our parents, to cry on their shoulders and seek solace in their words of sympathy and comfort. But that desire was simply a dangerous temptation, the devil on your shoulder telling you to give up. In order to avoid that temptation—a Biblical temptation if there ever was one—we basically had to forsake our parents, at least for the summer. There would be plenty of time to talk to our parents afterwards, when we could bathe in the glory of our success and humble them with our amazing accomplishments. Wait for that moment, the company urged: don't ruin it by succumbing to a moment of all-too-human weakness.

Despite all of these warnings and the resulting fear of what might happen if I ignored them, I found myself one afternoon feeling so small and lonely and vulnerable that I simply had to talk to someone. My survival depended upon it. And so I set about procuring a roll of quarters and finding a payphone in the shade that I could use to extend an electronic umbilical cord back to the source of my very existence: my own ever-loving mother.

A word about my mother: She's a wonderful woman—smart, thoughtful, and kind—but in general, she's not the sort of person who is swayed by bursts of emotional distress. Professionally, she is a software engineer and mathematician. Her thinking is very precise and rational, so she can always be counted upon to give straightforward, no-nonsense advice on just about any subject. But if warm, fuzzy emotional support is what you're looking for, she's not the first person you'd call. Unless she's your mother, in which case you have no choice but to take what you can get.

Now, I will freely admit that it is possible my mother was immune to emotional manipulation because I spent my childhood trying to emotionally manipulate her. In my defense I will just say that I was a kid, she was my mom, and that's kind of the way things work in families. Nevertheless, if I ever wanted to get anywhere with my mother, I pretty much had to lay out a well-reasoned, iron-clad argument—one she couldn't poke holes in with a few pesky questions.

A sample conversation between me and my mother when I was eight years old:

Me: "Mom, I need to go the 7-11." (Secret reason: I wanted to buy a Hostess fruit pie.)

Her: "Why?"

Me: "I want to buy a kite." (A total lie.)

Her: "Don't those always rip?"

Me: "Sometimes. But there's a green one I like." (Me doubling down on the lie.)

Her: "Why don't you make your own kite?"

Me: "That's too much work."

Her: "No it's not. It's easy. I'll show you. We can make it together." (Me: Noooooo!)

Me: "It's not the same."

Her: "You're right. It's better, because you'll have made it yourself."

Me: "There's a green kite I really want. It's got a dragon on it."

Her: "You can draw your own dragon if you want."

Me: "I can't draw."

Her: "No, you can't—not if you don't try."

Me: "But I'm really, really bad at drawing."

Her: (Sighing.) "Well, the whole thing sounds like a waste of money to me."

Me: "They don't cost very much."

Her: "Do you have the money?" (In our house, you had to save up if you wanted to spend money on anything.)

Me: "I will if you give me an advance on my allowance."

Her: "Well, why don't you wait until next week, when you have the money."

Me: "Because I want it now."

Her: "That's not a reason."

Me: "But there might not be any wind next week. I need to fly it today." (I can feel my argument breaking down.)

Her: "Well, if there's no wind next week, you won't need a kite, will you?"

Me: "But."

Her: "And if you want to fly a kite today, we can make one in less than an hour if we start now."

Me: "No thanks. Now I'm thinking I'd rather play basketball."

Her: "Okay. Have fun."

The point in this scenario is that my mother knew precisely why I wanted to go the 7-11. She knew I was lying, but instead of just calling me out on the lie, she would back me in a corner with a lot of questions. It infuriated me then, but now I understand that in a weird way she was always trying to guide me toward the "right" decision. She also wanted me to avoid the consequences of making the wrong decision. For example, the penalty for being caught consuming an illicit Hostess fruit pie—a sugar-laden demon snack if there ever was one—might have been grounding for a day, or extra chores, or a double load of spinach at dinner. If I ate the pie and she found out (as she inevitably would), she'd have no choice but to dole out the appropriate punishment. But if she could avoid punishing me in a way that allowed me to save face—in a way, that is, that guided me away from my natural inclination toward disobedience—then the correct outcome would be achieved.

Like I said: The woman is smart.

On the day I called her from the book field, I hadn't spoken to either of my parents since the day I informed them, in no uncertain terms, that I was going to be selling books door-to-door that summer, and there was nothing they could say that would stop me. Now I was calling with the secret hope that she would beg me to come home. I wanted my melancholy mood to upset her so much that she would plead for me to get on a plane and be there in time for dinner. I wanted sympathy and pity, some sign from my mother that the ordeal I was enduring was intolerable for her son. I wanted her to tell me to abandon all this book-selling nonsense and get back to where I belonged, on the beach with my friends doing absolutely nothing for anyone.

She was onto me from the start.

"Hi mom, it's me. I'm calling from a payphone and it's like a hundred degrees out, so if I pass out or suddenly run out of money, you'll know why."

"Well, it's nice and sunny here, but not too hot. I just got back from playing tennis."

"I wish I could play some tennis. There's not much in the way of fun here."

"That's why they call it work, honey. There'll be plenty of time for fun later."

"It doesn't feel like it."

"What's the problem?"

"Just everything."

"That doesn't help me. Can you be more specific."

"It's just boring and hard and . . . I hate it."

"But it's important work you're doing, right?"

"Sort of. Maybe. I don't know anymore."

"Think of all the kids you're helping. Education is a gift that keeps on giving."

"Isn't that syphilis?"

"It also applies to education and knowledge."

"If education were a gift, I think I'd feel more like Santa Claus. But I don't."

"Even Santa Claus has to work. Christmas doesn't do itself."

"Santa Claus doesn't sell door-to-door."

"No, he goes down chimneys. Would you rather do that?"

"No, but . . ."

"Is there a lot of corn in Iowa?"

"What?"

"Corn. Don't they grow a lot of corn there?"

"Yes, but . . ."

"There's nothing better than fresh corn. It's delicious."

"Yes, it is."

"How's your friend? Russell was it? How's he doing?"

"He's doing great, mom. Better than me, at any rate."

"Oh, I'm sure that's not true."

"Yes it is, actually."

"Well he is a couple of years older, isn't he? That makes a big difference at your age."

"Russ is peachy. I'm the one who isn't doing so hot."

"Well you haven't called us for money, so I take that as a good sign. Unless that's why you're calling now."

"No, that's not why I'm calling. I just needed to check in and say hi."

"Well, mission accomplished, then."

"Mom, I'm not sure I can keep doing this."

"By 'this,' do you mean your job?"

"Yes."

"Everyone has bad days, no matter what job their doing. I'm sure you're just having a bad day."

"More like a bad summer."

"You know, sometimes we make things more difficult on ourselves by trying to avoid doing whatever it is we're supposed to be doing. Might a little bit of that be going on here?"

"Maybe. But there's more to it than that."

"You'd be surprised how quickly things can turn around when you stop procrastinating."

"Yes, I know."

"Take your math homework, for instance. You always hated it, but once you got past the hate part and started to focus, you found out you were pretty good at math, and even liked it sometimes."

"This is different."

"What are you supposed to be doing right now? I'm going to take a wild guess and say it's probably not talking to me."

"No, it's not."

"Well then, what's stopping you from doing what you're supposed to be doing?"

"Nothing. Except that I hate it."

"I can't help you with that. All I can tell you is that if you stop thinking so much about how you hate it, and get back to doing it, maybe you won't hate it so much."

"That makes no sense."

"Not everything in this world makes sense. Least of all you, sometimes."

"Mom!"

"I'm joking. But you have to admit that sometimes . . ."

"Yeah, yeah."

"Look, honey, I'm sure what you're doing isn't easy, and sometimes you want to quit. But you made a commitment and you have to see it through. If you don't, you'll never forgive yourself."

"You sound like my manager."

"All I'm saying is that quitting is rarely the solution to anything."

"But sometimes it is."

"I'm not going to tell you what to do, but tomorrow is another day, and in my experience when you've had a bad day, the next day is usually better."

"It can't be much worse."

"Now you're just being dramatic."

"It's the truth."

"Really. What else is true?"

"What do you mean?"

"Well, isn't it true that you chose to spend your summer this way? Isn't it true that you knew it wasn't going to be easy? Isn't it true that part of you wanted it to be hard? And isn't it true that the challenge is what makes it rewarding in the end? I could go on."

"Yes. It's just . . . hard."

"Lots of things in life are hard, dear. You might as well get used to it."

"Okay, mom. I have to go. Thanks for talking."

"Of course, dear. Anytime."

"I love you."

"I love you too, dear. One last thing: Are you drinking enough water? Because dehydration can cause lethargy and mood swings."

"Mom, I have to go."

"It's also important to replace electrolytes. You might want to get yourself a Gatorade. The orange kind tastes best, I think."

"Okay mom."

"And I hope you're not eating too much fast food. All that sugar and fat and salt isn't good for you. That stuff can affect your mood too, which can of course affect your attitude."

"I'm out of quarters, mom. I really have to go."

"Okay. I hope your day improves."

"I'm sure it will, mom. Thanks. I love you."

"Love you too. Be safe."

"Of course. Goodbye."

"Bye."

Click.

This was not the first time I had been thwarted by my mother's lack of tolerance for self-pity. It was also not the first time that she knew what I wanted and ignored it, then proceeded to give me what I *needed*—which in this case was a bit of a kick in the butt and an admonition not to take myself and my circumstances so seriously. She was right, too—the best way to stop dwelling on my various misfortunes was to re-direct my attention to the job at hand, however distasteful that prospect may have seemed at the moment. At the time, I was of course disappointed that she wasn't more concerned about my welfare, and that she didn't respond to my complaints in a more emotionally satisfying way. I also can't say I felt "better" after talking to her, because she had effectively removed the option of quitting, and for the past few days it was the idea of quitting that had sustained me. Imagining what life not selling books in Iowa would be like had been a balm, or sorts, but also a torture. When you are sweaty and tired and trudging from house to house in search of a friendly face, the best way to ruin your day is to start thinking about girls on the beach.

And so, after talking to my mother, I hung up and resigned myself to the idea of seeing the summer through to the bitter end. Whatever happened, at the very least I could say that I tried my best and persevered in the face of insane adversity. Today may have been a bust, but she was right: tomorrow was another day, and with it came hope. But first, I had to admit that she was right about one other thing: I was extremely hungry and thirsty. So I decided to take her advice and go buy myself a Gatorade, after which I decided to ignore her and go to the nearest McDonald's for a Big Mac and some fries. True, my life to this day would probably be less problematic if I had taken more of my mother's advice over the years. But that would have required listening to her and admitting that she was right—which, at eighteen, was not something I was prepared to do. But the company was wrong, too: I had talked to my mother and the world had not ended. Nothing had changed. My parents were not the enemy. That realization alone was worth a roll of quarters and an afternoon of doubt and fear.

CHAPTER 33

Eight weeks into the book-selling summer, our original cohort of three-hundred eager young success junkies had dwindled to about thirty hardened veterans of the street. That's right: Ninety percent of the students who had started summer so full of ambition and courage had quit and gone home. Those of us who remained were committed to sticking it out, if only because the finish line was now only weeks away, and the payoff for all of our hard work was now within sight. Most of the books we sold were on a half-now, half-when-we-deliver-the-book basis. Many orders were held down with only a twenty-five percent deposit, with the rest due on delivery of the book or books people had bought from us. We sold these books with the promise that we would deliver them in mid-August, so most of the money we had made thus far was theoretical, tied as it was to collecting the remainder of the money owed to us upon delivery. Quitting now would just be throwing money away.

There was also the ongoing competition between our remaining crew to consider. Russ was particularly driven to be the best first-year salesperson in the company, and he had long ago left me and Dana and Jackie in the dust when it came to sales. He regularly sold several books a day, whereas I often got skunked—no sales at all—and usually only sold enough books to keep my head above water until the following week. Russ, on the other hand, was chasing excellence and achievement in the book field like a greyhound chasing a rabbit. He was a natural, and was already being recruited to return the following summer and train first-years in the art of advanced door-to-door persuasion.

Every Sunday, we got together with the rest of our group and shared our sales stats. For many of us, including me, revealing how much (or how little) we had sold in a given week was a source of extreme shame. When you spend sixty or seventy hours a week knocking on doors, talking to hundreds of people, and suddenly have to reveal the truth—that you only sold five or six books, with a pittance for down payment—all of the agony and procrastination and despair of the previous week are revealed for what they are: useless and non-productive wastes of time and energy that should have been spent in other, more sales-centered activities. In the heat of most afternoons, for instance, I usually took a long nap under the shade of the biggest tree I could find, in the emptiest park I could find, where I could loiter and procrastinate to my heart's content. This always seemed like a good idea at the time, because I was usually exhausted and sweaty and full of self-defeating ennui. But on Sundays, when I had to reveal my pathetic sales numbers, those delicious hours of work-avoidance and daydreaming were suddenly a source of extreme guilt—because, you know, I could have been knocking on doors all that time, and could have been selling more books.

Russ did not nap. The way he talked about it, he went full bore all day long, and rarely took breaks for fear that he would slow down and, come Sunday, get beat by someone else in the final sales tally.

Yet that's precisely what happened, every week.

Every Sunday, Russ discovered, much to his dismay, that he had been beaten by the same person—a woman from Boston University—and it drove him nuts. If he sold fifteen books in a week, she sold twenty. If he sold twenty, she sold thirty. She was a phenom, and we were all in awe of her. None of us could imagine selling as many books as she did, and she did it consistently, week in and week out, so it wasn't like she was on some kind of lucky streak. She was just that good.

"She has better territories," Russ would sometimes lament, but it wasn't true. She worked primarily in lower-income neighborhoods, where neither one of us had been able to sell much of anything at all. In fact, we'd given up on those neighborhoods.

How did she do it? We asked her that question constantly, and she always had the same basic answer: She grew up in the kinds of neighborhood in which she was selling; she knew these people; and she knew how to talk to them. It was as simple as that; she had a strategic advantage over us, one we could not overcome. We did not grow up in those types of neighborhoods, and had no idea how to talk to people who lived there, so what did we expect? It was all about trust and rapport. Her advice to us was to stick with what we knew and make the best of it—and, she couldn't help but imply, to accept that her 'best' was always going to better than ours.

We envied her because there was a kind of mythology in the book world around selling in poorer neighborhoods. In theory, the sales proposition of the *Volume Library* was that it was basically a high-school education in a four-pound package. It opened up a lifetime of educational opportunity and, as everyone knows, the best way to escape from poverty is to get educated and find a decent job. It was a slam-dunk sales proposition, because who wants to live in poverty? And, presented with a $79 lifeline out of such wretched circumstances, who wouldn't grab it? In Davenport, there were multiple neighborhoods that looked great on paper from a pure socio-demographic standpoint: poor-ish (though not entirely destitute) places where the American Dream was gasping and sputtering, but hadn't yet died. No matter how hard Russ and I tried, however, neither of us could sell a thing in those neighborhoods. Jackie had better success in those areas, but by the fourth or fifth week of the summer, the rest of us had stopped trying.

The last week of our bookselling summer was devoted to delivering all the books we had sold and collecting the remainder of our orders upon delivery of said books. Prior to delivery week, the Southwestern Company shipped the books to us, and we had to store them somewhere, then deliver them. At our house, since there were four of us, that meant many dozens of boxes. Luckily, we lived in a large house and the owner was still away, so there was plenty of space in an extra room on the first floor.

The way the accounting on the *Volume Library* worked was this: We "bought" the books from the company at a discount—$39—sold them for $79, and pocketed the difference. The company did not make us pay for the books before they were delivered—but, before we could go home, we had to settle our account. So, if we sold 100 Volume Libraries, paying $39 apiece for each one, we owed the company $3,900. In theory, then, we would collect $7,900 from our customers, pay the company its $3,900, and go home with $4,000 in our pockets.

At our final Sunday get-together before deliveries began, it came time to tally everyone's numbers and see where everyone ranked in our summer-wide sales competition. I expected to be in the bottom half, since Russ had long ago left me in the dust sales-wise. Besides, my bread-and-butter was the children's books, not the *Volume Library*, so though my net sales stats weren't awful, my profit numbers were abysmal compared to those who had successfully peddled the more expensive *Volume Library*. Dana and Jackie were somewhere in the middle of the pack as well. Russ was always very near the top. His goal for the summer was to be the best, and the only person who stood between him and that title was the woman from Boston University, who continued to tally extraordinary numbers that simply could not be beat. Going into that Sunday, Russ had already accepted that the best he could rank was second place. It irked him, but that's the way it was, and it was too late to do anything about it.

Then, something strange and disturbing—and frankly, sad—happened.

It started when our friend/nemesis/colleague failed to show up for the final meeting. This was odd for several reasons, not the least of which was that the final meeting was her chance to bask in the glory of victory. Over the course of the summer she had enjoyed needling Russ and me over our inability to out-sell her, and we had already prepared ourselves for the ribbing to come. It was all done in fun, but there was always an edge to this woman's sense of humor, a seriousness beneath the joke that indicated she was in it to win in a way that we were not. Her attitude suggested that she had something to prove—that she was the best, had always been the best, and would always be the best, no matter what—and she carried it off with a level of swagger and moxie that suggested her success was no accident: She simply worked harder than everyone else, and always had. In short, she was a perfect exemplar of the Southwestern ethos of success—a focused, disciplined, relentless door-knocker who delivered results, not excuses. Her success was a direct consequence of her work ethic, which was grounded in equal measures of faith and perseverance.

The meeting took place in a conference room at a hotel somewhere outside of Springfield, Illinois. We all took our seats, and our district manager, Mike, said a few words about how extraordinary we all were simply for having survived the summer. Most didn't, which was a testament to the quality and resilience of our character. Just by being there in that room, that day, we could all consider ourselves "success stories," he said. Though, as he was about to reveal, some of us had succeeded better than others.

As expected, my results landed me in the bottom third of the pack. Dana and Jackie had performed better than me, so they ended up somewhere in the middle.

Then it came time to reveal the top three rookie salespeople of the summer. Mike drew out the suspense as best he could, beauty pageant-style. Having conceded the No. 1 spot, Russ was desperate to come in at No. 2. There was a sigh of relief when the No. 3 spot was announced and it . . . was not Russ. Then Mike revealed the No. 2 spot, and again it wasn't Russ. I could tell by looking at him that Russ was concerned, because he had run the numbers beforehand—and, unless someone else had sold a ton of books in the final week, he knew he had the No. 2 spot locked up.

And yet.

Then the drum roll and announcement of the No. 1 rookie salesperson of the summer came. It was . . . Russ!

This was impossible. We thought it was a mistake.

Our BU colleague's name wasn't anywhere on the list. Even if she hadn't sold a single book in the final week of the summer, she still would have beaten everyone else hands down. But for some reason her name wasn't even mentioned.

Then the story came out: This woman, whoever she was, evidently hadn't sold a single book during the entire summer. She had lied and submitted fake invoices for everything. In fact, the rumor went, she actually spent her weeks in Boston with her boyfriend, and flew into Chicago every weekend so that she could come to the Sunday meetings and keep her ruse going. Furthermore—and this is the hardest part to believe—she apparently allowed hundreds of boxes of books to be delivered to a physical address somewhere, books that she was contractually obligated to pay for! But, since every sale she claimed was bogus, the books were just sitting there waiting to be shipped back to the company. She had simply abandoned them, and us, and everything else before it all came crashing down on her. In the end, she reportedly owed the company somewhere in the neighborhood of $10,000, and was currently "on the run," nowhere to be found.

I share this story because I have thought of this woman often over the years, and have always felt sorry for her. Why did she do it? No one knows. All I know is that in order to draw out her deception as long as she did, and to play the role of unbeatable sales queen week in and week out the way she did, she either had to have been paralyzed by circumstances that did not allow her an elegant exit, or have thought, in her mind, that admitting failure was the worst fate of all. That's certainly the message the company beat into our heads: that quitting was the coward's way out, and if you quit book-selling, you would probably be a quitter and failure for the rest of your life. If you believed that, and if the family and culture that had propelled you thus far all reinforced that same idea—that failure was not an option—then the prospect of imminent defeat would of course spark some sort of psychological short-circuit. The maxim "fake it 'til you make it" can only take a person so far; at some point you have to stop faking and come up with the goods. She couldn't, and ended up twisting herself into knots trying to avoid the inevitable reckoning.

While some in our group denounced this woman's actions as a betrayal of our collective trust, I refused to pass judgment because I felt too much sympathy for her. I understood at least some of the pressure she felt. I too hated the job and wanted to quit, but couldn't—or wouldn't—because to do so would have been a humiliating admission of defeat. After all, I had signed up for the whole mess in order to impress Russ and prove to my parents that I could pay my own way through college. My ego would not allow me to quit, because I was convinced it was better to go down in flames trying—or at least appearing to try—than to admit that the whole project had been a colossal clusterfuck from the get-go. I too pretended to work harder than I really did, and though I did not fudge my receipts, I was not above lying to Russ and Dana and Jackie that I had sold more on a given day than I really had, just to save face.

The reason I didn't quit—the difference between me and the woman from BU, I'm convinced—was that I had Russ and Dana and Jackie on my side, all of whom were fighting their own demons and frustrations, and all of whom were there, every day, to bitch and kavetch with. We were a team, and we kept each other's spirits up in the most trying of circumstances. She, on the other hand, was alone. With no one to talk to who understood her plight, the depth of her despair must have been enormous. Had I been alone, I'm certain I never would have survived the summer. So, though what she did was preposterous in one sense, it was entirely understandable in another.

Again, I don't know what motivated her, or why she let the ruse continue for so long. For all I know she was a lying, scheming sociopath who had manipulated and deceived her way through high school and into college, but who miscalculated when she signed up to sell books, and had to devise a scheme to cover her lying ass. It's possible. After all, she lied to my face so many times—indeed, to everyone's face—so convincingly and so often that it seemed entirely natural. She was a fantastic liar, one of the best I've ever seen. And who knows, maybe she went on to have a stellar career in politics, public relations, or marketing—one of those fields that rewards people who have a loose relationship with the truth and gift for plausible bullshit.

Whatever truth lay at the heart of her story, it always struck me as sad and unfortunate. There is no shame in quitting a job you hate, and there is no honor in enduring a shitty work situation. In fact, recognizing such situations and extricating oneself as quickly as possible is excellent career advice in the long run. It's much better advice than the trudge-forward-in-the-face-of-ridiculous-absurdity nonsense peddled by the Southwestern Company—or, for that matter, any other corporate entity that needs compliant, non-questioning mules to carry the load. Invoking the suffering of Christ doesn't help, either. Convincing people that the demands and sacrifices of a lousy job are some sort of Christ-like test of character is just despicable. People who do it are manipulating people's faith in order to serve their own interests, and using a grotesque distortion of Jesus's teachings in order to justify their own greed and avarice. The suits at the Southwestern Company were (and still are) masters of this sort of spiritual bait-and-switch, equating faith in Jesus with fealty to the company, and invoking the specter of spiritual shame to bully impressionable college students into submission. The question they never allow anyone to ask is: What would have happened if Jesus walked away? Answer: He would have lived, and may have gone on to provide an entire lifetime of wise teachings sans the miracle madness of his popular legacy. Which could have benefitted us all.

So next time you find yourself in a horrible job situation with no apparent way out, my advice is to start working on your exit strategy immediately. Yes, a shitty job can build character—but it can also destroy one's inner resolve. The longer you stay in a job you hate, the worse you end up feeling about yourself, and the worse you feel about yourself, the more likely you are to do something stupid and irrational and self-destructive. Better to cut the cord and face the consequences than to hold on so tight that you get dragged through the mud.

Unless, of course, wallowing in the muck is your thing.

CHAPTER 34

The end of the book-selling, door-knocking, street-walking, sweet-talking, sweat-dripping, soul-killing, sell-til-the-sun-goes-down part of the summer called for a celebration. Russ and I thought it would be fun to go to a dive bar, get shit-faced and play some pool. Maybe a little foos ball. Video games were fun too, particularly "Pac Man" and "Asteroids."

Dana and Jackie didn't like that idea. They wanted to go dancing.

So we compromised—and went dancing.

In 1979, discotheques were hot, because the movie *Saturday Night Fever* was hot, and there is a great American tradition of mimicking life on the big screen in ways that simultaneously glorify and diminish the fantasy that people in messy reality are chasing. The trouble was, there were no discotheques in Davenport or Bettendorf. Go figure. Dana and Jackie had researched the matter and concluded that the best place in the Quad Cities to go dancing was across the river in Moline, Illinois. None of us had ever been to Moline, because not many people go to Moline by choice. Moline is the kind of place most people either drive through very quickly on the way to somewhere else, or live and die there without thinking about it too much. Because if you think too much about living in Moline, chances are you will end up wanting to live somewhere else. That's why people in Moline dance, because the alternative—doing nothing, ever—is too depressing to contemplate.

I jest, of course. Moline is probably a fine city. I wouldn't actually know, though, because the only place in Moline I've ever been is a discotheque somewhere near the edge of nowhere, on the outskirts of oblivion, a stone's-throw away from the sixth circle of hell, which Dante called "heresy." The dictionary definition of "heresy" is: "any belief or theory that is strongly at variance with established beliefs or customs." In many cultures, dancing is viewed as "fun," and often accompanies celebratory events—weddings, for instance—where the joy is so overwhelming that people cannot sit still. Unless they're Catholic, in which case they dance because their ass is numb from sitting so long on a hard wooden bench. Or Jewish, in which case they dance because that's what they've always done, and to do otherwise now would be, well . . . heresy.

I always hated dancing. When I was in seventh grade, my mother made me attend "cotillion"—an upper-class tradition that teaches socially awkward twelve-year-olds how to do the fox trot without staring down directly into a girl's breasts. The purpose of cotillion is to teach children the manners and etiquette they will need to mingle in high society, relieving them of the anxiety that comes with social ignorance. Unfortunately, all it did for me was ratchet up my social anxiety to the point where a simple dance with a girl became a nightmarish obstacle course of potential embarrassments.

Then I met Russ. And attended the University of Arizona, where "country swing" dancing was definitely a thing. And Russ, of course, was the country-swing king, having won the university's dance competition several years in a row.

Russ loved dancing. Even more than that, I think Russ loved the idea of teaching Dana to dance—which he had, on and off all summer long. Now it was time to take all that training to the dance floor. So Russ was 100-percent on-board with the idea of going dancing, because dancing was in his wheelhouse of skills. Besides, he argued, I had to brush up on my own country-swing moves if I wanted to have any chance of getting laid when we got back to school. And I believed him. During my freshman year I had already witnessed how the girls at school shunned guys who couldn't dance. I didn't want to be one of those guys. So reluctantly, against my better judgment, and in direct opposition to my true nature, I agreed that a little bit of dancing might not be the worst thing in the world.

Dana and Jackie insisted that we all wear the nicest clothes we had—because, you know, this was a celebration. Russ and I were dressed in khakis and Polo shirts, the official uniform of collegiate douchedom, and Dana and Jackie were each wearing the only dress they had brought for the summer. It was mid-August, and by nine o'clock the heat of the day was dissipating, which means it was still 85 degrees and ungodly humid. There is a theory that the reason the Midwest—particularly Iowa—is so humid in the summertime is because of all the corn. Farmers water the corn, the corn releases moisture into the air, and the heat turns it all to steam, creating the perfect meteorological recipe for pit-dripping misery. The "ungodly" part refers to the oppressive and omnipresent nature of all that heat and humidity combined. Such a combination should not exist in a world ruled by a kind and merciful god. Conclusion: Such a god does not exist; the world is actually ruled by some sort of sinister sauna king who delights in the misery of others, and who loves to crank it up every now and then just to see people suffer.

The city of Moline is only four miles away from Davenport, but it seemed like we drove for hours. This was back in pre-historic times when one couldn't simply ask Siri for directions. In order to find a place, you had to have an address, a paper map—and, if you were driving at night, a flashlight. Maps don't include addresses, however, so you had to first find the street, guess the right direction by the numbers on the houses, and drive until you reached your destination. Not all destinations have the address in numbers visible from the front, so it was possible to drive past your destination five or six times before realizing that something was amiss. If you were looking for a discotheque in a warehouse-y part of a town you didn't know—especially if it was the sort of place hip people just magically "knew" about—you could drive around for quite a while arguing about how you got lost, who was to blame, and how to get un-lost.

Somehow we eventually found the place. From the outside it looked like an old grain elevator or some other architectural cast-off from the agrarian past. Inside, it was all mirrors and lights, jagged reflections and swirling colors moving into and out of sync with the relentless pulse of 1970s-era disco music: Donna Summer, Diana Ross, Earth, Wind & Fire, the Pointer Sisters, the Ohio Players, Sister Sledge—all of whose songs seemed to blend together seamlessly on a cushion of thump, thump, thumping that never stopped, even for a second, lest the vibe somehow dissipate and, given a second to think, people might decide to go somewhere else.

Once we stepped inside, it took about a nanosecond to realize that we were the only white people in the place—and that we were severely underdressed. The clientele was all black, and if the invitation to this party had a dress code, it was something akin to "ostentatious," or "dazzling." Indeed, if white people "dress to impress," it seemed to us that black people "dress to amaze"—that is, wear clothes that strut every ounce of your stuff in blazing sartorial glory. The women wore gauzy, flouncy dresses made of material that seemed to move like liquid around them as they danced. Their shoes were bright and daring, shiny bursts of red and yellow with heels so long you could roast a marshmallow on them. Jewelry dangled from their ears like tiny chandeliers, their necks shimmered with gold and pearls. Even more attention went to their hair and makeup: eyelashes so long they blew a gentle wind every time someone blinked; makeup so thick you could eat it with a spoon; hair so big and hard you could bounce a bowling ball off it.

But it was the men who amazed me. Everywhere I looked, I saw guys dressed in exquisitely tailored suits hung on lean, muscular frames. I thought getting "dressed up" meant putting on a blazer and a tie, but these guys took it to a whole new level. They all seemed to be wearing trim three-piece suits with elegant vests and crisply creased trousers that flared ever so slightly at their feet, framing the sort of aggressively stylish patent-leather shoes worn by pimps (Love Train, for instance) and movie stars. Tufts of colored silk poked out of every vest pocket, and gold chains of various sizes dangled here and there, as if they were carrying half-a-dozen pocket watches apiece. Some men wore chains of gold around their necks, but most seemed to care more about their hands, which were perfectly manicured and decorated with rings so heavy and thick it was wonder they could lift their arms. Actual cufflinks and fold-back cuffs spoke to the expense of their shirts, and they all wore ties knotted as neatly and cleanly as Russ's exquisite double-Windsor, often accented with a gold and pearl-encrusted tie clip that held the knot in perfect symmetry with the shirt collar. Afros were already out by then, so most of these guys had short hair shellacked with some sort of shiny gel—and they all smelled . . . wonderful. Too wonderful, sometimes, as the "more is better" motto by which they dressed seemed to extend to the volume of cologne they were wearing. Then again, these guys were competing with a roomful of other people dressed to the nines and perfumed to the tens, so a little excess was understandable.

Despite the fact that we were a conspicuously caucasian presence in their world, no one gave us any dirty looks or suggested that we leave, though Russ and I both thought it might be better if we did. The regular patrons of this establishment all seemed amused by our presence, and strangely entertained by the fact that we had not yet run for the exit. The looks Russ and I got from the men suggested that they wouldn't hassle us as long as we didn't do anything stupid.

As soon as Russ realized that we'd at least be tolerated in this club, he did something quintessentially Russ-like and insisted that he and Dana start dancing. Dana wasn't sure it was such a great idea, but when Russ insists, it's hard to say no. They had been practicing, he argued, and now it was time to strut all that hard work on the dance floor.

Russ wasn't interested in just any kind of dancing, of course; he was interested in demonstrating championship-style country swing adapted for a disco beat. That meant lots of fancy moves and impressive spins. One move, called "The Pretzel," required an intricate and simultaneous twisting and turning of various body parts, any one of which could snap a finger or dislocate a shoulder. Done properly, however, The Pretzel is an undeniably impressive move.

Jackie wanted to dance too, and indicated that she and I should follow Russ and Dana. But at about the same moment I agreed to go out on the dance floor, I realized that the gurgling in my stomach had not gone away. It had started earlier in the evening, and for a while I had felt a bit queasy—I assumed from the start-stop-and-jerk style of Dana's driving. Sometimes, sitting in the back seat with her at the wheel was like sitting in the back of a garbage truck. She did not believe in smooth acceleration and deceleration; she believed in fast starts, quick stops, and lots of frantic lane-changing in between.

Anyway, I was suddenly and shamefully aware that a bout of diarrhea was coming, and that I had to make my way to a bathroom. Feeling exponentially sicker by the minute, my mind flashed on the large chicken burrito I'd had for dinner. It was inside me now, but soon wouldn't be, I feared. I apologized to Jackie and immediately mounted an urgent search for the nearest toilet.

For a place that big, the bathroom was ridiculously small. It only had one toilet stall, one urinal, and a small sink. Someone was already using the commode when I arrived, so I had no choice but to stand there, waiting, while my stomach churned, my intestines protested, and my mind reeled. Great, I thought, our big night out and I have to get food poisoning or some kind of stomach bug, in an all-black nightclub somewhere in Moline, Illinois, in a bathroom so small you could smell a fly fart. Then, as I waited, it began to dawn on me that I was getting nauseous and needed to throw up. What's worse, I wasn't sure what was going to come first, the puke or the purge. I was fairly sure things were going to start coming out of both ends, though, and there was nothing I could do about it. The guy in the john ahead of me was taking his time—my time!—so I leaned my head against the the wall and closed my eyes. As the seconds ticked by, I focused all my concentration on preventing my body from exploding out of every orifice. I could feel the bile in my throat rising, the swill in my gut worming its way down, the dread of my ultimate humiliation working its way to the surface. Soon—very soon—I would lose control, I knew. One can only override the body's demands for so long; in the end, the body does what the body is going to do, whether you like it or not.

Finally, at long last, the gentleman ahead of me finished his business—a very complicated transaction, judging from the time he spent on it—and I rushed into the vacated stall. I locked the door and eyed the toilet, trying to decide which path of egress—back or front—was more urgent. My body made the decision for me: immediately, I kneeled in front of the toilet and hurled. After several heaving waves of nausea I felt marginally better, if only because I had moved beyond the dread of puking to the actual act. The relief was short-lived. No sooner had I stopped throwing up than another insistent urge came at me from the other end. I fumbled at my belt buckle and pulled my pants down just in time. A violent gush of regret and disease came rushing out of me with such explosive force that I gripped the rim of the toilet bowl, fearful that some sort of bizarre diarrheal liftoff might propel me up to the ceiling. As it all came out, in wave after wave, I gritted my teeth and closed my eyes, hoping it would all be over soon, but knowing in my gut—quite literally—that I was going to be there for a while.

For a few moments I was able to dissolve into my sickness and forget where I was. As the initial attack on my intestines began to subside, however, I heard voices and realized that I was not alone.

"Oh man, that's nasty."

"They gotta get some windows in this place."

"That's some sick shit."

"Too much hooch?"

"Nah, like really sick."

"Hey man, you okay?"

It took a moment to realize the voice was talking to me. I grunted that I'd be fine in a minute, and apologized for any inconvenience I might be causing.

"That's okay, man. You do what you gotta do."

Five or ten minutes went by, but the situation on my end (pun more or less intended) did not improve. After each bout of gastric distress, another one immediately started to lock and load, making it impossible to even consider getting off the toilet. More people shuffled in and out. Some made a gagging noise and immediately left. Others stood in line to take a piss and discussed their disgust of the smells I as producing. Also, what those smells might mean.

"Dude's been in there a while."

"Is he still alive?"

"He might be passed out."

"Maybe we should call a doctor or an ambulance or something."

What struck me about the conversation outside the stall was how nice these guys were being about my situation. Some even thought it was funny, and most seemed genuinely concerned about my welfare. It took a while for me to realize it, but their biggest fear seemed to be the possibility that I might have overdosed on something, and that I might actually be dying. Hard drugs like heroin or cocaine simply didn't exist in my universe, so I assumed they were assuming that I was drunk. Unfortunately, their concern for me was a bit more urgent.

"We can't just let him die in there."

"I'm gonna call Joe."

"Yeah, I think we got a situation here."

It soon became apparent that a plan was forming to rescue me. Despite my protestations—I was sick, I told them, but it was just food poisoning—they seemed unconvinced. They'd never smelled anything so rank, and it seemed clear to them that at one point or another I was going to need a doctor's attention. I began imagining the worst: Soon, an ambulance would come and they were going to haul me away in a sea of flashing lights. A large crowd was going to gather in front of the club to find out what was going on, and soon my private shame would go public. News cameras would be there too, reporting on the white guy who commandeered the toilet in an all-black nightclub and had to be rushed to the nearest hospital. What had happened?, they would wonder, answering their own questions with pure, baseless speculation. Drugs would be part of the picture, certainly, as would race and class and the question of what the hell I was doing there in the first place? A bad burrito would not be part of the story—when, in fact, a bad burrito was the whole story.

Then I heard a voice I recognized. "Tad, you in here?"

"In here," I replied.

"That your friend?," a deeper voice asked.

"The guy seems pretty sick," another voice added.

"Talk to me. What's going on?" Russ asked.

"Bad burrito."

"Hershey squirts?"

"Yep."

"How bad?"

"Pretty bad."

"Bad enough that we should leave?"

"Bad enough that I need to leave."

"Okay. I'll have Dana bring the car around. Think you can make it?"

"I'll try."

Precisely how we got out of there, I don't recall. There was sudden motion, a flurry of apologies, faces, a blast of humid heat as we stepped outside, the receding pulse of disco music, Dana and Jackie waiting in the car for us out front, and, for me, an overwhelming sense of relief as we accelerated into the night. I apologized for ruining the evening, and thanked everyone for understanding how delicate my predicament had been. The only good thing about it was that I didn't have to dance. It was also the last time we tried to do anything "fun" together. For whatever reason that summer, fun and I did not seem to get along.

CHAPTER 35

The following morning, at breakfast, Russ and Dana were acting a bit strange. The night before had been an odyssey not soon forgotten, so I figured we were all decompressing a bit, trying to regain our bearings.

But that wasn't it.

After our breakfast came, Russ announced that he and Dana had some news they wanted to share with us. And that news was: "Dana and I are getting married."

It's hard to explain how shocking and bizarre and surreal this declaration was. How it happened is a mystery to me still, since Russ never talked to me about his true feelings for Dana. Clearly, they were stronger than mine. But I saw no hint of looming matrimony, no whiff of eternal love between them during our summer together. If anything, their relationship felt more like a brother/sister thing. Russ would tell her sick jokes, fart in front of her, and say crass things that he knew would get a rise out of her—and she would dutifully comply, telling him what a pig he was and how much his antics disgusted her. That she always laughed at him should have been my first clue. Only later in life have I come to appreciate the wisdom of marrying a fart-tolerant woman. Which makes sense. After all, marriage involves a lot of eating, so pairing up with someone who isn't all hung up on maintaining civil decorum at the other end of the digestive process can make life much easier.

We lived with Dana and Jackie for a total of about four weeks, and during that time became quite comfortable with each other's habits, both good and bad. Russ may have been impressed by how easy it was to spend so much time with these gals, and may have extrapolated that if he married one of them, the comfort and laughter could go on forever. Still, asking Dana to marry him was an insane proposition. After all, they were both going into their senior year, at colleges located thousands of miles apart. So at best it was going to be a long-distance relationship in the era before the internet, when long-distance phone calls cost twenty bucks an hour and it took the post office three days to deliver a letter. Not that those types of relationships can't sometimes pan out; they can, if lack of communication is a cornerstone of the relationship. But they usually work when not being able to communicate regularly with someone allows for enthusiastic fantasizing about what kind of person they really are. When you only interact with someone once a week via a hand-written letter, there's plenty of room for projecting one's wishes and desires onto that person. After a while the fantasies get wilder, the connection between the person to whom you are writing and the fantasy you have concocted grows increasingly distant, and pretty soon you're basically having a love affair with an ideal that no actual human could ever live up to. It's Narcissism 101—falling in love with a reflection/projection entirely of your own making.

With Dana, however, Russ had already removed the two most crucial elements of a successful long-distance romance: mystery and ignorance. He knew exactly who Dana was, because he'd spent every day for an entire summer with her. He'd seen her at her best, her worst, her most vulnerable, and her most human. Then again, maybe that's why he asked her to marry him—because after all that, he still liked her.

Even harder to understand than the fact that Russ asked Dana to marry him was that she accepted. She never provided an explanation. In fact, she refused to talk about it. Which was strange, because Dana liked to talk about everything.

After breakfast, I tried to get the truth out of Russ. "Dude, I know it's none of my business, but what the hell are you thinking?" I asked. He did not have much of an answer, either.

"She checks all the boxes: pretty, smart, sense of humor, good family," was his reasoning, near as I can recall. "And I figure if we can get through this, we can get through anything."

He didn't seem to recognize that "this"—bookselling in Iowa—was an adventure that took place entirely outside the context of our regular lives, and that once we all returned to college, much of the magic and camaraderie of the summer would naturally dissipate. He wanted to hold onto it somehow, and one way to do that was to hitch his heart to someone who had also seen him at his best and worst.

"What about our pact? You know, the one about not having sex with our roommates?"

"I haven't broken that pact," he insisted. "She won't have sex with me. Yet."

"But she will marry you?"

"Apparently. Go figure."

I never got a straight answer from Dana about why she had accepted Russ's marriage proposal. But I did get a strange proposal from her. At the end of the summer, during our final get-together with the few remaining students who had not quit, the drinks were flowing and everyone was comparing notes about future plans. Russ announced to the group that he and Dana were engaged, which received a dutiful round of applause and at least a few gasps of astonishment. I was not among those who were applauding, because I thought the whole thing was a big fat mistake. Part of me might have been jealous as well, because flirting with Dana was suddenly a lot less fun. She and I teased each other mercilessly, and now that she was engaged to Russ, things had immediately gotten weird and murky and complicated.

Sometime during the evening, while everyone else was congratulating Russ, I stepped outside to get some air. Actually, I went outside to stew in my own skepticism. While I loved both Russ and Dana, and wished them well if marriage was really what they wanted, I could not shake the feeling that both of them were making a hasty, ill-considered decision. I had decided, though, that it wasn't my responsibility to dissuade them, and that for the most part I should keep my doubts to myself.

Outside, on the front lawn, I stood alone, beer in hand, looking up at the stars. It had been a strange summer, to be sure, but the whole Russ/Dana marriage thing was in a whole separate category, improbable bordering on absurd. Russ and Dana were two years older than I was, however, and that much closer to "adulthood." Thoughts of marriage to anyone were a long way off for me, but maybe, I reasoned, that's the kind of thing one starts to think about toward the end of school. My own parents had gotten married immediately after graduating from college, so disaster wasn't a foregone conclusion. But still, my gut told me it wasn't going to work out.

I had been standing outside for a few minutes when the front door opened and someone came out. It was Dana. She was clearly drunk. As the music and laughter continued inside, she walked toward me, then stood in front of me and put her arms around my neck. Looking up at me, eyes at half mast, she said, "Kiss me."

"It's a little late for that, isn't it?" I replied.

"Not *too* late," she said, coquettishly.

"But your future husband is thirty feet away, telling everyone how happy he is that you two are going to raise children and grow old together."

"And he can't see us," she said slyly. "Come on, just one kiss."

"What are you doing, Dana?" I asked.

"I'm trying to get you to kiss me," she replied. "And I don't know why it's taking so long, because I know you want to."

Yes, I did want to kiss her. But at that particular moment, doing so would have meant betraying my best friend. It also meant taking advantage of a woman whose inclination toward indiscretion was fueled by liquor, not like or love or loneliness. And if, God forbid, she and Russ did manage to get married someday, the fact of my betrayal would be a dirty and uncomfortable secret between Dana and me forever. It wasn't worth it.

But Dana was strong and persistent. She pulled my face toward hers and, to avoid kissing her on the lips, I kissed her on the forehead.

"You missed," she said.

"I'm not going to kiss you."

"Yes you are," she said, and started tickling me.

"Stop it," I said, grabbing her wrists. "Let's go back inside."

"No, let's stay out here and kiss," she slurred.

"Why do you want to kiss me?" I asked her. "More to the point, why do you want to kiss me now?"

"Because you're here, I'm here, and it's nice outside, so why not?"

I could give her a million reasons why not, but the most salient one was inside, toasting his engagement to her with a plastic cup full of 3.2 beer.

"I can't kiss you," I said.

"Why not?"

"Because I am an extraordinary kisser," I said. "Possibly the best kisser you have ever known. And if I kiss you, the sheer blissful awesomeness of it will spoil every other kiss in your life. From now on you would be comparing my kiss to other kisses—the kisses, say, of your future husband—and they'd all come up woefully short, as they inevitably must. I can't do that to you, or to him. So no, I'm not going to kiss you."

"Now I really want to kiss you," she purred.

"Of course you do. Who wouldn't?" I said. "But now is not the time or place."

"Now is all we've got," she said, suddenly sounding like a soap-opera siren schooled in the art of romantic Zen.

We never did kiss. Russ and Dana's "engagement" lasted a month at most—long enough for old college routines to establish themselves and for the foolishness of the idea to sink in on both sides. Part of me wishes I had a less active conscience and fewer scruples, which would have allowed me to take advantage of the situation outside that party, when Dana was trying to figure out if she really, truly wanted to marry Russ. But I'm glad I didn't, because if I had, I would have lived the rest of my life wondering if I'd somehow had a hand in breaking them up. Avoiding that yoke of guilt was probably one of the smartest things I did that summer.

CHAPTER 36

As I mentioned a hundred some-odd pages ago, one of the most difficult things about selling books for the Southwestern Company was the initial sales proposition: If you give me money now as a down payment, Mrs. Jones, I promise to bring you the book you just bought in a month or two, at which point you can pay for the rest of it.

These days, I know, it is difficult to imagine anyone accepting a deal like that. But back in 1979, before everything in the world could be delivered to your doorstep in a day, the proposition was not quite as absurd. Expectations of instant gratification were not yet engrained in the collective psyche, so people were accustomed to waiting for things. Still, making them wait a month or two was stretching it.

Nevertheless, whenever we sold a *Volume Library* or set of children's books, our task was to extract as much money as possible at the point of sale, and the only evidence that the transaction took place was a pink receipt we gave them in lieu of the actual book itself. Trust was the biggest issue. And the battleground of trust was the amount a customer was willing to pay upfront for a book they may or may not receive in the distant future. If they trusted you completely, they'd give you 100% up front. But hardly anyone would agree to that, because deep inside their heads was a voice that told them they were fools to trust some smooth-talking kid who just showed up at their door twenty minutes ago. Then the negotiation would begin: Would they be willing to put down 50%? 25%? 10%? Some of the more confident and experienced sales people would take no less than 50%, period. But those of us who were desperate to record a sale would often dip into the 25/10% territory, if only to avoid the embarrassment of having nothing to show for our hard work. Occasionally, too, if someone was absolutely strapped for cash but really wanted the book—and you trusted them to pay you when the book was delivered—you might break down and agree to a zero down-payment with full payment due upon delivery.

The down payment, then, was really a negotiation of trust. But the trust went both ways. The higher the down payment on the front end, the more likely customers were to pay in full when the books were delivered. Why? Because they had already made a significant investment in it.

But—and first-year book people always find this out the hard way—the less money people put down on a book, the less likely they are to pay up the balance when the book is delivered. People who gave you no money down or a paltry 10% would often claim they had no idea what you were talking about when you showed up at the door to deliver their shiny new book—even if you showed them the receipt they had signed and reminded them of the wonderful conversation you'd had, and the fiduciary promise they'd made to you.

So, while on the front end it was easier to convince people to buy a *Volume Library* if you let them give you a small down payment, it was exponentially more difficult on the back end to receive payment in full.

According to Southwestern mythology, delivering those long-awaited books to our eager customers was supposed to be a joyous occasion. On the cusp of a new school year and hungry for knowledge, families with a new *Volume Library* in their midst were the happiest families of all. Having waited so long for their ticket to a better life, that ticket—an awesome educational tool that could enrich everyone in the family—had finally arrived! You, the angel who brought this miracle into their lives, were their savior. Flush with emotion, we were told to expect an overwhelming degree of appreciation and gratitude when we showed up at a customer's door to deliver this amazing gift. We could also expect to receive generous tips, we were told, because people are just nice that way. If they invited us in for dinner, we were told to decline—because every minute spent with that customer was a minute some other lucky family had to wait before experiencing the joy of cracking open a brand new *Volume Library*. (Note: That particular moment of satisfaction was sometimes tainted by the fact that when people opened up a new *Volume Library*, the binding did sometimes crack.)

Needless to say, like everything else, it rarely ever went down the way the suits in corporate described it.

Far from joyous, delivery week was, for us, absolute chaos. The logistics of it all were compounded by the fact that there were four of us living in one place, and we only had one car.

The way the system worked, each of us tallied all the books we had sold during the previous two and a half months, then sent in an order to the company. The company then shipped the requested number of books to us, which we had to store somewhere, then deliver.

Though it didn't always feel like it, the fact was: the four of us had sold a lot of books. So many books, in fact, that they began arriving on pallets from UPS. On a single day in mid-August, we received close to one-hundred boxes of books, and had nowhere to put them. No officially sanctioned place, that is. So, taking the route of least resistance, we decided that the owner of our mini-mansion—who was still in Europe, and had not informed us when he was going to return—wouldn't mind if we used all that empty space in his enormous living room to store all those books until we could deliver them all. It would only be for a few days, we told ourselves, and there weren't any other good options.

When the books arrived, we stacked the boxes in the living room as neatly as we could. But there were so many boxes that they ended up taking over half the living room. Stacked six feet high and several feet deep, the boxes created a formidable wall of cardboard. They were an eyesore, to be sure, but ours were the only eyes that could see them, so we told ourselves it was okay, because it was temporary. No one ever needed to know.

The maid, however, was not happy. When she saw what we were doing, she yelled at us in Spanish that we were "muy loco," and complained that she was going to have to clean it all up. She threatened to call the owner of the house and tell him what was going on. She also tried to throw us out, insisting that we had broken the rules of the house and had taken advantage of her kindness. Which was true. She had turned a blind eye to Russ and me staying in the house, and we had repaid her by invading her domain, which was the entire lower floor of the house. Hauling all those boxes up the stairs would have been a Sisyphian nightmare, though, so we had to put them somewhere on the first floor.

Eventually, we talked her down and agreed to stack as many of the boxes we could into a small vestibule off the main foyer. The rest we loaded into Dana's car or hauled upstairs.

A *Volume Library* was about the size of a large dictionary and weighed about five pounds. Only four of them fit into a box, so each box weighed twenty pounds or more. Each morning during delivery week, we hauled as many boxes as we could down from the house and into Dana's car. The plan, since we only had one vehicle, was to deliver the books territory by territory. Dana and Jackie's territory first, then Russ's and mine.

Problems with that plan arose right out of the gate. On the first day of deliveries, Dana and Jackie set off on their own, while Russ and I enjoyed a much-needed day off. When the girls returned in the evening, however, they did not look happy.

"No one's home," Dana complained.

"They're all on vacation or something," Jackie echoed. It was the middle of August, after all.

The company had not prepared us for this. According to Dana and Jackie, they had covered Dana's entire territory, but were only able to deliver about a third of her book orders. They'd circled back to homes that were empty during the day, but still couldn't find anyone home in the evening. This was bad, because in order to collect the money due to us, we had to get cash or a check from a live human being, preferably the same one who ordered the book in the first place. If no one was home, a book could not be delivered, and money could not be collected.

Most of the customers Dana did manage to locate were gracious enough to keep up their side of the bargain. But she had encountered the dilemma all of us would eventually face: customers who denied ever buying a book; customers who admitted that they'd ordered a book, but claimed they couldn't afford it now and wanted to cancel their order; customers whose spouses were not happy that their beloved had spent $79 on a book without them knowing about it; customers who said they'd never seen us before and were going to call the police; and finally, customers who had moved or otherwise disappeared, never to be seen again.

Delivery was supposed to be the easy part. You arrived with the book, the customer cheerfully handed you a check for the balance, and you went on your merry way. In practice, however, delivering books was turning out to be just as challenging as selling them in the first place.

The Southwestern Company did not care. The company insulated itself from any problems on our end by calling us "independent business operators," which basically meant "you're on your own." We bought our books for $39, sold them for $79, and pocketed $40 in profit—out of which we had to pay for rent, food, gas, licenses for solicitation, and everything else. The Southwestern Company got its $39 no matter what, off-loading all the risk onto its army of compliant college students. If we couldn't get full payment for a set of books, that was our problem. In the end, we could return books we ordered but weren't able to sell, but only if the boxes hadn't been opened. It reminded me of my days delivering newspapers as a young lad of thirteen. In that arrangement, I "bought" newspapers for a discount and "sold" them to customers at the full subscription rate. But it was up to me to collect all the money—by going door-to-door, asking for it—and if for some reason I couldn't collect the money owed to me, I had to absorb the loss, not the paper. The San Diego Union always got its money—again, by off-loading all the financial risk on the backs of teenagers who woke up at 4:30 a.m. to go deliver their precious scribblings. There were plenty of months delivering newspapers that I had customers move on me without paying, refuse to answer the door, or otherwise neglect to pay their bill. (I used to think: Oh, this is how people get rich—by reneging on all of their responsibilities!) It always struck me as a particularly disgusting and feckless way to run a business. Cowardly, cruel, and amoral, too. I mean, what kind of business takes advantage of teenagers who are trying to scrape up some spending money by delivering newspapers?

And yet, here I was working again for precisely that kind of company. Why? Because I was the ideal victim for these types of companies: someone who is ambitious, energetic, and trusting; someone who believes in the ethic of hard work; someone who perseveres in the face of adversity; and someone who has absolutely no power to fight back if and when they get screwed.

Nevertheless, the economics of book-selling were what they were, and there was no getting around it. Until delivery week, we had all spent most of our up-front, down-payment money to survive. Whatever profit we earned from our summer of toil had to be collected in that final week, when all those people we received a down payment from—50%, 25%, 10%, nothing—had to be persuaded a second time that the books really were worth it.

Not everyone could be convinced. And for those people, I fantasized saying something like: "But you ordered the book and promised to pay for it upon delivery, Mrs. Jones. This is your signature right here on the receipt, isn't it? And here I am, delivering the book as promised. But now you're telling me you no longer want the book? That ordering it was a mistake in the first place, and your husband is mad at you for spending money you don't have? That's unfortunate, for a number of reasons. Technically speaking, what you're doing is breach of contract, of course. But I can see that you're not a technical person, so let me explain it to you in more down-to-earth, human terms. Do you realize what a monumental hassle it is for me if you decide, now, that you don't want that *Volume Library* you were so excited about just a few weeks ago? It means I have to schlep it back home, box it back up and mail it back to my company, at my own expense, on my own time. I realize you don't care about me, Mrs. Jones, or the trials and tribulations I have gone through this summer to make this amazing educational opportunity available to you—but Jesus Christ, you are really forcing me to question the essential goodness of humanity here, and if this goes on for much longer I am going to turn into a cynical, angry, vengeful little fuck who thinks that people with money, privilege, and an utter lack of moral character are trying to screw him at every turn? You wouldn't want that now, would you, Mrs. Jones? And by "that," I mean an army of disenfranchised young people who see through the hypocrisy of "the system," and after trying to work in good faith within that system discover that it is rigged against them—by capitalists who don't care about the people upon whose backs they profit; by sociopaths who will do whatever they have to in order to get ahead; by narcissists who only care about themselves; and by half-witted housewives who make promises they don't intend to keep! Please, oh please, don't turn me into one of those people! Please, just cough up the extra forty bucks you owe me, take your goddamn book, and go enjoy the ineffable pleasures of learning. Don't fight me on this. Because if I were another type of person—even angrier, and less morally grounded—I might want to seek retribution in some other way. Some devious, evil way that you might not appreciate. Property damage can be expensive, after all, and your nice little bass boat is parked right there in the driveway. Anyone could just walk up in the middle of the night and set it on fire, for instance, and there'd be nothing you could do about it. You should park your car in the garage, too, because when it's sitting on the street like that, anyone could come by and jab a switchblade into your Firestones, causing a hassle all around. Also, I'm not sure how that nice new paint job on your porch would respond to a few gallons of spilled bleach. Which is to say, I hope you sprung for high-quality paint, because any number of substances—tar, anti-freeze, battery acid, motor oil, dog urine, Kool-Aid, hydrogen peroxide, fountain-pen ink, egg goo, spray paint—could potentially undo all that hard work. I'm not saying that's going to happen, mind you—I'm just saying that if you don't pay me, and it did happen, you'd have no one but yourself to blame. Have you heard of karma? It's a concept of social and spiritual justice that many people believe in. The basic idea is that if you are a good person with good intentions who treats people with kindness and respect, good things will happen for you in the future—if not in this life, in the next one. On the other hand, if you are a bad person with bad intentions, who does bad things that hurt other people, bad things will eventually happen to you. Why? Because the universe hates shitty people. The trouble with karma, of course, is that the spiritual payback it promises often takes a few lifetimes to kick in. You might be a horrible person in this life, and in the next life you may be reborn as a grubworm or an armadillo. Which is fine, in the cosmic sense. But in order for karmic justice to work in the here and now, it often needs a nudge. A little help. Karma needs caretakers. Caretakers of karma sometimes take things into our own hands, because some people need to experience karmic payback immediately in order to get the point. Do you see what I'm getting at? What I'm trying to say here is that you have an opportunity to send either a good ripple of karma throughout the universe, or a bad one. But you have to make a choice about whether to pay me or not. Pay me, and your karma is likely golden. Don't, and I can't promise that karma won't come around and bite you in the ass very soon in this life. It's your choice, of course. No one is trying to make you do anything you don't want to do. I'm just explaining what the consequences of your actions might be, in case you haven't quite thought it through. That's one of the advantages of having a *Volume Library* in your home, of course—it gives you the intellectual tools to think about these things in a more constructive, realistic way. So what do you say?"

That's the kind of vindictive rant that went through my head dozens of times a day during delivery week. But more often than not we did not even get to confront the people who ditched us, either because, as Dana had said, they were either on vacation, or moved, or wouldn't answer the door when we came to their house. Over the course of a week and a half, we would circle back to these deadbeats three or four times, at all hours of the day, in hopes of finding them at home. Because, as I explained before, if we couldn't get an actual human being to give us cash or write a check for the balance they owed us, we got no money.

On paper, after paying the company, I should have been able to collect about $3,200 from the number of books I had sold. My goal for the summer was to make $3,000 so that I could return to school, pay my own tuition, and have enough pocket money left over to enjoy life for a change. When all was said and done, however, my profit for the summer only amounted to about $1,700. Not bad, but not nearly as much as I hoped or expected. Still, it was money in my pocket—except that it wasn't money yet, because mostly what I had was an envelope full of uncashed checks.

In the old days, before ATM machines were invented, if someone wrote you a check, the only way to cash it was to deposit it into your own bank account and wait a day or two for the transaction to be recorded, or go directly to the bank that issued the check and cash it there. Since none of us had a bank account in Davenport, the only way any of us was going to walk away with actual money in our pockets was to go around to every bank in town and cash our checks in person.

To do this efficiently, we all four divvied up our checks by bank and spent an entire day going from bank to bank, cashing checks. At each bank, we presented the checks written to us by various customers and walked out with a wad of cash—a few hundred-dollar bills, but mostly twenties and tens. A few checks bounced, but we didn't have time to go back to those customers to get a new check, so we wrote them off as yet another loss among many. At the end of the day it didn't matter though, because we all had bank satchels full of cash and were feeling so flush and full of ourselves that the only thing left to do was to celebrate.

The only logical place to celebrate was back at the diner where it all started, where we'd met Madge and Love Train, the unimaginably odd pair of locals who had welcomed us to Davenport and helped us in those first fraught days of panic and despair. Since then, we'd survived so many misadventures and humiliations and heartbreaks that it seemed like years had passed since we last set foot in the diner on that fateful day just two-and-a-half months prior. But we had survived. The four of us, working as a team, had managed to outlast almost everyone in the book-selling business who had started with us. More than three-hundred college students had begun the summer with ambitions similar to ours, working in small to mid-sized towns all over the Midwest, trying to make enough money to get through another year of college. Only a handful remained at the end, so we were justifiably proud of ourselves for not quitting, as so many had, and for supporting each other through thick and thin without tearing each other to pieces.

The camaraderie of that summer was extraordinary, to be sure. We had all experienced stratospheric highs and catastrophic lows, moments when we wanted to quit or, more often, periods where we just didn't care anymore and couldn't muster the energy or drive to continue. Whenever anyone was down, the rest of us worked together to bring them back up, to vanquish the "doubt and fear" alluded to in the the Bookman Song and restore their faith in, if nothing else, our collective ability to deal with any raging shit-storm of nonsense that the world threw at us.

And here we were, with satchels full of cash, high on victory, getting ready to go back to school with a giant notch cut deep into the belt of our own personal accomplishments. Along the way we'd gathered a great deal of street savvy as well. There was no way we were going to downtown Davenport carrying thousands of dollars in cash. So we each grabbed a twenty out of our stash and hid the rest in the house. To be safe, I slipped my money into a seam at the bottom of my backpack, so that even if someone did go rummaging through my stuff, they wouldn't be able to see it.

When we arrived at the diner, Madge didn't recognize us at first. When she'd met us, we were two guys alone in the world; now we were two guys accompanied by two attractive women, and we weren't hauling backpacks or conspicuously red sales cases with us, either. We reminded her who we were, and her eyes lit up.

"I've been worried about you boys!" she exclaimed as she poured us all glasses of water.

We assured her that we were fine, and thanked her again for helping us out at the beginning of our adventure. We introduced her to Dana and Jackie as our "angel savior," the only person other than Love Train who had helped us when the chips were down and everything seemed hopeless. She blushed and said, "I always knew you boys would land on your feet."

We asked about Love Train, but she said she hadn't seen him in weeks. He'd asked about us once or twice, she said, but had disappeared for the time being, an occurrence that was entirely consistent with his character, she said, because "no one knows what goes on in that man's head."

Shortly after our food arrived, Dana posed the question: "So, knowing what you know now, would you consider selling books again next summer?"

"No way in hell," I immediately responded.

Dana agreed that for her, selling books was a "been there, done that" situation, and that she would not consider returning. Like Russ, she was heading into her senior year and anticipated graduating and getting a real job, one with an air-conditioned office and bathrooms accessible at any hour of the day.

Jackie surprised us by saying that she wasn't sure, but she might consider it—if nothing better came up in the way of summer employment for her the following year.

Russ was last to answer. I assumed he felt the same way as me, but he allowed as how Mike had already tried to recruit him to come back next summer, and that he was considering it. Yes, he was graduating and could get a different job, but he had been offered something higher up the Southwestern food chain, something that included recruitment, management training, and more money. He hadn't made a decision yet, he said, but now that he had one summer under his belt, he felt like he could really "kick some ass" next summer.

I was gobsmacked. The only reason I was even there was because of Russ. And now that he was entertaining the idea of an encore next summer, I knew he was going to start pressuring me to join him. Because we were a team. Because the only reason we had survived is because we'd stuck together. Without me, could he even do it? Maybe. But I did not want to find out. I knew unequivocally in my heart that I was never going to subject myself to this kind of torture again, even though in hindsight it was easier to remember the good moments than dwell on the many agonies and tribulations that had characterized most of my days in the book field.

Russ could feel my apprehension, I think. "But I don't have to make that decision yet, so I'm not going to," he said with a smile. I was relieved, because I was in no shape to have that discussion yet. I wanted to celebrate our victory, not strategize ways to make myself miserable again.

CHAPTER 37

After dinner, we went home to pack. The next day, we were scheduled to hit the road. Protocol demanded that we head back to Nashville to return books we'd been unable to deliver and settle accounts with the Southwestern Company. After that, we'd be heading our separate ways.

The following morning was bittersweet. Our district manager Mike had arrived close to dawn to make sure we weren't dawdling. As usual, the meetings in Nashville were scheduled in a way that made everything seem like a rush. And just as usual, Mike's primary function was to ratchet up the tension until everyone was pissed at him. It was an eight-hour drive from Davenport to Nashville (seven if you didn't stop for lunch or bathroom breaks) and Mike wanted us there by mid-afternoon so that we could get processed and be on our way. That meant wrapping things up in Davenport and hitting the road as soon as possible.

But packing was no picnic. Besides our personal stuff—four backpacks and a few souvenirs we'd collected along the way—we also had several dozen unsold books to return. Dana's car had a large trunk, but not large enough for everything. So backpacks and as many books as possible went into the trunk; Mike took the rest of the unsold books in his car.

Before we left, we each decided to grab a ten-dollar bill out of our cash stash for gas and food on the way. Also, Mike needed to see our money to make sure that we'd cashed all our checks and were ready to go through the de-briefing process in Nashville. I dug my satchel out—a bright red bank pouch with a fat brass zipper—and showed it to Mike.

"Nice work," he said. "You be careful with that now. If I were you, I wouldn't let that bag out of my sight until you get to Nashville." I assured him that I wouldn't, and we shook hands. Mike looked at everyone else's satchel of cash and mumbled his approval, no doubt because a portion of it was going to him in the form of a commission. Whether he wanted to admit it or not, we four were his big success story of the summer. He had been against Russ and me hooking up with Dana and Jackie in the beginning, because he thought we might distract each other from the important business at hand. But almost everyone else had dropped out on him, calling his leadership skills into question. The fact that we had all four survived the summer was evidence that he wasn't an entirely worthless manager, though in reality he was about as close to worthless as a human being can get. The truth was, he had nothing to do with our eventual success, and had opposed all the decisions on our part that had made our success possible. In fact, if you had to identify a formula for our eventual triumph that summer, it would have been: We did the opposite of whatever Mike said.

Then it was time to leave. "Time to saddle and ride, troops," Mike declared in his peculiar Southern drawl. For close to three months, Davenport had been both our home and office. We hadn't been there long, but we'd knocked on pretty much every door in the city, so we felt like we knew it better than most of the people who lived there. None of us liked it much, so we weren't particularly sad to leave, but departures of any kind are always muted by melancholy, if only because they remind us that the moments leading up to goodbye are over. Having shared this strange experience with each other, we were all headed back to school with a store of secrets and stories that virtually no one else in the world would understand—or, in some cases, even believe. Russ and I were headed back to the same school, and would be living in the same fraternity, but we too had experienced entirely different realities in the book field. He had experienced much more success than I had, and was seriously considering coming back the following year. I was going to put the whole experience behind me and go apply what I'd learned to whatever future lay ahead of me. I did not need to do it again.

It was about 10 a.m. when we eased onto I-74 going south toward Nashville. Mike had wanted to be on the road by 8 a.m., and had jetted ahead of us as if he were daring us to keep up. With Davenport receding in the rear-view mirror, Russ started singing the Bookman Song and we all joined in. For once, the line, "It's a great day to be a bookman, and be of good cheer," was accurate. Our collective mood that morning was somewhere between buoyant and ecstatic. The summer was over, we had all succeeded in our own way, and all we had to do now was drive all day with the windows open and the radio blaring. It felt the way freedom is supposed to feel—light, expansive, and open. The air was charged with possibility, with that heady feeling that life is there for the taking, and all you have to do is grab it. A twinge of melancholy made the moment that much more poignant. We had all been through an extraordinary adventure together, and now the adventure was over. What lay ahead of us all now was a return to our regularly scheduled lives: school, career, marriage, kids; the whole looming specter of adulthood. None of us knew where our individual paths would take us, only that for a few months in the summer of 1979, our paths had crossed in the most extraordinary of ways, and we had shared an adventure unlike any other. No one outside our tiny confederacy could ever understand what we had gone through, much less the ambivalent mix of emotions our undertaking had instilled in us—the stratospheric highs, the subterranean lows, the peculiar blend of hope and despair that characterized so many of our days walking around the neighborhoods of Davenport looking for a friendly face. It was all so wonderful and weird. Fate had thrown us all together, and by some odd miracle we had managed to stay together, through thick and thin, under circumstances that had overwhelmed so many others. I certainly felt fortunate (the Southwestern executives would have said "blessed"), because I knew there was no way I would have survived the summer without them.

A few miles south of the Quad Cities, I reached for the bright-red bank satchel that held all my earnings for the summer: $1,700, in cash. I wanted to look at it, to re-count it, to feel it—because there's nothing quite like looking at a fat stack of cash that's yours, that you earned, and that you are now free to spend any way you choose. I was going to buy a new stereo system and lots of vinyl records. I was going to take women on real dates to nice restaurants. I was going to enjoy having enough money to, well, enjoy things—concerts at school, new clothes, Orange Julius's whenever I wanted them: the possibilities were endless.

I reached down between my feet to grab the satchel, but . . . it wasn't there. I patted the seat on either side of me, but it wasn't there, either. Panicked, I scanned the entire back seat, but no satchel. I knew I hadn't put the satchel back in the trunk, because I had made a mental note to keep it close to me at all times. Then I had terrible, awful, sickening realization: When I was showing the money to Mike and took a ten-dollar bill out to pay for gas and food along the way, I had briefly placed the satchel on top of the car. I jutted my hand out the window and felt around on the roof of the car. Nothing. We were going seventy miles an hour, though, so what did I expect?

"Turn back. We have to turn back," I blurted.

"What's wrong?" Russ asked.

"My money. I think I left it on top of the car."

"You have got to be fucking kidding me."

"No way," Jackie said.

"It's not here, I'm telling you. Maybe it's in the trunk, I don't know. But I have to find it or I'm going to puke," I pleaded.

Russ instructed Dana to pull over. We looked through every corner of the trunk and everywhere in the car—under the seats, in all the side crevices—but the satchel was nowhere to be found. My brain was starting to fritz, and Russ could see it.

"Okay, look, if you did leave it on top of the car, it had to have fallen off somewhere between here and the house, probably the first time we made a turn," Russ reasoned. "The most logical thing to do is go back to where we started and retrace our route."

Everyone agreed. Dana got off at the next exit and we turned around, back toward Davenport, back to the beginning. We'd only been on the freeway for about ten minutes, and away from the house for about twenty. Hoping against hope, and praying—yes, praying—that the forces of the universe had not decided to punish me in such a brutal and humiliating way, I scanned the other side of the freeway for flashes of red, in case my summer profits had somehow remained on the roof until we picked up speed on the freeway.

No such luck.

When we arrived back at the house, there was no sign of my bank satchel. We retraced the route we had taken out of town, but couldn't find it. We went back and forth a couple of times between the house and the exit out of town, but my money was nowhere to be found. Slowly, the sickening reality of my situation began to sink in. The house where we'd been staying, while grand in its way, was actually situated in a fairly sketchy area, on the edge of the sort of neighborhood where outsiders get warned to leave, if they know what's good for them. For the better part of an hour, $1,700 in cash had been lying on the ground somewhere in that neighborhood, in a bright red bank pouch that screamed "notice me!"

After re-tracing our route several times, it became more apparent with each futile pass that the money was gone. We were in a bind, though, because we had to get back on the road to Nashville.

"We should at least report it to the police," Dana suggested.

"Maybe someone found it and turned it in," Jackie offered.

"Not likely," I said.

"Still. What else can we do?"

When I explained to the officer taking my statement that I'd lost a bright-red bank pouch with $1,700 in it, and where, he laughed. Not an amused chuckle, mind you, but a full-throated belly laugh triggered by what he saw as the absurdity of thinking that there might be a possibility, however slim, of recovering the money; funnier still, of thinking—hoping—that some good Samaritan with a heart of gold might waltz through the door and hand it over.

Then he got real: "Son, I'm not going to lie. Chances are, your money is gone. Chalk it up to a lesson learned. Leaving large quantities of cash on the roof of your car is never a good idea," he said, barely able to contain his mirth. "Look on the bright side. You probably made some kid's day."

The optimist's creed: Look on the bright side.

There was no bright side, as far as I was concerned, only clouds and darkness. My entire summer had gone up in smoke, just like that. All that training and work, for nothing. All that fear, heartache, despair, and suffering, for nothing. I was going to return to school with nothing—*nothing*—to show for my efforts. And the story of how I arrived at this terrible state of nothingness would make me a laughingstock, the butt of a thousand jokes. Far from feeling a sense of pride at accomplishing the near impossible, what I now faced for the rest of my life was a kind of bottomless dread. How could this happen to me?, I wondered. Is it possible that I am the unluckiest person in the world? And that no matter how hard I try—at anything—the cosmic deck is stacked against me? From here on out, every time I experience even a modicum of success, will the rug of fate be pulled out from under me? And if so, what is the point of striving? (Later in college, I was of course drawn to the writings of Boethius, author of *The Consolation of Philosophy*, who wrote that our lives are largely guided by the bitch-goddess Fortuna, a capricious manipulator of people's destinies who, depending on her mood, could either steer someone's life toward the great and good, or crash it on a pile of rocks just for the fun of it.)

Then, just as I was beginning to move past my rage and lean into some acceptance of my fate, Russ offered an olive branch of hope.

"I'll bet Mike has your money," he said. "In fact, now that I think about it, this whole thing has Mike written all over it. He's the guy who told you to 'be careful' with your money, after all. It would be just like him to take it, just to fuck with you. To teach you some messed-up lesson about paying attention, in case some inconsiderate asshole decides it would be funny to steal your money and make you think you lost it. I'll bet he has it in his car, and he's going to give it back to you in Nashville. It's the only thing that makes sense."

He was right! It did make sense! Mike was always doing stupid shit like that just to needle us. And what better way to get under my skin than to make me think I had lost all my money? After he had warned me? And while we were getting ready to go, didn't he suddenly have the urge to take off, to get going ahead of us? That would make a lot more sense if he had taken my money and wanted to get on the road before I noticed. The joke would only work if I spent a while stewing on the possibility of losing it all. In my mind's eye I could see him handing over the bank pouch when we stopped for lunch. He'd smirk at me for allowing him to pull a stunt like that, and imply that I was stupid for trusting an asshole like him, even for a second. The more I thought about it, the more I became convinced that the whole sorry episode had to be the work of Mike's deranged brain. And to top it off, when he gave my money back he'd say something insanely self-congratulatory, like "You should thank me, because now you'll never lose anything again by leaving it on top of your car."

There were no cellphones in 1979, so there was no way to call Mike and let him know that we were on to him. By now he was at least an hour ahead of us; all we could do was get to Nashville as quickly as possible ourselves.

For the next eight hours, I seethed at Mike and plotted various revenge scenarios. I imagined punching him in the face, sticking his head in a toilet bowl, burning his car, stealing *his* money and tossing it into the burning car, but only after switching out the real money for a duffel bag full of paper—to make him *think* I had burned it!

But somewhere along the way I realized that an angry, insane outburst like that was precisely what he was hoping for, so that he could laugh at me for taking the whole thing so seriously. Getting angry at him would be an admission that he had fooled me, that he had gotten under my skin. I wasn't going to give him that satisfaction. No, I was going to pretend everything was cool, and when he gave me my money back I was going to look him in the face and say, "Seriously, you're going to have to do better than that if you want to fool me."

It was the only way to one-up him and regain my dignity.

Late in the afternoon, as the outskirts of Nashville rolled by in a seemingly endless array of options for those in need of fast food and auto repair, I braced for the encounter to come. We were supposed to meet Mike at the Southwestern Company's headquarters, where we'd finish up our paperwork, settle our accounts—and, though we didn't know it yet, get pressured like crazy to return the following summer.

When we pulled into the parking lot, Mike's car was already there. He was waiting for us in the lobby, and when he saw us, he started yelling. "Where the fuck have you guys been!? I was about to send out a search party. We're, like, two hours behind schedule." He looked genuinely pissed.

I gave him a few moments to dramatize the gravity of the situation, figuring it was all just a theatrical preamble to his golden moment—the moment he handed me my "lost" bank pouch and chided me for being such a gullible fuck-up.

But the moment never came. We told him what we thought had happened, and how we had gone back to look for the money—something he should have understood and anticipated, because he was the one who stole it, making it necessary to go back and look for it in the first place!

He looked at us like we were crazy. "I hate to burst your bubble, but I don't have your money," he said.

What?

"You've got to be fucking kidding me," he added, exasperated. "I told you to be careful! I told you not to let that money out of your sight! How could this happen! This is not good. Not good at all!"

And just like that, the thin thread of hope to which I had been clinging for the past eight hours . . . snapped.

CHAPTER 38

Long story short, I never found the money. It did not magically materialize out of nowhere in one of those "I could have sworn I looked there" moments. No call from the Davenport police ever came. The money was just gone. Lost. Forever. And with it went any tangible evidence that I had done anything worthwhile over the summer.

It's hard to think of a worse way to make absolutely no money in a summer job than door-to-door book sales. The money was everything. It was redemption, proof to people who thought I was crazy for selling books in the first place—particularly friends and parents—that there was a method to my madness, and that their skepticism was misplaced. With $1,700 in my fist, I could shake my bounty at the doubters and dismiss their negativity as the product of small-minded people who sneer at those who take radical risks even as they secretly admire them. With no money to show for my efforts, though, their skepticism was validated. The "nattering nabobs of negativism," as *New York Times* columnist William Safire once called them, could shake their heads and tsk-tsk me and tell me they told me so. They could congratulate themselves for not being as stupid as me, and for not allowing themselves to get into the sort of position I had put myself in. The money would have made me the triumphant hero of my own story; the lack of it—and the way I lost it—made me a laughingstock.

As it turned out, most of the end-of-summer "processing" at Southwestern headquarters happened the following day. Students from all over the country milled around, trading war stories and plans for the upcoming school year. These were the successful book-sellers, mind you, the rare students who had made it through the summer and were now basking in the glory of a job well done. It was a fraternity of sorts, a brotherhood of men and women who had endured an extraordinary gauntlet of trials and tribulations to get where they were, and those experiences bound them together in much the same way "hell week" binds fraternity pledges together in a common bond. Everyone in that building had been through a "hell summer," and, having survived it, they were now free to enjoy that delicious illusion of superiority that overtakes people who think their suffering is a moral badge of honor. High-fives and fist bumps were the order of the day for returning veterans of the book field who already knew each other, and everyone was in a hyper-cheerful mood, as if the lyrics of the Bookman Song had been distilled into a drug and injected in their veins. Bragging about how much money they made was suddenly everyone's favorite sport. Rumors floated around about veritable demi-gods who had cracked the magical $10,000 barrier, and virtually everyone seemed to have made at least a few thousand dollars.

My $1,700, even if I had it, would not have impressed anyone in this crowd. Rather, I was in that pitiful cohort of people whose most laudable accomplishment was not quitting. As word of what had happened to me got around, however, I turned into something else—a pariah, an omen of bad luck, a sad ball-sack of a human being whose tragedy was so terrifying that people didn't even want to look me in the eye for fear they might catch whatever devilish contagion I carried. Others had suffered and endured, and that they understood. But I had been *devastated*. The worst thing in the world anyone in that building could possibly imagine had happened to me, and there was nothing anyone could say or do to make it better. So they said nothing, or mumbled something like, "Dude, that's harsh." The mood around me was funereal. I was the guy with the menacing cloud of financial death hanging over my head, the dark basement of doom in a house full of happiness and light.

No one wanted to get near me; it was too uncomfortable. And I didn't blame them, because I too felt like a part of me had died. I was in shock. How could this have happened?, I wondered. Did I somehow invite it? Did I subconsciously make it happen? Did I do something to deserve it? Or was I just the unwitting victim of chance? Of my own stupidity? I couldn't blame anyone else, after all. It was my doing. I had screwed up. And now I was going to have to deal with the consequences.

One of those consequences was that I ended up *owing* the company several hundred dollars to settle my account. Russ paid the balance on my behalf out of his earnings, mostly because he felt sorry for me, I think, but also because the company's bean-counters weren't going to let me leave the premises until their spreadsheet said I could.

The other consequence was a bit more amusing. Even before I had lost the money, I had decided there was no way I was going to sell books again. But a large part of the Southwestern de-briefing process was an aggressive hard-sell on the idea of returning—to improve on past results; to take advantage of everything you've already learned to make some *real* money in the future; to polish the sheen of your already amazing character; to fulfill the potential you know in your heart is still untapped; to strengthen your relationship with the Lord, who above all things wants his worshippers to sell a ton of marginally literate educational books, the kind with shitty bindings, shoddy research, out-of-date scientific data, questionable historical interpretations, and so many spelling and grammatical errors that you'd swear it was written by a bunch of drunken teenagers.

The funny part was that the Southwestern veterans had a script for this whole process, one they followed as faithfully as they did the tried-and-true book-selling script. Yet when applied to me, that script became self-evidently absurd.

"Tad, doesn't it feel good to have accomplished so many of your goals?"

No, nothing feels good at the moment.

"When you get back to school, Tad, how do you think people are going to react when they learn what you have done this summer?"

They are going to laugh, then drown me in pity. I will never hear the end of it.

"What are you going to do with all the money you have earned?" (The set-up question to: Just think how much money you could take back to school next summer.)

I am going to buy myself a cool glass of tapwater and drink it. Then I am going to take a long walk and cry.

"Be honest, Tad, aren't there a lot of things in the book field you'd do differently if you had the chance to do them over?"

Yes, I wouldn't have put my money on top of a car and driven away.

"And don't you owe yourself the opportunity to be the best salesperson you can be?"

I owe myself $1,700, that is all.

In order to get around the fact that they were talking to an emotionally crushed human being who had experienced something too horrific to fight with mere positivity, they even concocted the story of someone in the company *who had done the very same thing*—but, rather than give up, this courageous fellow had of course returned the following summer and become one of the company's top salespeople. Making up stories on the spot about fictitious people who have gone through similar experiences is a skill good salespeople develop in order to manufacture a false sense of empathy, which they then use to manipulate people into trusting them. I knew the game, and I wasn't playing.

"I want to talk to this person," I said.

"Well, he's no longer with the company. He's retired."

"You must have his contact information," I pressed. "I just want to talk to him, to ask him if it was worth it."

"He was one of our best."

"Really. What was his name? And when did he do his selling? The 1940s?"

"Look, the point is . . ."—the classic re-direct. Anytime a salesperson says, "the point is," it's because you've trapped them into a logical corner out of which they must now escape. It works because it suggests that they are in control of the conversation, and that you don't quite "get" what they're trying to tell you. All a salesperson is ever trying to do is sell you something, though, so chances are you "get it" perfectly well—so well that "the point is" they must now change the subject, lest you completely derail their sales pitch.

"Look, I'm going to save us both some time here," I said. "I will never sell your books again, under any circumstances." To which I added, in words more or less along these lines: "Not because selling door-to-door isn't a character-building experience—it is, or at least it can be. No, I will never sell Southwestern books again—particularly the *Volume Library*—because it is a horrible product. Most of the sections look like they've been slapped together from old textbooks, and much of the information—particularly in the sciences—is so out-dated that it verges on the comical. Besides which, this company's core values are based on coercion, manipulation, lies, and deception, all of it delivered with a smug, self-righteous smile. You know the smile I'm talking about; it's the one that you're giving me right now, the one where the corners of your mouth are turned up, but your eyes are dark little thunderclouds of fury. And why are you so angry? Because you are lying and we both know it, but you don't like the fact that I'm calling you on it. You will deny that you are lying, of course, but that doesn't change the truth. So tell me again, where can I find this mythical salesperson of yore with whom I can commiserate?"

I was lucky. They gave up on me relatively quickly, having concluded no doubt that even if I wasn't a completely lost cause, my attitude going forward was likely to be hostile and counter-productive. They were all about inspiration and positivity; I was, in that moment, about as negative as Nietzsche at a Bible convention. So no, I would not be selling their books again, and no, I would not be recommending the experience to others. They had failed me. I had failed them. And with so much failure in the air, what was the point of continuing? If I was going to be a failure in life, I'd rather fail doing anything else, anywhere else.

CHAPTER 39

The following morning, Russ, Dana, Jackie, and I said our goodbyes. It didn't take long. Dana and Jackie were driving back to Kansas together, and Russ and I had a plane to catch back to Tucson. (My parents paid for my ticket—a humiliating admission of defeat—and Russ paid for the cab to the airport.)

Strangely, there wasn't much to say. On some level we all realized that we'd shared a collection of unique experiences that most people would not understand or believe, and that talking about them now, at that moment, was a waste of time. The moment was too big for small talk, and too small to say anything of import that hadn't already been said.

"Well, that was interesting," Dana said, perfectly capturing the spirit of disbelief we all shared that the summer was finally over. Having endured so much in such a short amount of time, it seemed as if life from there on out would be a breeze. No test in college could possibly compare to the one we had just completed, and no future challenge would ever feel as insurmountable. All of us had been pushed to our physical and emotional limits, and we had learned that our individual reservoirs of grit and determination went much deeper than any of us could have imagined. I personally had no desire to dip further into my emotional reserves anytime soon, as I was still numb from the shock and dismay of losing all of my summer earnings. But knowing those reserves were there, somewhere, deep inside, ready to provide support and strength in cases of extreme emergency, provided a sense of comfort and confidence. If we could survive this, we thought, we could survive anything.

Now that it was over, though, we didn't quite know what to do with each other. There was also the open question about whether and to what extent we'd try to stay in touch after we all got back to our regular lives. There was no Facebook in 1979, so if you wanted to remain in contact with people you had to send letters back and forth, or spend money on long-distance phone calls.

Or marry them.

Russ and Dana's flash engagement was the giant flaming elephant in the room. They would of course be staying in contact with each other because, eventually, there would be a wedding to plan. Russ also wanted Dana to visit him in Arizona, so travel plans between them were being hastily made on the side. To Jackie and me, this felt like a betrayal of sorts. In order to survive the summer, we had all made a pact to remain in the "friend zone." Russ and Dana had violated that pact. It was understandable, and sort of cute, but their whole relationship was a mystery. Exactly when and how did they fall in love? Neither Jackie nor I had seen it coming. On the surface it always appeared that Dana thought Russ, despite his charms, was far too arrogant and disgusting for someone of her more refined tastes, more like an annoying big brother than a partner for life. Yet now she was going to marry him? And all summer long Russ had made it his mission to tease Dana mercilessly. Sometimes it was hilarious, yes, but at other times he clearly went too far, most often when he failed to read signs that she was not in the mood for his horseplay and shenanigans. There was also the inconvenient fact that they both had at least one more year of college to complete, and that meant managing a long-distance relationship during a period in American history when inter-state communication was neither instantaneous nor cheap.

But that was their problem.

Still, it meant that in all likelihood I too would be seeing Dana again at some point in the future. It was also tacitly understood that Jackie was not going to be invited to that party. Not that she wasn't a lovely person, just that the connective tissue between us was not strong enough to include Jackie. Back at school, Russ and I would be living in the same fraternity house. If Dana came to visit, I would of course see her. The connection was natural. If Jackie suddenly showed up, it would be entirely unnatural and forced, because our friendship had been a by-product of our circumstances. The bizarre dynamics of the book field had made it possible for us all to be friends. But outside the book field, we were an uncomfortable foursome, one made even more unwieldy by the fact that two of us were pairing off with each other, and the other two—Jackie and me—were not.

The parting was awkward, so we kept it brief. Promises to stay in touch were made, though deep down we knew they were probably empty. In fact, after that day I never heard from or communicated with Jackie ever again. I did see Dana, once, when she came to visit Russ in Arizona. But shortly after that visit she evidently came to her senses and broke the engagement off. I never saw or heard from her again, either.

Returning to school that year was difficult, to say the least. The triumphant narrative I had hoped to trumpet upon my return to school was muted by the fact that a) I had nothing to brag about, and b) contrary to the inspiring jibber-jabber of so many Southwestern executives, no one really cared what Russ and I had done during the summer. Our experience did not even top the list of "worst summer jobs" undertaken by our fellow fraternity members. That honor went to two brothers who spent the summer scraping up road kill on the highway between Tucson and Phoenix. The challenges of the book field could not compete with vivid descriptions of cow carcasses bloating and decomposing under the hot desert sun. Nor could our stories rise to the level of horror and disgust evoked by the terrible smell of a squashed and rotting skunk, or the dread of a seemingly dead rattlesnake suddenly writhing to life in the hands of an unsuspecting fraternity brother. There was also a guy who spent his summer in Texas climbing to the top of oil rigs and capping off methane fires, and another who hunted and killed wild pigs (javelina) in the desert around Tucson. Selling education books door to door did not carry quite the same swagger and machismo. Our tales of weariness and woe seemed silly by comparison.

Selling books door-to-door was supposed to be a character-building experience, and perhaps it was. A certain amount of adversity can certainly be character-building, but too much adversity can crush a person—and during that summer in Davenport, I came very close to being crushed. To the person who lives by the motto "no pain, no gain," an almost—but not quite—soul-crushing experience is just about right. To build muscle, one has to push the muscle to the point of fatigue—of failure—to tear down the muscle fibers so that they can rebuild themselves stronger than they were before. The danger lies in glorifying the "pain" part of the process to the point where the pain itself becomes a source of pleasure, and the people who enjoy punishing themselves thus begin to think it's a good idea to inflict their passion for pain on others.

When I agreed to sell books door-to-door in the summer of 1979, I wanted to test myself, to see how much adversity I could endure. I also wanted to make money and improve myself by following the lead of an older and presumably wiser person whom I admired and sought to emulate. I certainly succeeded in testing myself; unfortunately, I made no money and am not at all sure I improved as a human being. In fact, coming face to face with so much humanity in such a short time at such a young age made me quite skeptical of the human race's ability to rise above its own base nature. On the other hand, meeting people like Love Train and Madge and the Grim Reapers—and even Frank the Vietnam vet—opened my eyes to dimensions of human nature to which I was not previously aware. Who knew that underneath the flashy façade of a pimp would lie a strangely generous soul who loved to laugh, or that beneath the shell of menace, a motorcycle gang is just another group of people trying to make their way in a world where they do not quite fit in, and where loyalty and friendship and principle matter more than looks or brains or money?

In America, most people would rather hear a pretty lie than face the ugly truth. Indeed, the worlds of politics, advertising, entertainment, sales, marketing, public relations, and religion are all based on telling people what they want to hear, not what they ought to know. And there are millions of people out there who, despite their better instincts and all evidence to the contrary, end up believing that the person knocking on their door—or talking to them through the TV, or calling them on the phone, or yelling at them on the internet—is telling them the truth, promising a solution to all of their problems if they, the unwitting customer, will simply buy what the man with the golden words is selling.

Chances are the words are misleading, and the truth—whatever it is—lies elsewhere.

EPILOGUE

Over the years I have often wondered what happened to the $1,700 I lost on that soul-crushing day in Davenport. Where did it go? Who found it? What did they do with it? I'll never know. But in order to cope with the loss of all that money and most of my dignity and self-respect, I have imagined numerous scenarios, all of which end in a way that soothes my singed and skewered psyche. The stories I tell myself are a way of converting tragedy into triumph, of re-imagining what might happen in a world that truly is run by an omniscient puppet master whose moral logic is both infallible and inscrutable. They are a way of illustrating how faith *should* function in a world where all the pieces of the puzzle somehow fit together—a way of connecting the cosmic dots to satisfy the human yearning for explanation and evidence. Above all, the stories I tell myself are a way of exerting control over my own narrative, of transforming the bleakest day of my life into something a little less bleak—something close to redemption.

Here is one such story:

Jamal Tyrone Pearson was scared. It was 4:00 a.m. on a dark, moonless night, and he was biking home from his friend Billy's house, where things had not gone well. Not well at all. Billy had done stupid things before, but this time he had gone too far. He was out of control, and Jamal was afraid that when Billy got out of the hospital, he might do something genuinely awful—something his hot-headed friend would regret for the rest of his life.

The night before, Billy was already in a foul mood when Jamal came to the door, but he wouldn't say why. Jamal had seen that wild, unhinged look on Billy's face before. When Billy was really pissed off about something, he clenched and unclenched his jaw like he was chewing on a piece of rubber, and his eyes were deep and empty, as if he'd disappeared into a cave inside himself and refused to come out. When Jamal knocked on the door, Billy opened it and motioned with his head for Jamal to come in. Billy didn't say anything; he just plopped back down on the couch and stared at the TV. On the screen was a re-run of a stupid new show called *Fantasy Island*, about a crazy rich dude and his midget assistant who grant wishes to other rich people on a magical island where everyone's fantasies come true and all their problems get solved at the end of every episode. It was a rich person's show if there ever was one, thought Jamal—wish fulfillment for anyone who could afford it.

Jamal and Billy hung out for a while, watching TV and drinking a few beers and not saying much. But Jamal could tell that Billy was getting restless. His leg was shaking the whole time and he was constantly drumming his fingers on his knee, as if sitting still was painful and the only way he could keep from exploding was to keep some of his body parts moving.

At some point Billy decided he could take no more and turned off the TV.

"Let's get out of here," Billy said.

"Where to?" Jamal asked.

"Dunno. Just out."

Billy had a yellow Pontiac Firebird with a four-hundred horsepower V8 under the hood that he'd been working on for years. When it was running, the car was a monster, as loud and fast as a car could get without being completely illegal. And Billy drove it that way, peeling away from stop lights as fast as he could, turning corners like he was a stunt man in the *Dukes of Hazzard*, driving like the lunatic he was when beer and weed fogged his brain and there were no cops around. Jamal had feared for his life several times when Billy was behind the wheel, because there were times when Billy didn't seem to care if he lived or died. In fact, Billy seemed happiest when he was cheating death, when he was begging for fate to take a swipe at him. That's why he got into fights, why he stole stuff from 7-11, and why, now, he was driving toward the edge of town at an alarming speed, not talking, jaw clenched tight, eyes focused on the road ahead as if he were expecting his Firebird to suddenly grow wings and fly.

"Hey, slow down man, you're freaking me out," Jamal pleaded at one point. Billy responded by pushing the accelerator all the way to the floor.

"Gotta blow the carbon out," Billy said matter-of-factly.

Jamal knew where they were going. About two miles outside of town there was an abandoned barn where kids in their school went to drink and smoke pot and shoot .22s at bottles and cans lined up on an old, rotting log. From a distance, Jamal could see that a fire was already going outside, and, as they approached, the silhouettes of seven or eight people came into view.

Billy pulled up in a cloud of dust, making sure to let everyone know that he had arrived. Upon seeing him, one of the girls gathered around the fire abruptly got up and headed into the barn. Another girl—the only two there—followed her into the barn, while the rest of the crowd gathered around the fire just stood and watched. Billy ran past the fire watchers and into the barn after the girls. Jamal, worried about what Billy might do, followed him. When Jamal reached the barn door—on opening, really, because there was no actual door—he saw Billy yelling at one of the girls. Her name was Mary, and she and Billy had been dating, sort of, for a few months. Which is to say, she had been having sex with Billy since the beginning of summer, and had yet to realize how big a mistake that was. Billy had hit her before, Jamal knew, and was capable of worse.

Jamal kept his distance, but he saw what the argument was about: Mary was beginning to show, and Billy was angry that she hadn't yet gotten an abortion, and angrier still that she seemed to want to keep the baby. Mary didn't say anything; she just put her head in her hands and cried while Billy berated her, hands flailing, his skull bobbing up and down as if he were trying to hammer her into the ground with his forehead. Mary's friend Karina tried to persuade Billy to calm down, but when she stepped between him and Mary, Billy pushed her away.

"Look at me!" Billy commanded at one point. When Mary pulled her hands away from her face, Billy hit her with the back of his hand and kicked the bale of hay on which she was sitting.

"Dumb bitch," he spat as he strode out of the barn, past the gathering around the fire and back into his car. To let everyone know how mad he was, Billy did two donuts in the dirt, spraying gravel and dust everywhere, then fishtailed a couple of times and went barreling down the dirt road, away from the barn and into the darkness.

For a while, Jamal could see Billy's headlights bouncing around in the void as he drove away, and he could hear the roar of the Pontiac's V8 as Billy channeled his rage into the car's accelerator. On most nights, standing outside on a farm in Iowa is one of the most peaceful experiences one can imagine. But on this night, the vast expanse of solitude surrounding Jamal was pierced by the fading snarl of Billy's engine as he slammed through the gears and raced away. The night was so still that Jamal could still hear Billy's engine in the distance for several minutes, a cry of rage that refused to subside, a howl of animal indignation that reverberated through the darkness with an eerie hint of impending doom.

Then something happened: there was a pop, then a kind of crunching thud, followed by an otherworldly mechanical whine that blared at an alarmingly high pitch. Then nothing. Just silence, empty and terrifying. Jamal and at least two of the boys gathered around the fire realized instinctively that something bad had happened, but none of them seemed eager to investigate. They all hated Billy, and figured that whatever happened to him, he deserved it.

Jamal convinced one of the boys, Zack, to drive out and take a look, if only to make sure Billy wasn't dead. Another boy, Trevon, decided to tag along in case Billy was indeed dead, in which case he'd have an opportunity to see his first corpse.

The scene was horrific. Billy had apparently hit a deer, then veered off the road and smashed sideways into a telephone pole. The deer lay bloody and mangled on the side of the road, it's neck broken and legs askew. The sharp stench of scorched rubber and crushed metal hung heavy in the air like a warning, and one of the car's headlights shot a beam of light into a tall row of corn growing alongside the road. Lit this way, the stalks of ripe corn looked vaguely human, like a crowd of silent witnesses gathered to see what all the commotion was about.

Billy, still behind the wheel—he actually wore his seatbelt—didn't look much better than the deer he had killed. Blood poured from a wound in his forehead, and he too looked like he was dead. In fact, Jamal and his friends didn't know Billy was alive until they pulled him out of the car and laid him on the ground. He was still breathing, but barely, and there was so much blood that they weren't sure he could survive much longer. By the time they found a phone and called an ambulance, he'd be gone for sure, they figured, so the three boys picked Billy up and put him in the back seat of Zack's car.

"That fucker better not stain my seats," Zack declared as they hoisted Billy's limp and surprisingly heavy frame into the car.

On the way to the hospital, Billy floated in and out of consciousness. Nothing he said made any sense, but that was often the case even when Billy's brain was operating at full capacity, so the gibberish coming out of his mouth wasn't quite as alarming as it might have been otherwise. At the hospital, Billy's words began to sound more menacing. Sitting in a hospital bed, his head bandaged and an IV tube attached to his arm, Billy began muttering—then yelling—"Stupid bitch! I'm going to kill her! That fucking cunt is doing to die!"

Over and over again, Billy vowed to end Mary's life—for defying him, for making him angry, for causing him to total his car, for sending him to the hospital, for almost killing him—and to do it as soon has he could walk out of the hospital. Jamal was in the room when Billy started ranting, but soon left when it was apparent that Billy wasn't in his right mind, assuming he had one at all. Jamal sat in the waiting room with Zack and Trevon for a while, but from the reception area they could still hear Billy yelling, off and on, whenever a new wave of indignation overcame him. The doctors had tried to sedate him, but Billy's anger seemed to be no match for the meagre cocktail of Tramadol and morphine seeping into his veins.

At some point Billy did succumb to sleep, and all three of the boys—Jamal, Zack, and Trevon—agreed that they should leave the hospital. It was close to 3 a.m., and the night had not gone the way any of them had planned. They were all exhausted, and there was nothing more they could do. They had saved Billy's life, of that they were certain; whether they would live to regret it remained to be seen.

Zack dropped Jamal off at Billy's house to retrieve his bicycle. Zack offered to put the bike in his trunk and drive Jamal home, but Jamal declined. He liked to ride his bicycle around town late at night, especially when he was troubled and his mind was reeling, searching for answers to questions he never wanted to ask in the first place. On this night, Jamal had become increasingly concerned about what Billy might do to Mary when he got out of the hospital. Billy had made his intentions perfectly clear: He wanted to kill her. Immediately. Whether Billy would actually follow through on his threats was an open question. What scared Jamal most was his growing suspicion that Billy was entirely capable of murder, and that if he didn't do anything—if Jamal ignored the hot knot of dread in his stomach—Mary might soon be dead. And it would be his fault, because he saw it coming and did nothing.

Jamal did not sleep. Instead, he lay in bed trying to figure out how to warn Mary, and how to talk Billy down once he got released from the hospital. Jamal did not want to confront Billy, for fear that his angry friend might turn on him for getting in the way. But he couldn't allow Billy to get near Mary, either, because there was no telling what he might do to her.

At breakfast, Jamal's twelve-year-old little brother, Aaron, began peppering him with questions.

"Where'd you go last night?"

"What did you do?"

"How come there was blood on your shirt?"

"Did you get in a fight?"

"Who with?"

"Where?"

"Did you win?"

"Where did it happen?"

"Did he kick your ass? Because it sure looks like he did."

"Are you going to get him back?"

Jamal did not answer. "Shut up and eat," he said as he stared down into his own bowl of cereal, tired but still buzzed from the previous night's drama.

One thing Jamal had noticed about his younger brother was that over the past couple of weeks he'd started wearing clothes Jamal had never seen before. He'd also taken to wearing a pair of Ray-Ban sunglasses outside, which were expensive and not the sort of accessory one would expect a twelve-year-old to wear, which was precisely why Aaron liked them. According to Jamal's friends, in the past few weeks Aaron had also developed a habit of stopping at the local 7-11 every afternoon and buying his friends Slurpees, a conspicuous act of generosity that Jamal found highly suspicious.

"Hey, where did you get that shirt?" Jamal asked, changing the subject.

"It's Jimmy's. He gave it to me," Aaron replied.

"What about those sunglasses?"

"I found them."

"Where?"

"In the park."

"And how is it that you're suddenly so flush that you can afford to treat your friends to Slurpees every day?"

"Birthday money," Aaron replied.

"Your birthday was in April."

"I saved."

"Bullshit."

"I only did it a couple of times," Aaron protested.

"That's not what I heard."

"Whatever."

"You better not be getting mixed up in any of that street shit," Jamal warned.

"I'm not."

"Then where did you get the money?"

Aaron did not answer.

"I swear to god, A, if I find out you're into something stupid, I'm going to ring your scrawny little neck."

The truth is, Aaron was bursting to tell Jamal about the money; he just didn't know how. The secret was eating him alive. Finally, he caved and said, "If I tell you, will you promise not to tell anyone else?"

"That depends if I need to save your ass or not," Jamal replied.

"Just swear you won't rat me out."

"Okay. I swear."

At that, Aaron motioned for Jamal to follow him. They went upstairs into Aaron's bedroom, where Aaron closed the door and motioned for Jamal to sit on Aaron's bed. Aaron then got on his knees, reached inside his closet and pulled back a corner of the carpet. From underneath the carpet flap he pulled out a red cloth bank pouch with a large brass zipper on top. Aaron pulled the zipper open and handed the pouch to Jamal. Inside was a fat wad of cash almost two inches thick, mostly twenties, neatly stacked and bound with a rubber band.

"Where did you get this?" Jamal asked, alarmed.

"I found it in the street."

"How much is here?"

"About $1,700, more or less."

Jamal took the bills out of the pouch and riffled the stack with his thumb. "You know someone is going to come looking for this, right?"

Aaron nodded.

"And if they find out you have it, they're going to beat the shit out of you, or worse—right?"

Aaron cleared his throat. "That's what I thought too," he said. "But I've had it for two weeks, and nobody has said anything about it. There's no chatter on the street. Nothing. It's like someone lost it and forgot about it."

"Nothing?"

"No. And I swear, I only used a couple twenties. It's almost all still there."

Jamal put the money back in the pouch and zipped it shut. "Look, little man, I'm glad you told me. This is dangerous. You should not be hiding this much money in your room."

Aaron nodded that he understood, and he did. Every day since he'd found the money, he'd been a nervous wreck for fear that someone would hunt him down and kill him.

"Tell you what I'm going to do," Jamal said. "I'm going to take this and find a safe place to stash it. If anyone asks you about it, you don't know anything, okay?"

"Okay."

"And if anyone does ask about it, you tell me immediately, understood?"

"Sure. But when do I get it back?"

Jamal held the pouch in his right hand and pointed it at Aaron's face. "Look, I'm doing you a favor here. If I let you keep this, eventually you are going to go out and buy something you shouldn't, and people are going to get suspicious, wondering where you got the money. The smartest thing to do now is forget you ever found it, and hope whoever lost it is dead or in jail. Got it?"

"Uh huh."

"Good. Now get out of here."

"But this is my room," Aaron pointed out.

"Right," Jamal said, and stood up to leave. "Oh, and whatever you do, do not tell mom about this. This is our secret, so let's keep it that way."

Jamal went directly to his room and counted the money. As Aaron had said, the pouch contained more than $1,600 in small bills. It was probably drug money, Jamal thought, though he'd never heard of any drug dealers carrying cash in a bright red bank envelope. There were a few uncashed checks in the pouch as well, all made out to "The Southwestern Company," which was weird, and contradicted the drug-money theory. No drug dealers he knew accepted checks.

That and the fact that no one seemed to be looking for the money indicated to Jamal that maybe, just maybe, this was cash that could not—and would not—ever be traced by whoever lost it. Because if they could find it, wouldn't they have done so already?

Jamal thought for a while about what he should do with the money: where to hide it, and for how long. Six months? A year? Two years? He didn't know. Spending it anytime soon was of course out of the question. If Jamal were suddenly flush with cash, people would get suspicious of him too unless he confined his purchases to bubble gum or candy, which was pointless.

Then, in a sudden flash of clarity, Jamal knew exactly what he had to do with the money. It was risky, but it was also right, and in this case the rightness outweighed the risk.

Jamal immediately put the pouch in his backpack, strapped it on, hopped on his bike, and started riding toward Karina Pritzker's house. Karina was the girl who, the night before, had befriended and defended Mary from Billy's rage. Mary often escaped to Karina's when Billy lost his temper, and Jamal guessed that's where Mary was now. At the barn, before the crash, Billy had yelled at Mary and hit her, so she was likely licking her wounds at Karina's, frightened, wondering what to do next. Jamal liked Mary—he thought she was sweet and kind deep down—and he thought Billy had always been a jerk to her, something she did not need or deserve given that her life was already such a mess. Her father was in jail (for armed robbery, if Jamal remembered correctly), and her mother had succumbed to the twin evils of heroin and prostitution. Mary was caught in between, and had turned to Billy for some measure of security and affection, even though Billy could be relied upon to provide neither, preferring instead to rule Mary's life through fear and intimidation. If Mary had to be hit every now and then to keep her in line, so be it. Billy knew no other way to communicate. Though Billy was Jamal's friend, Jamal hated the way Billy mistreated Mary and so many other girls who had crossed his path over the years. At the moment, however, Jamal was concerned that Mary might not survive Billy's wrath if he got out of the hospital and found her. He didn't plan to let that happen, but his solution depended on Mary's willingness to believe that the father of her unborn child wanted them both dead.

It didn't take much to convince her. Mary was terrified of Billy, and wanted nothing to do with him anymore. At Karina's, Jamal found her in a borrowed bathrobe, curled up in a ball on the couch, eating Fruit Loops out of the box. Still shaken from the night before, Mary bit her lip and wept when she learned that Billy was still alive. She had secretly allowed herself to hope that her problems with Billy might be over after the crash. She didn't really want him dead—that would be mean—but she did want him out of her life, and the only way that could happen was if he disappeared somehow.

But there was another way, Jamal pointed out: What if *she* disappeared?

"Mary, you need to trust me. If you stay in Davenport, Billy will find you and hurt you," Jamal explained. "You need to get out of here. You need to go somewhere—anywhere—else and start a new life. There's nothing for you here, and if you stay, you'll be endangering both your own life as well and the life of your unborn baby."

Jamal unzipped his backpack and took out the bright-red bank pouch. "Don't ask where this money came from," Jamal said. "Just take it and use it to get out of here. Gather your things now and get to the bus station as fast as you can. Pick a place to go, somewhere far away where Billy can never find you, and use this money to get a fresh start. Do you understand what I'm saying?"

Mary nodded that yes, she understood, but refused to accept the money.

"I could never pay you back," she protested.

"You don't have to," Jamal said. "This isn't a loan, it's a gift. There's more than $1,600 in here, enough to keep you going for a while until you get on your feet. Use it, and don't look back."

Mary didn't know what to say. No one had ever done anything that nice for her before, and no one had ever expressed that much concern for her welfare. She didn't know if she could trust Jamal, either, since he was Billy's friend. He'd always been kind to her, and she had no particular reason to distrust him, but she still wasn't sure. Trusting the wrong people was a weakness of hers, and she didn't know how to avoid it.

"Look Mary, I'm going to leave this money with you," Jamal said. "Do whatever you want with it. But I'm telling you, as a friend, Billy is dangerous, and if you want to keep that baby, you need to think about how to protect it."

Jamal stood up and handed the money pouch to Mary.

"And one more thing," he said. "If you leave, don't tell anyone where you're going. Not even me and Karina. Understand?"

After Jamal left, Mary and Karina opened the red pouch and stared at the money inside. They sat in silence for a while, each girl trying to wrap their mind around what had just happened. People didn't just walk through the door and give other people piles of cash out of the goodness of their own heart. That kind of thing only happened in the movies. And yet, that's exactly what Jamal seemed to have done, for reasons they couldn't quite explain and didn't entirely trust. Where did the money come from, after all? And why was Jamal so eager to give it to her? Was it secretly Billy's money? And if she took it, would Billy then come looking for her until the end of time? But if Billy had that kind of money lying around, why was he always broke? Maybe it wasn't his after all. Maybe it came from somewhere else. And maybe, just maybe, Mary didn't want to know where it came from. Because if she knew, maybe the whole situation would get too complicated, too fast, and she wouldn't know what to do. And lately, not knowing what to do had become a recurring theme in her life.

Finally, Karina broke the silence and said, "He's right, you know. This is your chance. Maybe your only chance."

Mary did not want to think that it had come to this. But the more she did think about it, the more she realized that Jamal and Karina were giving her permission to do what she had been wanting to do for a long time but thought was impossible: trade her current life for another, better life. She didn't know where she could go, exactly, but anywhere was better than Davenport. And once this thought entered her head, she suddenly found herself filled with a heady sense of urgency and purpose. It was a strange, unfamiliar feeling, an odd mix of exhilaration and apprehension. And she liked it, a lot.

Without a word, she handed Karina the box of Fruit Loops and ran into the bathroom to brush her teeth and change. She was fully clothed when she emerged, and held a toothbrush in her hand. "Can

I steal this?" she asked. "And can I borrow some clothes? And a backpack?"

Quickly, the girls assembled a travel bag for Mary—some extra clothes, toiletries, a sandwich, an apple, and a few cookies—and put the money pouch at the bottom, where it would be harder to find. Karina then drove Mary to the Greyhound bus station and dropped her off.

"Do you know where you're going to go?" Karina asked as Mary got out of the car.

"Not yet," said Mary. "But I'll figure it out."

"Don't tell me. Just send me a postcard when you're safe," Karina said. "I'm going to miss you, but I am really happy for you. Good luck, sweetie."

Mary blew Karina a kiss and headed toward the ticket office. The bus destinations were posted in alphabetical order on a large board—Akron, Albuquerque, Birmingham, Boston, Chicago, Dallas, Denver, etc.—and Mary scanned them all, looking for a sign, some sort of indication or clue about where her destiny might take her, or where she should go to find it. Half the cities on the board she'd never even heard of, and even the city names she recognized were places she knew nothing about. The farthest away from Davenport she'd ever been in her life was a weekend in Des Moines with Billy, who had driven there to pick up a fresh stash of weed. "Travel" for fun was something other people did, people who had money and time to escape the drudgery of their day-to-day lives. Danger, not drudgery, was forcing her to contemplate just such an escape. But to where? Mary scanned the board of cities but none of them spoke to her. She found this frustrating, because she wanted her decision to be a conscious, deliberate one, not a random choice made under pressure with little or no information. Still, if she had to, she was prepared to get on a bus, any bus, and see where it took her.

Her chest began to tighten as she moved down the alphabet—Nashville, Portland, Raleigh—and saw nothing but city names that sounded unfriendly and uninviting, places in other parts of the country that looked as suspicious to her as a stranger in an alley. Impatient and overwhelmed, she finally decided to hell with it and asked the ticket agent, "What's the farthest away from here I can go?"

"Depends on which direction you travel," the agent said. "Miami to the east, and San Diego to the West."

San Diego? The name sounded suddenly and strangely familiar. Then she remembered: Hadn't she met a guy from there on a bizarre night earlier in the summer, one of those nights when Billy had hit her and she had gone to the women's shelter to get a decent night's sleep? And hadn't he described it as kind of a magical place, with warm beaches and sunsets over the ocean—the ocean!—and no such thing as winter or snow, just summer all year long? Yes, he had. And she remembered it because, as he was describing this wonderful place to her that evening, she had momentarily allowed herself to wish that she was there too.

This was the sign she'd been looking for, Mary decided. She then leaned toward the agent behind the counter and said, "One ticket to San Diego, please."

The last anyone ever saw of Mary Lynn Thompson, she was sitting on the beach, staring out at the Pacific ocean, wondering what lay beyond the horizon. Tiny shore birds with spindly stick legs skittered across the wet sand in front of her, and several children down the beach were making a sand castle with plastic buckets and shovels. The sun sparkled off the water like glitter, and the surf's soft rumble calmed her nerves, rinsing her thoughts of worry. For the first time in Mary's life she actually felt hopeful about the future. She had been given a chance to start a new life, and she didn't want to blow it. No one in San Diego knew her real name. Ever since she arrived, she had been telling people her name was Kate. Or Jasmine. Or Lisa. She knew she'd have to settle on a new name at some point, but for now the freedom to be anyone she wanted to be was intoxicating. In California, reinventing herself every day felt almost normal, as if everything that had happened in her life leading up to that point was irrelevant, because it was in the past, in another time and place far away and out of mind. Yes, she had Billy's baby in her belly, but he didn't want it, so she felt justified in keeping it from him. He would have been a horrible father and husband anyway, so she felt as if she had done both herself and her baby a huge favor by leaving Davenport. What she would do after the baby was born, she did not know. She knew she wanted to finish high school, or maybe get her GED and learn how to cut hair and give people manicures—something practical that brought a little beauty into the world.

But there was plenty of time to figure all that out. For now, it was enough to just sit on the beach and stare at the line where the water met the sky, and wonder what magical, miraculous thing might happen next.

www.ingramcontent.com/pod-product-compliance
Lightning Source LLC
Chambersburg PA
CBHW030431010526
44118CB00011B/594